This book is dedicated to the late, great Rashmi Thakrar who passed away, too soon, in 2017. He was Shamil's father, Kavi's uncle and the first Dishoom person that Naved ever met. He was (until the very end) our most joyful cheerleader, and tireless finder-in-chief of obscure nuggets to turn into fully formed ideas. He's the reason why Dishoom is so full of stories.

He believed that for something to truly succeed it must have a little poetry at the heart of it.

He also believed in reincarnation. We'd like to think that he is somewhere reading this dedication and diving into this book with delight.

DISHOOM

"FROM BOMBAY WITH LOVE"

Shamil Thakrar

Kavi Thakrar

Naved Nasir

Photography by
Haarala Hamilton

BLOOMSBURY PUBLISHING
LONDON · OXFORD · NEW YORK · NEW DELHI · SYDNEY

CONTENTS

Novices to Indian cookery, seek enlightenment here.

WELCOME TO BOMBAY

First impressions

You may not find Bombay an easy sort of place. At least, not to begin with.

As you step off the plane, you first feel the heat, then a ripe waft of warm air. Then, an unfeasibly new, shiny airport and an invariably old, surly customs official. After your perfectly good papers have been shuffled, scrutinised and shuffled again, you head into town, perhaps in one of the noisy little black and yellow 1960s design Fiats that still function as part of the swarm of taxis in Bombay.

Next, as an appropriate introduction to the rhythms of the city, you experience the traffic. For at least a little of the time, your sweaty and smiling taxi-walla cheerfully weaves in and out of lorries and scooters, narrowly missing them. The rest of the time you and he are stuck, engine off, your arm resting on the hot metal window sill, sitting in the jaded torpor of standstill hooting traffic. Perhaps you are on a flyover, able to peer into the open windows of the little flats on either side. You will have noticed that there are people everywhere, crowded onto motorbikes, into cars, onto the streets.

More than likely, you will eventually arrive at your destination. If you're coming to south Bombay, you will probably travel past high-rises, permanent makeshift slums, crumbling old houses, a brand new sea-link flyover and an Aston Martin dealership, to arrive somewhere near the bottom of the pendant of reclaimed land that is the city.

By now, you may have an initial impression of Bombay. It's a crowded place, of course. Glass and steel alternates with corrugated iron and then gives way to fading Art Deco and wild, slightly oriental Gothic. It's not really the same as the rest of India. It's somewhat monochromatic, with less of the colour that people seem to associate with the country. It is clearly a city of massive and closely juxtaposed extremes.

However, as you spend more time in Bombay you might begin to see past your first impressions, past the crowds, past the extremes and into the layers: Portuguese then British colonial rule, massive inward migration from both land and sea,

development of enterprise and wealth, myriad and unexpected ethnicities, religions, cultures and languages. It's certainly the biggest, fastest, densest and richest city of India. But it is also the most cosmopolitan; it is startlingly full of accumulated difference. In a way, it seems that this accumulated difference, and its complete internalisation, has become the nature of the city itself. So many different voices from so many different places telling so many different stories joined together to become Bombay.

And then, gradually, you discover the simple joy of morning chai and omelette at Kyani & Co., of dawdling in Horniman Circle on a lazy morning, of eating your fill on Mohammed Ali Road, of strolling on the sands at Chowpatty at sunset and of taking the air at Nariman Point at night.

Once you have found your places of refuge, Bombay first becomes human and then – without you noticing exactly when – it completes the seduction and becomes delightful.

Meet your hosts at the charming Irani café, Koolar & Co.

For me, the Irani cafés are a significant part of this seduction. Once liberally sprinkled across the city, only twenty-five or so remain, all of them old, comfortable and worn. All who know them well seem to have fond memories of them – as places for bunking off school, or debating politics and philosophy with the idealistic energy of youth, or for escaping, deeply, into a book, all accompanied by chai. The Irani cafés were places for growing up, and for growing old, whoever you were.

In the course of your time here in the city, you'll get to know these cafés and their ramshackle charm. You'll become familiar with their proprietors (invariably kindly and eccentric uncles or aunties), their food and, of course, their sweet milky chai. Might I suggest that you start in Koolar & Co.? This little café occupies a narrow wedge of a street corner on King's Circle up in Matunga, which is on the way to south Bombay. Amir-bhai is the owner and his family have had the café since 1932. He is genial and quirky,

like his café. He is also generous in sharing his reminiscences over a plate of tasty but slightly odd "honey half-fry" eggs (eggs only slightly fried and drizzled with honey), which I've never eaten anywhere but here.

Koolar & Co. has a specific importance for me. Not far away is a small ground-floor flat in an unremarkable building, where my mother and I spent a few months of my very early life. My family had been thrown out of our home on another continent, and Bombay was our refuge when we had nowhere else to go. We actually celebrated my first birthday here in Koolar & Co. and apparently we had a little cake. This would certainly be a memory I would lovingly treasure if I had it.

Meanwhile my father was getting our papers in order so that we could join him in London. Although we eventually settled there, I often returned to Bombay, and to that little flat. I used to stay with my grandmother ("Baa"), who had an enormous love for the city. My memories of that flat are vivid. If I close my eyes, I can still see our little blue Formica-topped dining table, with the crackling boxy Grundig radio that my grandfather ("Dada") used to listen to intently, next to the little toaster that toasted one side at a time.

Without Baa's influence, my cousin Kavi (also her grandson) and I literally wouldn't be doing what we're doing at Dishoom. We both have distinct memories of being in Bombay with her. At Chowpatty or Crawford Market, or strolling up to Nariman Point at sunset with my grandfather, who could walk endlessly. Sadly, Baa and Dada are both no more, but a memory that I treasure lovingly is the utterly unselfconscious, wide grin on Baa's face when she ate a kala khatta gola ice at our pop-up on London's South Bank back in 2011. Even as she was in her eighties, she used to love showing off Dishoom to her old friends from Bombay. When she did so, it made my heart sing.

Chef Naved has been with us since the very beginning. He already had a successful career in some of India's finest hotels. We were lucky indeed that he agreed to move from Bombay to London in 2010 to dream up a menu for a restaurant that didn't yet even exist and which, furthermore, had a silly name. In fact, he nearly refused the interview because of this name. "Dishoom" is the word for the sound effect used in an old Hindi movie when the hero lands a fine punch. If we're candid, it is an odd choice of name for our restaurants. It was our good fortune that this normally level-headed man threw all caution to the wind and gave us a chance. Thus, Naved's delicious recipes first filled our restaurants, and now fill this book.

4

5

6

Through the course of these pages, Naved, Kavi and I will take you on a day-long tour of south Bombay. Naturally, we will include a lot of food. We'll show you the various places for eating and drinking – from street vendors to restaurants to cafés – that have inspired Dishoom's recipes; places for which we have reverence, and places that give us comfort. However, it will also be a tour of the other parts of Bombay with which we are deeply in love. There are the stories and histories, but also the people, the beautiful buildings, the little institutions and the small oddities in between, some of which, very sadly, may not be here to enjoy for much longer. We make no claims that this is anything other than a tour of our own favourite places, curated with a disregard for balance or completeness. We will certainly have missed out important things, and we may also be too excited for your taste about Bombay's jazz age.

By the end, we hope you will feel as if you've been to Bombay with us, and seen what we see, and tasted what we taste. You might even one day do this little tour for yourself. You'll certainly know more about the city than when you first picked up this book, although any knowledge may be random and your view of the city excessively rose-tinted.

"By the end, we hope you will feel as if you've been to Bombay with us, and seen what we see, and tasted what we taste."

You may also gain an insight into how we started and grew Dishoom. This book is very much a reflection of everything that we pour into the restaurants. Most obviously, there is the Bombay food and drink that you'll taste and the Irani cafés that you'll visit. Beyond that though, almost every little thing we do at Dishoom – from the detailed design of our spaces, to our celebration of Bombay's big cultural events, to the stories we tell – is somehow rooted in this Bombay that we love, some may say, obsessively. We do a five-day version of this tour (which we call the Bombay Bootcamp) with anyone who has worked at Dishoom for more than five years. We find it helps those who work with us to become just as obsessed.

Finally, and perhaps most importantly, we hope you will be replete with recipes and stories

to share with all who come to your table. There is nothing that we love more than feeding you all in our restaurants, and we are extremely happy to be sharing our Dishoom recipes, so that you can cook them in your own kitchen.

An early morning stroll to see the city from a lovely viewpoint

Before you sink your teeth into the *bun* (bread) and *maska* (butter) of this tour, first head to leafy Malabar Hill to enjoy the pleasant breeze and get your bearings. Look for the playground with the giant old woman's boot opposite the Hanging Gardens. (As it happens, this is where Kavi's father, as an unruly six-year-old, was separated from his parents when Prime Minister Nehru unexpectedly appeared close by for a stroll with his sister and drew crowds. Kavi's father was of course eventually found.)

Just beyond the playground is a vantage point from which you can admire the generous sweep of the bay. The Portuguese clambered ashore in the sixteenth century when there was little more than a clutch of seven tropical islands at the edge of the Arabian Sea. Imagine this view without buildings and with a lot more sand and palms. The place was named "bom bahia" ("good bay" in Portuguese) which eventually became Bombay.

The Portuguese acquired the islands from the Sultan of Gujarat but in 1661 they felt compelled to include Bombay in the dowry for King Charles II of England, who was reluctant to marry their princess Catherine of Braganza. Apparently the groom thought his bride looked a bit like a bat,

but he was pragmatic and the dowry helped him see otherwise. Then, a few years later, the King privatised the territory, leasing it to the British East India Company for £10 per year. Even this early, Bombay was characterised by international transactions and an expensive arranged marriage.

Over the next few centuries Bombay continued to develop ever more vigorously in this commercial vein. The East India Company was aggressively focused on making its joint stockholders in London wealthy beyond reckoning, and the city evolved to support this. Through trade and transactions, the generation of wealth became the very point of Bombay from early in its life. As a consequence, the city developed its other essential characteristics – being utterly mixed-up and utterly full of life.

Dreams of profit attracted the bold, enterprising and colourful from all over the subcontinent and from all over the world. Fortunes were made and lost in opium, cotton and land speculation. Bollywood became the manufacturer of the nation's aspirations and fantasies. The city brought people in, swallowed them up and made them its own. In *The Moor's Last Sigh*, Salman Rushdie describes Bombay thus: "In Bombay all-India met what-was-not-India, what came across the black water to flow into our veins... Bombay was central; all rivers flowed into its human sea. It was an ocean of stories and everyone talked at once."

Inevitably the population expanded and, at first, the islands' perimeters did not. Ambitious plans were made both to unite the seven islands by filling in the swamps, and then to claim more land from the sea. Most of these plans were eventually

7 View of the bay from Malabar Hill
8 Children playing in the giant old woman's boot

realised (with notable exceptions), although there was never enough land to keep pace with the relentless demand for it. You'll recall that Bombay is a pendant of land hanging from north to south into the ocean, which surrounds it on three sides. Like Manhattan, but with no bridges as valves to release the pressure. Instead there are the super-dense crush-load local trains daily conveying millions north to south and back again, fifteen people to a square metre. The roughly twenty million inhabitants of the city jostle and hustle and squeeze for space daily.

Notice for a moment how spacious this park feels and how misleadingly tranquil Bombay looks from here. Look across the bay. You'll be walking and eating your way through the city that lies before you. Down to your left you can see sandy Girgaum Chowpatty, where you'll stroll and snack at sunset. Further south you can see the gentle curve of Marine Drive to Nariman Point, which at night becomes the Queen's Necklace. You'll walk there too, eat ice cream, and see the beautiful Art Deco buildings facing the sea. You'll learn about the city's Gothic architecture, the cotton boom of the 1860s, Bombay jazz and Led Zeppelin's visit to Colaba. You'll also eat vada pau from the street and slowly cooked trotters on the crowded Mohammed Ali Road. We suggest you end with a stiff drink at the Taj, which you'll likely need by then. And of course, you'll be visiting some Irani cafés.

"Look across the bay. You'll be walking and eating your way through the city that lies before you."

The story of Bombay's old Irani cafés

The Parsis are a proper Bombay success story. They are an ancient and distinct community from Iran which has not only been absorbed into the city, but has shaped it and is completely identified with it. At the same time, the community has held onto its identity and traditions with integrity. The Parsis originally landed and settled north of Bombay in Gujarat a thousand years ago, but came to the city as it grew. (Gujarat is also where Shamil and Kavi's family is from.) They were enterprising and valued education, and became wealthy and influential through trade in cotton, opium and other goods. They were also strongly civic-minded and philanthropic. Over the centuries, Bombay has owed a significant part of its infrastructure and public culture to the Parsis' generosity.

In 1854, a Parsi named Dinshaw Maneckji set up a fund to help fellow Zoroastrians in Iran join the thriving Parsi community in Bombay. The people in this second wave of immigration came to be known as "Iranis" and it is they who established the cafés from the late nineteenth century onwards.

The story of the disappearing Irani cafés has a certain wistful poetry. Iranis cross the Arabian Sea to Bombay to escape religious persecution. They

10

work in the homes of established Parsi families, leaving to set up their own cafés, often on street corners which happen to be shunned by Hindus for some superstition. These Irani cafés become an irreplaceable Bombay institution. One which earns a fond place in the hearts of Bombayites, regardless of caste, class, religion or race, by providing a cheap snack, a decent meal, or just a cup of chai and cool refuge from the street. Fans turn slowly. Panelled walls are hung with sepia family portraits and mirrors. Wealthy businessmen, sweaty taxi-wallas and courting couples sit close to each other on rickety bentwood chairs at chipped marble tables. Students eat breakfast while high-court lawyers read their briefs. Families have lunch and writers find their characters.

As the decades wear on, eventfully, the Irani cafés peak in number in the 1960s and then start closing down. From none to four hundred and back down to twenty-five within a century. Children of café owners become accountants and doctors, or the land becomes too valuable to keep. Café Coffee Day, clad in cheerful Western plastic, becomes the choice for bashful teenage trysts. Bombay becomes Mumbai and cafés become sweet memories. Tears are shed, but modernity creeps in quickly with its petty pace and has little regard for what we all once found precious. Brave new India looks to a shiny future, and doesn't pause much to remember its own stories.

In fact, this very park was once home to one of Bombay's most loved Irani cafés. Café Naaz used to sit up here on Malabar Hill, enjoying the same view that you are now enjoying. Many a Bombay teenager went on a shy or secretive date here. If they really wanted to impress, they could pay a little extra for the best views of the bay. But after wrangles over an expired lease, the café closed, and the space is being redeveloped. Cafés like Naaz are now gradually disappearing from the collective memory of the city.

The importance of shared spaces

The Irani cafés were not just a source of romantic nostalgia. They were also important. Nineteenth-century Bombay is often and rightly described as a cosmopolitan city, but eating out was uncommon and almost always segregated. Religions had strong and specific prescriptions on diet, with caste an additional division. Further, the colonists created racially exclusive spaces. Those with brown skin couldn't enter the Yacht Club or the Bombay Gymkhana and generally weren't allowed to eat in the dining halls of hotels. (The great Parsi industrialist, Jamsetji Tata, changed this when he opened the Taj Mahal Palace hotel where the rule was clear that no one could ever be denied access for being Indian.)

The Irani cafés, opened by outsiders, simply could not hold any such biases. They quietly subverted all the rules by welcoming all comers. And, unlike the Taj, they were affordable. A few paise could buy you a cup of chai and bun maska or a biscuit. Over time, many local Iranis became reliable places for a cheap, sustaining meal. They also became meeting and relaxing places for the

9   Advertisement for Ideal Restaurant, 1939
10 Quiet corners in B. Merwan
11 Lunch at Britannia Restaurant
12 Rules at Dishoom Shoreditch
13 Ladies' rooms are often found in Irani cafés

"The Irani cafés were not just a source of romantic nostalgia. They were also important."

great number who lacked the luxury of space at home (or even those, like hookers, who were shunned elsewhere). They played a significant role in enabling women and children to participate in eating out by incorporating family rooms or cabins (which also had the unintended benefit of sheltering illicit liaisons). In this way, these cafés set up by immigrants became Bombay's first real public eating and drinking places.

If Bombay was already full of all kinds of people, Irani cafés further helped to mix them physically in the same spaces and helped enhance the cosmopolitan culture of the city. When people break bread together, barriers break down.

These shared spaces and this cosmopolitan culture were extremely valuable. Shared spaces beget shared experiences and shared experiences mean that people are more likely to tolerate each other's differences, less likely to hate and less likely to explode into violence towards one another.

In 1947, the joyous awakening of the nation to life and freedom was stained with the blood from Partition. The violent rupture of the subcontinent into India and Pakistan resulted in perhaps a million deaths.

However, Bombay came together rather than falling apart. Naresh Fernandes – a passionate advocate of the need for shared spaces in Bombay – writes in his book, *City Adrift*, that "Freedom came amidst a shortage of milk and sugar as Bombay devoured piles of celebratory sweets. At midnight on 15 August 1947, B.G. Kher... head of the provincial ministry, raised the tricolour... and declared, 'Citizens of free India, you are now free'. After a shastri, a moulvi, a Catholic bishop and a Parsi priest said appropriate prayers, Kher touched a switch and the buildings behind him burst into light. A mighty roar went up and brass bands blared out raucous tunes. A river of revellers swept through the streets, waving tricolours, riding in trams and on top of them. While Delhi and Calcutta were wrenched apart by riots sparked by the anxieties of Partition, Bombay was joyous and peaceful. Reported *The Times of India*, 'Hundreds of thousands marched cheering through the illuminated streets of Bombay, uninterruptedly shouting slogans in a multitude of tongues, which turned the city at midnight into a Babel.'"

Dishoom: from Bombay with love

Back in 2010 when we first opened Dishoom, we (perhaps sensibly) thought our job was simply to serve Londoners good food and good drink. However, as we deepened our knowledge of the Irani cafés and their role in Bombay's civic culture, we became increasingly conscious that breaking down barriers was important to us too.

We love serving you dishes cooked in Parsi, Muslim, Hindu and Christian traditions, which all jostle on our tables for space. We like to do it deliberately and self-consciously. As you enter our restaurants, you might spot a statue of Ganesh – the elephant-headed Hindu god who removes obstacles – sitting companionably alongside an Asho Farohar, the symbol of Zoroastrianism. We also feel very strongly that Dishoom has to be a place where the hard-up student (taking full advantage of our bottomless chai) can sit easily next to the wealthy steel magnate (who might order bottles of champagne), and where the Muslim family can share a table with Hindu teenagers.

Some years ago, we received some hate mail. Somebody wanted to book a table, and then didn't. Not because of our booking policy, but because of the pictures of smiling Muslim children on our website observing Ramadan, and because we are Hindus who celebrate Eid with storytelling and feasting. He called us backstabbing traitors, colourfully insulted our mothers and sisters, and worse. We wished the writer no ill, but as we all read the message together as a team, it bolstered our conviction. That year, we also noticed a tweet from our Eid feasting. A picture of three hands, three girls – Aisha, Geeta and Sarah – who had henna applied to their palms to celebrate Eid. It was the polar opposite of that hate mail, but both pushed us towards increasing our efforts.

Accordingly, we've had the privilege of bringing Hindus and non-Hindus together to throw colour at each other with abandon at Holi, and to dance together at Diwali. We bring Muslims and non-Muslims together over food and music for Eid, and Christians and non-Christians together for Christmas Carolling. Chef Naved (a Muslim) and Shamil (a Hindu) fast together every year for Janmastmi and Ramadan and lead our teams in breaking fast together. (To be clear, Shamil only manages one day of Ramadan fasting!)

Each August, we celebrate the Hindu festival of Raksha Bandhan ("the knot of protection"). We take inspiration from the great Indian poet

"We love serving you dishes cooked in Parsi, Muslim, Hindu and Christian traditions, which all jostle on our tables for space."

Rabindranath Tagore, who appropriated the ceremony (normally for brothers and sisters) to unite Hindus and Muslims in Bengal in 1905. He asked them to tie white *rakhis* (threads) on each other ("we are brothers and sisters and will not be separated!") in successful protest against the British decision to divide the region. Thus, each year, we encourage our team and our guests to tie a *rakhi* on someone of a different faith, nationality or culture as a symbol of solidarity and peace. For each *rakhi* tied, we donate £1 to Seeds of Peace, a remarkable charity that brings young people from conflict regions (including Israel and Palestine) together in summer camp, to listen to each other and to forge the mutual understanding that might actually bring peace.

One of the best things we've ever done at Dishoom had its origins in Ramadan. Some of us were sitting around a table replete with food (not an uncommon event at Dishoom). Most of us knew that charity was one of the foundations of Islam, but we learnt that the holy time of Ramadan is particularly associated with giving to those less fortunate than yourself.

Our food-laden table was beautiful, but in that context it gave us pause for thought. We decided that our *zakat* (charity) for the month of Ramadan would be to feed children in need for every meal we served. We put this into place and worked with the charities Magic Breakfast in the UK and The Akshaya Patra Foundation in India to provide nourishing, free meals to school children who would otherwise go hungry. Both of these charities do a valiant job breaking down the corrosive social barriers that arise when kids are too hungry to learn, or when girls don't get sent to school at all.

Later that year, at Diwali, a special time for Hindus, we decided to make our *zakat* a permanent feature of what we do at Dishoom. Since then, for every meal we serve, we donate another to a hungry child, and we've so far donated over seven million meals to children in the UK and India. A meal for a meal. This is, without doubt, one of our very proudest achievements.

ABOVE: In Irani cafés, you are typically seated on bentwood chairs from central Europe

RIGHT: B. Merwan on Grant Road dates from 1914 and is still open

KYANI & CO.

"Your early morning wander should, without too much doubt, begin at this utterly charming Irani café, which is most certainly our favourite place for breakfast in Bombay."

BREAKFAST

"8 o'clock"

BREAKFAST AT KYANI & CO. FOLLOWED BY A STROLL AROUND DHOBI TALAO

TO HELP YOU ACCLIMATISE gently to the pace and heat, the noise and dust, you must rise early. Bombay is at its most beautiful in the morning. The air shimmers. Birds circle endlessly in the sky. The pavements, sometimes freshly rinsed by rain, have yet to become crowded with dusty feet. It is the time when the city feels most at peace.

Resist the temptation to ignore your alarm. Yawn, stretch deliciously as you look out of the window, do a few Surya Namaskars (in India, the sun should surely be saluted) and walk out into the street as the city starts to wake. Start in the neighbourhood of Dhobi Talao.

Your early morning wander should, without too much doubt, begin at the utterly charming Irani café, Kyani & Co., which is most certainly our favourite place for breakfast in Bombay. It is a refuge from the street, a place to idle a while before a day's activity.

Navigate the short flight of steps from the pavement into the café (use the dangling knotted rope if you need to steady yourself), and seat yourself at one of the tables. Your chair will be a slightly rickety but elegant bentwood chair from Czechoslovakia which, like many of its kind, probably journeyed to Bombay before India's independence. The scent of freshly baked bread rests in the air, stirred gently by the ceiling fans. If you're early, it will be calm and quiet and you can enjoy your chai and the newspaper in peace.

Gradually the café will be filled with office-goers, relieved to be out of the absurdly crowded Bombay local train, and students from the nearby St. Xavier's. They slurp chai from their saucers and eat before their day's exertions. Plates of omelette, akuri and bun maska will appear in enthusiastic bursts from the kitchen, conveyed by generally amiable, but slightly impatient waiters.

A breakfast of akuri or omelet-pau and a cup of sweet, milky Irani chai will nourish you well for

"Bombayites (Mumbaikers, if you must) have been enjoying pau dipped in chai in Kyani since it opened in 1904."

the day's relaxed activity. Don't hold back. Ask for extra chai and extra pau if need be. Savour the eggs, then dunk the buttery pau freely into your chai. Enjoy the warm indulgence with a smile and without shame.

Look up and you might notice eccentric Christmas decorations (left up long into the year) hanging peaceably alongside old family portraits, Zoroastrian symbols and a sketch by the late, great Bombay artist M. F. Husain. Before he exiled himself from India after painting his controversial nudes, he was a frequent visitor here for chai and bun maska. All are welcome at the good-natured Kyani & Co.

Bombayites (Mumbaikers, if you must) have been enjoying pau dipped in chai in Kyani since it opened in 1904. Sitting here, you can almost imagine the café as it might have been in the early twentieth century. No doubt the streets were a little quieter back then, but in truth, it really hasn't changed that much. Kyani is the sort of place of refuge that, once located, might help you to feel comfortable in a city. Farokh-bhai, whose family has owned the café since 1959, is a kind and reassuring presence at the owner's desk. He's the third generation of the Shokriye family to roll up Kyani's shutters each dawn.

Wipe any ketchup from your lips and scoop the last crumbs from your plate. Say your goodbyes to Farokh-bhai (perhaps doing his accounts at the owner's desk, perhaps seated at a table making

"Kyani is the sort of place of refuge that, once located, might help you to feel comfortable in a city."

1 A cup of sweet, milky Irani chai and some bun
2 The charming interiors of Kyani & Co.
3 Paintings and pictures on the balcony of Kyani & Co.
4 Faded sign of the now-closed Bastani café
5 A dangling rope at the entrance to Kyani & Co. helps patrons enter
6 The owner of Kyani & Co., Farokh-bhai, at his desk
7 Metro Cinema, opened in 1938

his way through the newspaper). If you are still feeling peckish, or plan to feel peckish later, then ask him for some of his delicious mawa cake to take with you. For a certain type of Bombayite, milky sweet mawa cake from an Irani café is as evocative of memory as Proust's madeleine.

Now be sure to wander across the road, where you can see a reminder that most of the Irani cafés of Bombay have gone for good: the faded shutters of Bastani, another legendary café, permanently and sadly shut. Both cafés once did a steady trade in their Irani biscuits and confectionery. Charm is so often lost in the headlong rush to modernity. We're just grateful that the modernity that has overwhelmed so much of the city has not managed to overwhelm it completely.

You'll need to walk off your breakfast, so take a stroll now around Dhobi Talao. Despite the area's name, the local *dhobis* (washermen) have long since moved elsewhere, and the *talao* (lake) has been filled in and built upon, and built upon, and built upon. This is a familiar story in Bombay. People are many, land is scarce.

This morning's walk begins at Metro Cinema, which overlooks an enjoyably chaotic junction where five major roads converge. (For your safety,

consider using the subway to cross the road, even though it may take several attempts to find the right exit.) Metro Cinema is a local landmark. Built in 1938, it is a good example of Bombay's very own form of Art Deco. After a few days in Bombay, you'll become familiar with it. Art Deco first made the journey to India from the West in the early 1930s and this most cosmopolitan of cities was quick to catch on. The first batch of Deco buildings in Bombay, which lined the western side of the Oval Maidan, effectively faced off the grand Gothic revival structures on the eastern side. They flaunt their colourful façades in front of the stern and stony Gothic structures, and enjoy the sea breeze while blocking the older structures' sea view.

These Deco buildings were created by the first generation of Indian architects, graduates from the Sir J. J. School of Art (which is only

a few hundred feet from where you now stand). These students were surely also happy patrons of Kyani & Co. In taking a modern, global style and flavouring it with local motifs, Indian architects challenged the aesthetics of their colonial rulers. The style became so popular in Bombay that the city is second only to Miami in its quantity of Art Deco buildings.

If you're not in a hurry (and why should you be?), call in to the People's Free Reading Room and Library. Walk through the elegant entrance, and leaf through a newspaper at one of the designated wooden stands. Browse the collection of books covering all aspects of Bombay history, and admire the marble busts of local worthies (stony-faced or smiling). It is a pleasantly hushed and sleepy place.

Outside the Reading Room, turn left, pass the statue of Khan Bahadur Kavasji Petigara (the first Indian officer to head the Bombay Criminal Investigation Department, and the man whom Mahatma Gandhi insisted on being arrested by) and continue your stroll along the street to your left. You'll note the presence of numerous Goan restaurants on the side streets. This neighbourhood is home to many Goan folk. Indeed, Jer Mahal, the delightfully ramshackle and crumbling estate

"Under the watchful gaze of Buddha, Asho Farohar and the guru Yogananda, you must take the time to sample some of the finest baked goods Bombay has to offer."

8 Studies underway in the People's Free Reading Room and Library
9 The façade of a Parsi Fire Temple in Dhobi Talao
10 Danesh Nejadkay, the affable owner of Paris Bakery

that houses Kyani, also contains various *kudds* – social-club-cum-sleeping-places for gentlemen migrated from Goa. Each *kudd* belongs to a specific village, and acts as a sort of tiny outpost of a far-away community, wedged implausibly within the beams of an inevitably creaky old building.

You will reach an intersection at Princess Street where you find yourself with a Zoroastrian Fire Temple to your left and another Fire Temple immediately ahead. Enjoy the carvings and motifs on the Fire Temples which recall the ancient Persian roots of the religion. There are several more temples in the vicinity and you might even get the impression that this density of Fire Temples is normal in Bombay. In actual fact, it is due to the historically large number of Parsis in the area. The Parsi community is completely associated with Bombay's prosperity and culture, but is now much reduced in numbers.

Take a left down Dr C.H. Street, which also goes by the elegant name of Our Lady of Dolours Church Lane, and the less elegant Dukar Gully (pig lane) for the slaughterhouses and pork shops supplying the local Goans, who have a fondness for the meat. You will make your way to our final port of call in Dhobi Talao – Paris Bakery, an unassuming hole-in-the-wall, vending the most delicious cakes and biscuits in south Bombay.

Under the watchful gaze of Buddha, Asho Farohar and the guru Yogananda, you must take the time to sample some of the finest baked goods Bombay has to offer. Stock up on more mawa cake and exchange pleasantries with the big-hearted owner, Danesh Nejadkay – a man of great talent, and surely responsible for many a Bombayite's stubbornest pounds.

ABOVE: Perennial Christmas decorations inside Kyani & Co.

LEFT: Taking your morning chai at Kyani & Co. with the newspaper is a sublime delight

AKURI

Akuri – a simple dish, not unlike scrambled eggs – is an Irani café classic. Kyani & Co. serves the best akuri, along with a similar, slightly drier dish called bhurji. It is delicious mopped up with fresh, pillowy pau (Bombay's favourite bread buns) or thick slices of fresh, white loaf, but it will work just as well on toast.

Use the best quality free-range eggs you can find, and a good, ripe, flavoursome tomato – this will make all the difference. And do make sure you have cooked everything else – including the toast – before the eggs hit the pan; they'll be ready before you know it.

This recipe serves one as a generous breakfast, or two alongside some bacon, sausages, grilled mushrooms and masala beans (page 48). If you double the recipe, use a large frying pan so that the ingredients sizzle and the eggs cook quickly.

SERVES 1

~

1 medium tomato (about 70g)

1 tsp olive oil

A pinch of sea salt flakes

½ small green chilli, very finely chopped

About 6 coriander sprigs, very finely chopped

¼ red onion (30g), finely chopped

¼ tsp ground turmeric

A pinch of deggi mirch chilli powder

2 large eggs

1 tbsp vegetable oil

¼ tsp fine sea salt

TO SERVE

1 thick slice of white bloomer or sourdough

Butter, for spreading

A few coriander leaves

1. Heat the grill to high.

2. Slice the tomato in half. Place one half on a baking tray, cut side up, drizzle with the olive oil and sprinkle with the salt flakes. Place under the grill and cook for 10 minutes.

3. Put the chopped chilli, coriander and red onion into a bowl. Remove and discard the seeds from the other tomato half, finely chop the flesh and add to the bowl. Add the turmeric and chilli powder. Set the bowl to one side. Put the bread in your toaster now.

4. Warm a medium frying pan over a high heat. Crack the eggs into a cup or small jug, but don't mix them at this stage.

5. Add the vegetable oil to the pan and swirl to ensure the base is coated. Add the fine salt to the onion mix and toss well. When the oil is hot, tip the contents of the bowl into the pan and let the mixture sizzle for 40 seconds, stirring regularly so nothing burns.

6. Add the eggs and mix well to scramble. Count to five, then mix again. Count to five again, mix again. Repeat this, counting only to three each time, until the eggs are just cooked and still very soft.

7. Butter your toast, place on a warm plate and pile the eggs on top. Serve immediately, scattered with a few coriander leaves and with the grilled tomato on the side.

PARSI OMELETTE

Parsis are notorious for being fond of eggs. It's something of a cultural in-joke. Irani cafés like Kyani and Koolar devote whole sections of their menu to eggs in various permutations, and omelettes are a favourite. A Parsi omelette is typically flavoured with green chillies, onion, tomato and coriander.

It is important to chop the onion and tomato quite finely, otherwise it will be hard to roll up the omelette when you serve it. You'll need to use a big, wide frying pan to make sure the omelette is thin enough.

You can make this without using a grill – in a frying pan over a medium heat. Just carefully turn the omelette over when it is almost completely set, then remove to a plate, roll up and serve.

SERVES 1

~

2 large eggs

A large pinch of fine sea salt

¼ red onion, very finely diced

½ small tomato, deseeded and finely sliced

½ green chilli, very finely diced

About 6 coriander sprigs, finely chopped

1 tbsp vegetable oil

Coarsely ground black pepper

TO SERVE

A few coriander leaves

Tomato ketchup

Buttered toast

1. Heat the grill to high.

2. Crack the eggs into a jug or bowl and beat lightly with a fork until nicely mixed (but not frothy). Add the salt, red onion, tomato, green chilli, a few twists of black pepper and the chopped coriander. Mix well.

3. Warm a large frying pan over a high heat. Add the oil and swirl around the pan to coat the base. Add the egg mixture and shake the pan to ensure the mixture reaches the edges. Cook for 20 seconds then place the pan under the grill. Allow to cook until just set; this should take about 2 minutes.

4. Slide or invert the omelette onto a warm plate and roll it up. Serve with a few coriander leaves, tomato ketchup and buttered toast on the side.

KEJRIWAL

Fried eggs atop chilli cheese on toast is a favourite of the well-to-do Willingdon Club, the first such Bombay institution to admit Indians. It is reputedly named after the member (not to be confused with the Indian politician Arvind Kejriwal) who, not allowed by his wife to eat eggs at home, kept asking for the dish in his club.

The most convenient way of finishing the eggs here is to use a frying pan that can go into the oven. If you don't have one, fry the eggs until cooked in the pan, then top with the cheese, spring onions, chilli and pepper. The cheese won't melt quite as much, but it will still be delicious. If your frying pan is reliably non-stick you should need little or no oil.

SERVES 1

~

80g mature Cheddar, grated

1 or 2 thick slices of white bloomer, sourdough or brioche (depending on size and level of hunger)

2 spring onions, chopped

1 green chilli, very finely chopped

1 tsp vegetable oil (optional)

1 or 2 large eggs (one per slice of toast)

Coarsely ground black pepper

TO SERVE

Tomato ketchup

1. Let the grated cheese come up to room temperature; it needs to be quite soft and workable.

2. Heat the oven to 240°C/Fan 220°C/Gas 9. Place a baking tray inside to warm up.

3. Toast the bread until very lightly browned on both sides. Set aside to cool slightly while you prepare the topping.

4. Put a small handful of the grated cheese (roughly 10g), 1 tsp chopped spring onion and a pinch of green chilli to one side, to be used when you fry the egg(s).

5. Crack the egg(s) into a cup or small bowl, being careful to keep the yolk(s) intact.

6. Put the remaining cheese, spring onions and green chilli into a bowl, add plenty of black pepper and mix well. Using the back of a spoon (or your fingers), work the cheese mixture into a paste by pressing it firmly into the side of the bowl.

7. Spread the cheese mix evenly over the toast and press it in, using the back of the spoon, to create a firm, even layer that goes all the way to the edges of the toast. Place on the tray in the oven and cook for 6–8 minutes, until deep golden and bubbling.

8. While the chilli cheese toast is cooking, warm a frying pan over a high heat and, if using, add the oil. Gently tip the egg(s) into the hot pan and add some black pepper. Top with the reserved grated cheese, spring onion and green chilli. Place the frying pan in the oven and cook for 2 minutes, or until the cheese is melted and the egg white(s) are cooked but the yolk(s) are still runny.

9. Carefully slide the egg(s) onto the cheese on toast and serve right away, with plenty of tomato ketchup.

KEEMA PER EEDU

You'll find Irani cafés all over south Bombay serving little dishes of *keema* (spiced lamb mince) and freshly baked bread for breakfast, lunch and dinner. While this lamb dish, keema pau (page 109), sits on our all-day menu, at breakfast we serve a lighter variation using chicken mince – served *per eedu* (with an egg on top).

It is a fortifying combination of minced chicken keema, spiced chicken livers and eggs, salli potato chips for crunch, and some bread to mop up all the delicious juices. It's a real power breakfast, perhaps not for the faint-hearted, but if you're intrigued enough to try it once, you're likely to make it again. You could leave out the livers to simplify the dish (or if you just aren't keen on them), but we wholeheartedly recommend they stay in it.

Chicken mince can be a little hard to come by. If you can't find it in a local shop, buy skinless chicken thighs and put them through a mincer on its finest setting.

SERVES 4 GENEROUSLY

~

FOR THE CHICKEN KEEMA

500g chicken mince (see above)

25g garlic paste (page 353)

20g ginger paste (page 353)

3 tsp fine sea salt

2 tsp deggi mirch chilli powder

2 tsp ground cumin

2½ tsp garam masala (page 356)

80g full-fat Greek yoghurt

¼ tsp ground turmeric

70ml vegetable oil

175g Spanish white onions, finely diced

1 bay leaf

3 green cardamom pods

1 cinnamon stick

35g fenugreek leaves

A handful of coriander leaves

1. For the chicken keema, put the mince, garlic and ginger pastes, 1 tsp salt, the chilli powder, ground cumin, garam masala and 50g of the yoghurt into a bowl and mix well. Cover and leave to marinate in the fridge for 8–12 hours.

2. When you are ready to cook the keema, pour 200ml cold water into a bowl and stir in 1 tsp salt with the turmeric. Put to one side.

3. Warm a saucepan over a medium-high heat and add the oil. When the oil is hot, add the diced onions and sauté until they are dark golden brown; this will take about 15 minutes.

4. Add the bay leaf, cardamom pods and cinnamon stick and cook for 1 minute, shaking the pan a little, listening to the seeds crackle.

5. Add the marinated chicken mince, the final 1 tsp salt and the remaining 30g yoghurt. Sauté over a high heat for 10 minutes, then turn the heat down low and cook gently for a further 15 minutes.

6. While the keema is cooking, chop the fenugreek leaves and soak them in the salted turmeric water. When the keema has simmered enough, squeeze the moisture from the fenugreek leaves using your hands, then add them to the pan and cook for a final 5 minutes.

7. Add the coriander leaves, stir well, then turn off the heat. Let the keema sit, covered, for 5 minutes to allow the flavours to mingle.

TO ASSEMBLE AND SERVE

1 quantity spiced chicken livers (page 44), freshly cooked

4 soft white bread buns, sliced in half

Butter, for spreading

4 eggs

1 tsp vegetable oil (optional)

Freshly ground black pepper

Salli (page 173)

Coriander leaves, to finish

8. Cut the warm chicken livers into bite-sized pieces and stir through the keema. Toast and butter the buns. Crack the eggs into a small bowl, keeping the yolks intact. Warm a frying pan over a high heat; if using, add the oil.

9. Gently tip the eggs into the hot pan and add some black pepper. Fry the eggs until the whites are cooked, leaving the yolks still runny.

10. Divide the keema between warmed bowls and place a fried egg on top of each portion. Finish with salli and coriander leaves. Serve immediately, with the buttered, toasted buns.

CHICKEN LIVERS ON TOAST

This is Naved's mum's recipe; he has memories of eating it at home with lots of fresh roti. *Khaleji* (liver) has a robust flavour that stands up well to spices. Served on fire toast, spiced chicken livers are a great breakfast. A squeeze of lime makes them sing.

The oil will separate from the sauce towards the end of cooking. Don't be tempted to leave it behind in the pan – it will be utterly delicious mopped up with toast.

The spiced chicken livers are an important component of keema per eedu (page 42); the quantity below is sufficient for 4 servings of keema.

SERVES 2

~

250g chicken livers

25ml vegetable oil

1 garlic clove, very finely chopped

FOR THE SPICE PASTE

5g garlic paste (page 353)

5g ginger paste (page 353)

⅓ tsp fine sea salt

½ tsp ground cumin

⅓ tsp ground turmeric

½ tsp deggi mirch chilli powder

⅓ tsp garam masala (page 356)

40g full-fat Greek yoghurt

3 tsp vegetable oil

TO SERVE

4 slices of fire toast (page 48)

Lime wedges

Coriander leaves

1. Mix together the ingredients for the spice paste in a medium bowl.

2. Trim the chicken livers of any connective tissue or fat, and slice any particularly large parts in two. Add to the spice paste and toss to coat. Cover and leave to marinate in the fridge for 30 minutes.

3. When the marinating time is up, remove the chicken livers from the fridge to take the chill off them while you cook the garlic.

4. Warm a frying pan over a low heat. Add the oil and fry the chopped garlic for about 8 minutes, until golden.

5. Add the chicken livers with their marinade, stir well and turn the heat up. Sauté for 6–8 minutes until the livers and spice paste are both cooked, stirring frequently.

6. Pile onto warm fire toast and serve at once, with lime wedges and coriander leaves.

BACON NAAN ROLL

Our bacon naan roll has something of a cult following; it must surely be our signature breakfast dish. The freshly cooked naan is graced with a little cream cheese, tomato-chilli jam and fresh coriander, and wrapped around a few rashers of smoked streaky bacon. Make sure you prepare all the ingredients for the filling before the naan hits the pan.

Use good-quality flavoursome bacon – or sausages or eggs for the alternative fillings (see below). A combination of bacon or sausage with an egg makes a first-class filling.

SERVES 1

~

1 quantity naan dough
(page 364)

FOR THE FILLING

4 rashers of smoked streaky bacon

1 tsp full-fat cream cheese
(Philadelphia)

8 coriander leaves

A pinch of finely chopped green chilli (optional)

1 tsp tomato-chilli jam (page 59), plus extra for dipping

1. Follow the naan recipe up to and including the stage where you roll out the dough (as for step 5, page 364). (If you're making more than one naan roll, roll out as many naans as you need, keeping them on the oiled surface while you roll the others.)

2. Grill or fry the bacon until the fat is nicely crisped.

3. Cook the naans (following steps 6, 7 and 8, page 365).

4. To assemble, spread the cream cheese across the cooked naan and top with coriander leaves. Add the cooked bacon rashers and scatter over the chopped green chilli, if using.

5. Drizzle with tomato-chilli jam, fold the naan in half to enclose the filling and eat immediately, with extra tomato-chilli jam on the side for dipping.

Variations

Sausage naan roll: Prepare as above but for the filling, instead of bacon, grill or fry 2 good-quality sausages until nicely sizzled and cooked through, then slice them in half lengthways. Assemble as above.

Egg naan roll: Prepare as above but for the filling, instead of bacon, fry 2 free-range eggs in a little oil until the white is cooked and the yolks still runny. Assemble as above.

FIRE TOAST

This method allows you to get a good amount of char to your toast without making it dry or burnt. It goes splendidly with masala beans (see below), orange and star anise marmalade (page 56) or pineapple and pink peppercorn jam (page 58).

SERVES 1

1 large slice of sourdough bread

10g butter, melted

1. Warm a cast-iron griddle pan over a medium-high heat.

2. Place the slice of sourdough in the warmed pan and cook for 1–2 minutes, or until golden brown with darker stripes. Flip over and brush the cooked side with melted butter. Cook the second side for 1–2 minutes, then remove the toast from the pan and serve immediately.

MASALA BEANS

We did try to create a home-made baked beans recipe from scratch, but it just wasn't the same as good old Heinz. So, this is a simple recipe using the most classic of tinned baked beans, although not quite as you know them.

The beans are good served plain and simple, on fire toast; they also make a wonderful accompaniment to kejriwal (page 41) or a Parsi omelette (page 38).

SERVES 4

400g tin Heinz baked beans

30g onion-tomato masala (page 354)

¼ tsp garam masala (page 356)

½ green chilli, finely chopped

1 tsp chopped coriander leaves

A pinch of fine sea salt

TO SERVE

4 slices of buttered fire toast (above)

1. Tip the baked beans into a sieve and allow the sauce to drain off. Discard the sauce.

2. Place a saucepan over a medium heat, add the onion-tomato masala and warm until it starts to bubble. Stir in the garam masala and cook for 1 minute.

3. Add the beans, chopped chilli and coriander, stir well and simmer for 3 minutes. Pile the beans onto the fire toast to serve.

BANANA &
DATE PORRIDGE

This is a hearty winter-warmer porridge that does not call for sugar, because natural sweetness is provided by the bananas and the dates.

It can easily be made vegan by substituting whole milk with soya milk. To ensure that it does not become too sweet, count your dates carefully: three if your soya milk is unsweetened; two if it is already sweetened.

If you plan to make this porridge regularly, the banana-date mix can be made in bigger batches a day or two in advance and kept in the fridge.

SERVES 1 GENEROUSLY

~

2–3 Medjool dates, according to preferred sweetness

1 ripe banana

170ml whole milk or soya milk

30g steel-cut oats

1. Remove the stones from the dates. Peel the banana, slice off one third and set aside with one date half; these will be used to finish the porridge.

2. Chop the remaining dates and banana very finely. Place in a small pan and pour on 185ml boiling water. Cook over a low heat until you have a thick, mushy, reasonably smooth paste, stirring regularly and using the back of the spoon to crush any lumps; this should take around 10 minutes. You can also use a stick blender to deal with any stubborn lumps.

3. While the banana-date mixture is cooking, pour the milk into a bowl, tip in the oats and leave to soak for a few minutes.

4. When the banana-date mix is ready, add the milk and oats to the pan, bring to a gentle simmer and cook for 12–15 minutes, stirring regularly, until the oats are completely tender.

5. Slice the remaining third of the banana and finely shred the reserved date half. Serve the porridge in a warmed bowl, topped with the banana slices and dates.

GRANOLA

This is a wonderfully crunchy, buttery granola mix that is very simple to make. We recommend serving it topped with a generous dollop of vanilla yoghurt (see below), fresh fruits in season and a drizzle of honey, but it's perfectly lovely just with milk too. It will keep for up to a month if stored in an airtight container.

MAKES 10–12 PORTIONS

~

200g rolled oats

100g almonds

80g cashew nuts

75g pistachio nuts

45g desiccated coconut

70g sunflower seeds

70g pumpkin seeds

20g sesame seeds

100g acacia honey

100g unsalted butter

1 tsp ground cinnamon

1. Heat the oven to 210°C/Fan 190°C/Gas 6–7. Line two large baking trays with baking parchment.

2. Tip the oats, nuts, desiccated coconut and seeds into your biggest bowl and mix nicely.

3. Put the honey, butter and ground cinnamon into a small saucepan and warm over a gentle heat until the butter is just melted. Pour onto the dry ingredients and mix well.

4. Divide the granola mix between the lined baking trays and spread evenly, pressing down gently to compact it a little. Put the first tray in the oven and bake for 10 minutes. Take out the tray, mix the granola well, then press it down again (this helps it to form into lumps) and return it to the oven. Bake for a further 5 minutes before removing from the oven. Allow the granola to cool completely on the tray before you stir or move it. Repeat with the other tray.

5. Store the cooled granola in an airtight container or Ziplock bag and use within a month.

Vanilla yoghurt: Put 300g full-fat Greek yoghurt into a bowl. Split a vanilla pod, scrape out the seeds and stir them through the yoghurt, with ½ tsp caster sugar or 1 tsp runny honey. Cover and place in the fridge for 30 minutes or, even better, overnight, to allow the vanilla to infuse. *Makes enough for 4 servings*

BREAKFAST LASSI

Lassis are a very common drink in India, although, admittedly, not often seen at breakfast. The classic flavour choice is sweet or salted. In the Punjab, you can enjoy a full-fat milk yoghurt lassi – served in a big glass and topped up with freshly churned butter. It's unsurprisingly rich, and lovely and frothy when served over crushed ice.

This breakfast lassi is not dissimilar to a smoothie, with plenty of bananas and oats. For more lassi recipes see page 140.

SERVES 2

~

1 very ripe banana, peeled

100ml coconut milk

140g full-fat Greek yoghurt

50ml mango purée (fresh or tinned)

2 tsp steel-cut oats

3 tsp runny honey

A large pinch of cumin seeds

A pinch of fine sea salt

4 ice cubes

1. Put all of the ingredients into a blender, add 160ml water and blitz until completely smooth.

2. Pour into glasses and serve, with straws.

ORANGE & STAR ANISE MARMALADE

Star anise lends a beautiful smokiness to this easy marmalade, a pleasant surprise in amongst the familiar flavours of sweet orange and bitter rind. As it simmers, your home will be filled with the delicious aromas of star anise and citrus fruit – it's worth making it just for that.

MAKES ABOUT 450g

~

3–4 large oranges

4 star anise

225g preserving sugar

25ml lemon juice

1. Put a couple of small plates into the fridge to chill; these are for testing the setting point of your marmalade.

2. Roll the oranges around a little; this will help you juice them when they are peeled.

3. Using a standard vegetable peeler, cut the peel from the oranges (so you take some of the white pith with the rind); you will need 125g. Slice the peel into thin slivers, about 3cm long.

4. Squeeze the juice from the oranges into a measuring jug; you need 225ml juice.

5. Using a pestle and mortar, bash the star anise a little, so that some of the "points" fall off the "stars".

6. Place the orange peel slivers, 225ml orange juice and the star anise in a medium saucepan and top up with water so that the liquid comes 2cm above the peel. You need a pan large enough to accommodate the sugar (when it is added later) with room to boil.

7. Place the pan over a high heat, bring to the boil, then turn the heat down low and let the orange pieces simmer and soften for 45 minutes, until they are quite tender. Add a little more water or orange juice if the liquid goes below the level of the orange pieces.

8. Add the sugar and lemon juice, bring back to the boil and simmer until setting point is reached. To test this, take a plate from the fridge and dollop a teaspoonful onto it. Let it sit for a few seconds, then run your finger across the surface; if it ripples and feels gel-like, your marmalade is ready. If it's not quite there yet, simmer for a while longer, and use the second plate to test.

9. Pot into a warm sterilised jar while still hot, wipe the lip of the jar to ensure it is clean and then secure the lid. Store the marmalade in a cool, dark place and it will keep for up to 6 months.

PINEAPPLE & PINK PEPPERCORN JAM

The sweetness and tang of pineapple is enlivened by a mild, peppery kick. If you are a fan of tropical fruits, you must try this winning combination. (For another pineapple-pepper recipe, see page 312.)

MAKES ABOUT 800g

~

600g pineapple flesh (soft flesh only, exclude the hard core)

5g pink peppercorns

3g citric acid

500g jam sugar

70ml lemon juice

1. Put a couple of small plates into the fridge to chill; these are for testing the setting point of your jam.

2. Cut the pineapple flesh into 1–2cm chunks and place in a large non-reactive saucepan, along with the pink peppercorns and citric acid. Pour on enough water to just cover the pineapple. You need a pan large enough to accommodate the sugar (when it is added later) with room to boil.

3. Bring to the boil and then immediately turn down the heat and simmer until the pineapple is very soft; this will take about 1 hour.

4. Add the sugar and lemon juice, bring back to the boil and simmer until setting point is reached. To test this, take one of the plates from the fridge. Dollop a teaspoonful onto the plate, let it sit for a few seconds, then run your finger across the surface; if it ripples and feels gel-like, your jam is ready. If it's not quite there yet, simmer the jam for a while longer, and use the second plate to test.

5. Pot into a warm sterilised jar while still hot, wipe the lip of the jar to ensure it is clean and then secure the lid. Store the jam in a cool, dark place and it will keep for up to 6 months.

Illustrated on page 57

TOMATO-CHILLI JAM

Sweet, sharp and spicy. This is very easy to make, and gets along well with most breakfast dishes. It is also the signature sauce in our bacon naan rolls (page 47). It relies on good, ripe, flavoursome tomatoes. If they are in season, use fresh ones; if not, good-quality tinned tomatoes are a better option.

MAKES ABOUT 800g

~

800g tomatoes, roughly chopped if fresh; including the juice if tinned

60g fresh root ginger, finely chopped

15g garlic (3–4 cloves), finely chopped

8g green chillies (2–3), finely chopped

125ml rice vinegar

300g granulated sugar

1. Blitz the tomatoes using a jug or stick blender, in batches if necessary, until you have a coarse purée. Add all of the remaining ingredients except the sugar, and blend until well combined.

2. Pour the blended mix into a non-reactive cooking pot and add the sugar. Bring to a gentle simmer and cook over a low heat until reduced to a thick consistency; this should take about 30 minutes.

3. Pot into a warm sterilised jar while still hot, wipe the lip of the jar to ensure it is clean and then secure the lid. Store in a cool, dark place and the tomato-chilli jam will keep for up to 6 months. Once opened, keep refrigerated and use within a month.

Illustrated on page 46

YAZDANI

"Stroll unhurriedly through the narrow shaded lanes of Fort to
Cawasji Patel Street. Pause outside to admire the building, which is
exotic and beautiful. The restaurant occupies a former Japanese bank
building dating from around the First World War."

MID-MORNING SNACKS

"10 o'clock"

MID-MORNING SNACKS
AT YAZDANI, AND THE GREAT BOMBAY
COTTON BUBBLE

YOUR NEXT WALK will take you into the historical area known as Fort. Bombay was once protected by the walls of this fort; within them, it grew from a sleepy settlement into a thriving port city. However, in 1864 (in the midst of a raging cotton boom, about which more later) the city's Governor, Sir Henry Bartle Frere, tore down the ramparts, judging that space was desperately needed and that the city was now safe from passing marauders. The name, Fort, still remains.

Stroll unhurriedly through the narrow shaded lanes to Yazdani Restaurant & Bakery on Cawasji Patel Street. Pause outside to admire the building, which is exotic and beautiful. The restaurant occupies a former Japanese bank building dating from around the First World War. Note the many and varied signs and chalkboards. Some list the baked goods that daily draw hungry patrons from across the city. Others are marked with deliciously pithy statements such as "toast is ready" or "eat fresh ginger biscuits – get rid of your cough".

Now step up and in. Your warm welcome will be a gentle slap of heat. Thanks to the bakery's wood-fired ovens, which are enthusiastically stoked by hard-working young men in vests, it is usually even warmer inside the café than out. It is time for a champion mid-morning snack. You will find champions aplenty on the walls of the iconic bakery, proudly flexing their muscles, biceps threatening to bust out of the frames that hold their faded photographs. Many of the Irani restaurateurs were body-builders, pumping their iron in gyms across the city, like Markers in Mazgaon and Talwalkars at Charni Road. They beefed up their bodies on Viking double sets and leg-press machines until they were championship ready. Some restaurateurs had belted twelve titles by the age of twenty.

Yazdani's proprietor, Mr Zend M. Zend, was known as "Knock-out Zend". His prowess even earned him a place at the prestigious St. Xavier's College. He is no longer a prize fighter, but still has plenty of fighting spirit. Depending on the day, and whether or not he takes a shine to you, his manner can be jovial or intimidatingly stern. He quite often orders for customers without asking them what they might actually want. It's probably easier that way.

Ease yourself into one of the Formica-topped booth tables. You might find yourself jostling with local gents for a spot, inelegantly wedged in and forced to chat. Or you might enjoy a moment of serenity beneath the whirring fans. Despite the heat, you must order (or allow yourself to be ordered, if Knock-out Zend has form) a piping hot cup of chai, and brun maska to dunk into it. The simplest, most delicious of Bombay things: a crunchy, slightly crumbly crust encasing soft white bread, cut in half, given a decent slice of Amul butter, folded back together and cut into fingers just narrow enough to fit into your dainty cup. Dip the *brun* into the sweet chai, allow the butter to melt slightly and put in your mouth for immediate, simple and true delight. (You can also order the softer *bun* as well as *brun* but at Yazdani, the *brun* is the true champion.)

The heat may now be getting to you. Dab perspiration from your brow and wipe crumbs from your lips with one of the little squares of paper that serve inadequately as napkins. Say your goodbyes to Mr Zend, and step out to explore the Fort area, starting in nearby Horniman Circle.

Here you will see India's first Starbucks, which opened in 2012. If you're feeling hot and Mr Zend has left you in the mood for some cool Western indifference and a skinny iced caramel latte, then by all means pop in for a few minutes to enjoy the air conditioning. It's a flagship branch, and quite a nice one as they go. Naturally, the coffee chain from far-away Seattle will spread from Horniman Circle across the city like a rash. Globalisation is not new, of course. Decisions in faraway America have been shaping Bombay for years.

"Yazdani's proprietor, Mr Zend M. Zend, was known as 'Knock-out Zend'. He is no longer a prize fighter, but still has plenty of fighting spirit."

The quiet and pleasant garden sanctuary of Horniman Circle began life as the Bombay Green. In the 1850s, under the generous shade of the banyan trees which still stand today, the canny Indian cotton merchants used to conduct their daily trades. One day in 1855, twenty-two of them decided to contribute a rupee each and thus began the Native Share and Stock Brokers' Association which eventually became the great Bombay Stock Exchange, now located a stone's throw away on Dalal Street. The might and power of commercial Bombay has its roots right here amongst these trees.

Perhaps most aggressive amongst these twenty-two aggressive seekers of profit, was the infamous Premchund Roychund, who became known as the Cotton King. In 1861, in Charleston Bay, South Carolina, troops belonging to the Confederacy decided to open fire on the federal garrison at Fort Sumter. President Lincoln called on the Union militia to suppress the insurrection and thus began both the Civil War in America and the roaring financial exuberance of Bombay. Supplies of cotton from the Southern slave states to Britain's mills were disrupted and the panicked mill owners of Lancashire looked quickly eastwards to India and to the cotton merchants, right here in Bombay Green.

Cotton prices jumped from five pence to twenty-four pence per pound. Trade was frantically transacted. Bombay was quickly awash with cash beyond anyone's imagination. In turn the price of everything else increased: food, wages, rents and of course land. Speculation abounded, gripping rich and poor alike. While the poor were ripping the stuffing from their mattresses, rich merchants were trying to find a place to reinvest all of their sudden profit.

Bartle Frere was appointed governor of this increasingly crowded city in 1862 and decided to open up the activity of land reclamation from the sea to private interests. Accordingly, reclamation companies became the recipients of a large portion of the city's cotton fortunes via finance companies and banks, all of whom were controlled by the same people. Share mania ensued and inevitably, as you might expect from any decent speculative bubble, share prices became completely untethered from company profits.

In the middle of this all, blowing the bubble even bigger, was the ingenious Premchund Roychund. He established the Back Bay Reclamation Co. (amongst plenty of other ventures), and found novel and innovative ways to make himself and

1 Yazdani Restaurant & Bakery
2 Many and varied signs and chalkboards, listing Yazdani's wares
3 Mr Zend M. Zend, Yazdani's spirited proprietor
4 The garden sanctuary of Horniman Circle
5 The Cotton King, Premchund Roychund
6 View of Horniman Circle

other investors giddy with wealth, at least on paper. He was promoter and shareholder of various banks and controlled the Bank of Bombay. His banks would lend to investors, who in turn would buy shares in financial companies that he was promoting, which in turn would float other land reclamation companies, with investors in these borrowing money secured against the original shares. And so forth. The shares changed hands at ever more outlandish premiums.

On Palm Sunday in 1865, the American Civil War ended, cotton prices tumbled and the Bombay markets crashed, taking many with it. Thousands were bankrupted, rich and poor, including the city's prominent wealthy businessmen, and, of course, Roychund himself. The biggest cotton bull of all became a reviled man.

7

8

> ## "Shamil has a vivid memory of going to Jallianwalla Bagh with his grandparents as a child in 1978; he touched the bullet holes in the walled garden, and later had recurrent nightmares about General Dyer."

The formal gardens that you are now in were created in 1872, when Bombay Green became Elphinstone Circle, named after Lord Elphinstone, the Governor before Bartle Frere. However, after Independence the Circle was renamed in honour of Benjamin Horniman, the upstanding British editor of the *Bombay Chronicle*, which had its offices right here (in the red building on the same corner as Starbucks).

In 1919 General Dyer commanded his troops to open fire on peacefully protesting Indian civilians in Jallianwalla Bagh in Amritsar. They fired for ten minutes and only stopped when their ammunition had run out, murdering perhaps around a thousand men, women and children. Horniman bravely defied British censorship of the event by smuggling photographs to the *Daily Herald* in Britain, which shocked public opinion and helped turn it against Dyer. (Shamil has a vivid memory of going to Jallianwalla Bagh with his grandparents as a child in 1978; he touched

the bullet holes in the walled garden, and later had recurrent nightmares about General Dyer.)

Horniman was promptly deported for his efforts, although he made his way back to India a few years later. He resumed his previous position, and later went on to help start the first Indian tabloid, *Blitz*, which featured the early work of the political cartoonist R. K. Laxman, and famously covered the scandalous Nanavati affair (more on this later).

Look now to the Town Hall, the enormous neo-classical building that occupies the eastern flank of the circle, the opposite side from where you entered. This imposing structure was built in 1833, not least to show off the might of British colonial power. To the average impoverished nineteenth-century Bombayite, it must have seemed an alien palace beyond the realms of imagination.

Walk in and climb the stairs to say *sehbji* (a respectful hello in Parsi Gujarati) to the statue of Sir Jamsetjee Jejeebhoy at the top of the staircase, and *namaskar* to the statue of Jugonnath Sunkersett at the landing level. Jejeebhoy and Sunkersett were two of Bombay's leading *sethias*, or wealthy merchant-princes of the nineteenth century. They were smart, entrepreneurial and, unusually for natives in a colony, they held the city's commercial power in their hands. Our old friend Premchund Roychund was, of course, another *sethia*. Many of them first made their fortunes by trading opium with China, which gave them and their families the capital to invest in other things (including cotton).

9

10

7   The original offices of the *Bombay Chronicle*
8   The Town Hall, which also houses the
    Asiatic Society
9   Flora Fountain in the early 1900s
10 A statue of Bombay *sethia*, Jugonnath Sunkersett

It can be fairly asserted that Bombay was partly built on drug money. At any rate, the sheer amount of wealth that the *sethias* generated meant that they were instrumental in turning Bombay into the centre of commerce that it remains today. Very fortunately for the population of the city, the *sethias* shared their gains. They were generous philanthropists who funded the construction of hospitals, schools and museums; homes for sick or stray animals; drinking fountains; and countless other charitable ventures. Bombay owes a great deal of its public infrastructure to their gifts, and their names punctuate the older parts of the city.

On the main floor of the Town Hall you will find a marble statue of Bartle Frere, Governor of Bombay from 1862 to 1867. In addition to tearing down the Fort walls and privatising land reclamation, Bartle Frere had a comprehensive vision for Bombay as a modern city. He saw himself as a master planner, civic improver and empire builder. He wanted to create an indigenous school of architecture "as extensive and as distinct as the pure Hindu and Mahometan schools of former days". This intended Anglo-Indian style, modelled on Gothic revival forms but adopted to Indian conditions using Indian materials

and craftsmen, did not travel much across the country, but as you will see it was extremely successful in Bombay – not least as an exercise in self-congratulation by the British Raj. (After Bartle Frere left Bombay, he went on to have a controversial posting as High Commissioner in southern Africa, culminating in him being recalled to London for acting recklessly.)

In fact, for the last part of this walk, you should stroll down one of Bombay's most grand vistas. Head back west again, past Starbucks and to Flora Fountain. The fountain was built in 1864 as part of Bartle Frere's works, and was officially called the Frere Fountain. Yet the name never stuck and it was always known as Flora Fountain,

11 Bombay University
Convocation Hall
12 Gothic spires of the Rajabai
Clock Tower
13 Looking across the Oval Maidan,
host to many cricket games

after the Roman goddess of flowers and spring who presides over it. Go straight across the busy junction and you will come to the grand Oval Maidan. (You may recall that on the other side are a line of Bombay's finest Art Deco buildings.) The Maidan often hosts cricket games, which are lovely to watch on an idle afternoon.

Walk down the triumphal palm-fringed stretch of imposing Gothic revival buildings, including the Bombay High Court and University of Mumbai. This is a particularly enjoyable walk in the very late evening, when the absence of traffic, the floodlit Gothic buildings and the warm evening breeze through the palm trees combine to create delightful serenity. (Do look up Christopher London's very good book, *Bombay Gothic*.)

We'll end by returning to the story of the Cotton King. Next to the University Convocation Hall you will see the Gothic spires of the tall Rajabai Clock Tower, which was built in 1878. The clock tower was designed by the famous English architect Sir Gilbert Scott (who apparently had Big Ben in mind) and funded by none other than Premchund Roychund. Roychund named the tower after his mother, who was a strict Jain, and was beginning to lose her sight. Apparently, the evening toll of the bell helped her to observe her religious tradition of eating before sundown.

Today Roychund is just as well known in the city for being a dutiful son and building the tower for his mother as he is for his creative exploitation of the Bombay cotton boom.

Unverwechselbar: Pfister Sonne

der Geschmack aus
unseren Altdeutschen Steinbacköfen

URBAN HERITAGE AWARD - 2007

YAZDANI BAKERY

EARLY 20TH CENT. BUILDING
CAWASJI PATEL STREET, FORT

INDIAN HERITAGE SOCIETY - MUMBAI

SMOKEFREE

SMOKING HERE IS AN OFFENCE
M.C.G.M.

BRUN
BUN 8
MASKA
RS - 40/each

ABOVE: "Cutting chai" (a half cup of chai) from a chai-walla is just enough to refresh your senses

RIGHT: Yazdani Restaurant & Bakery is housed in a former Japanese bank

BRUN MASKA
BUN MASKA
EGG PUFF
MAVA PUFF
VEG PUFF
CARROT CAKE
MAVA CAKE
BREAD PUDDING
FIERY GINGER
BISCUIT

FIERY

ABOVE: A Parsi body-builder flexes his muscles on the walls in Yazdani

LEFT: Yazdani is known for its baked goods, delightful chai and heavily buttered brun maska

BUN (& BRUN) MASKA

Most Irani cafés started out as small tea-shops and bakeries, and it's still very common for them to sell baked goods. *Bun* and *brun* are staples of Irani cafés, but they're very difficult to make at home in a domestic oven. In Bombay *bun* is a soft white roll whereas its close cousin, *brun*, has a crunchy, crumbly outer shell, which soaks up chai very nicely. (*Maska* is the butter within.)

The closest thing that you can easily find will be a good-quality brioche roll for *bun* or a crusty white roll for *brun*. Simply slice the bread roll in half (warming it gently in the oven first, if you like) and place a thick slice of fridge-cold butter inside. Then dunk it into your spicy chai and allow the butter to melt slightly and the bread to become soggy.

Many Irani cafés will serve their bun with a thick, sweet jam. Koolar & Co. does a delicious variation with butter, cheese and honey. You can approximate this with the addition of sliced havarti cheese and a drizzle of clear honey.

KEEMA PUFFS

In Bombay a puff is a tasty little pastry parcel, stuffed with minced lamb keema, spiced vegetables or another first-rate filling, not unlike a small pasty. Sassanian in Dhobi Talao serves the best ones with mutton, chicken and vegetable variations.

These keema puffs will be very good with a little tamarind chutney (page 377) or even chilli chutney (page 378), but in Bombay you would eat them with good old tomato ketchup.

Make sure the filling is completely cold before you assemble the puffs, otherwise the pastry will be difficult to handle.

MAKES 12

~

1 sheet of ready-made puff pastry (320g), about 35 x 23cm

Flour, for dusting

1 egg, beaten with 1½ tsp milk (eggwash)

FOR THE LAMB FILLING

½ quantity lamb keema (page 109)

15g frozen peas

½ tsp fine sea salt

3 spring onions, finely chopped

1 green chilli, finely chopped

1 tbsp chopped coriander leaves

1. Take the pastry out of the fridge, remove any outer packaging and allow around 20 minutes for it to come to room temperature before using.

2. Heat the oven to 210°C/Fan 190°C/Gas 6–7 and line a large baking sheet with baking parchment.

3. For the filling, tip the lamb keema into a large bowl. Put the frozen peas into a small bowl, pour on enough boiling water to cover and leave for 2 minutes, then drain and add to the keema, with the salt, spring onions, chilli and coriander. Mix nicely and set to one side.

4. Unroll the pastry and cut in half (to create two squarish rectangles rather than two long strips). Lay one of the pieces on a lightly floured surface. Using a floured rolling pin, roll the pastry a little thinner, so that it is about 1cm longer and wider. Cut 6 even squares.

5. Place a heaped teaspoonful of filling towards one corner of a square, leaving a clear margin around the edge. Brush the pastry edges with eggwash. Fold the pastry over to form a triangular parcel enclosing the filling, then gently crimp the edges to seal. Repeat with the remaining pastry squares, then with the other half of the pastry sheet. Transfer to the lined baking sheet, leaving 2–3cm space between the puffs.

6. Brush the pastry generously with egg wash, then bake in the oven for 20 minutes, or until the pastry is puffed and golden brown, and the filling is piping hot.

Variation

Vegetable puffs: For the filling, mix ½ quantity vada pau potato mix (page 174) with 1½ tbsp chopped coriander leaves and 50g frozen peas, blanched in boiling water (as above) for 2 minutes and drained. Cut the pastry into squares and assemble and bake the puffs as above.

CHEESE & MASALA STICKS

Paris Bakery serves an excellent version of these little cheese-and-pastry twirls. They are just right for dipping into hot masala chai, and an easy snack to make: you only need ready-made puff pastry and a handful of store-cupboard ingredients.

The cinnamon sugar sticks are a lovely sweet variation (see below). You probably already have the ingredients to hand, so we recommend you make both, to satisfy sweet and savoury tastes.

MAKES 16–20

~

1 sheet of ready-made puff pastry (320g), about 35 x 23cm

Flour, for dusting

1 egg white, beaten

FOR THE TOPPING

1¼–1½ tsp chaat masala

40g mature Cheddar, finely grated

4 tsp chopped coriander leaves

1. Take the pastry out of the fridge, remove any packaging and allow around 20 minutes for it to come to room temperature before using.

2. Heat the oven to 210°C/Fan 190°C/Gas 6–7 and line a large baking sheet with baking parchment.

3. Unroll the pastry and cut in half horizontally (to create two short rectangles rather than two long strips). Take one piece of pastry and lay it flat. Slice into long strips, 1.5–2cm wide, leaving the strips where they are as you go (a floured pizza slicer is best for this). You should be able to get 8–10 strips.

4. Brush the pastry with egg white, then dust lightly with chaat masala and sprinkle over the cheese and chopped coriander (you might find it easiest to microplane the cheese directly onto the pastry). Lightly run a rolling pin over the surface to secure the cheese and coriander, then dust with a little more chaat masala for luck.

5. Trying not to dislodge the topping, lift a pastry strip by both ends, twist it around to create nice twirls in the pastry, then lay it on the lined baking sheet and give it a light press to make it stay in place. Repeat with the rest of the strips, then with the other half of the pastry sheet.

6. Bake for 15–18 minutes, or until the pastry is puffed, golden and quite crisp. Place on a wire rack to cool. Serve the pastry twists once they have cooled, with plenty of chai.

Variation

Cinnamon sugar sticks: For the topping, mix 4 tsp white granulated sugar with 1 tsp ground cinnamon. Roll out the pastry and cut into strips as above. Sprinkle with the cinnamon sugar (there's no need to press it in with a rolling pin), then twist and bake as above.

KHARI

These buttery, flaky pastry treats are very simple, yet moreish. They're often referred to as biscuits, although they're truly not. Kyani & Co. is known to serve the best versions.

Even easier than the cheese and masala sticks on the previous page, kharis have a little more "puff" as they're not folded before baking. You can mix and match the toppings across the kharis and sticks.

MAKES ABOUT 26

~

1 sheet of ready-made puff pastry (320g), about 35 x 23cm

Flour, for dusting

1 egg white, beaten

FOR THE MASALA TOPPING

1 tsp fennel seeds

1 tsp coarsely ground black pepper

¼ tsp cumin seeds

1–1½ tsp flaky sea salt

1. Take the pastry out of the fridge, remove any packaging and allow around 20 minutes for it to come to room temperature.

2. Heat the oven to 210°C/Fan 190°C/Gas 6–7 and line two large baking sheets with baking parchment.

3. Unroll the pastry and cut in half to create two long bands, about 11.5cm wide. Trim to neaten, if necessary.

4. Cut each piece of pastry into strips, about 11 x 2.5cm, leaving them where they are as you go (a floured pizza slicer is best for this). Brush the pastry with egg white and sprinkle over the masala spices and salt, ensuring you get even coverage with each ingredient.

5. Press the masala spices in very lightly with your fingers, then transfer the pastry rectangles to the baking sheets, leaving about 2cm in between each one. Bake for 15–18 minutes, or until the pastry is puffed, golden and quite crisp.

6. Allow the kharis to cool on a wire rack before serving.

Variation

Chilli-topped khari: In place of the masala topping, use 1–1½ tsp deggi mirch chilli powder and 1–1½ tsp flaky sea salt.

JEERA BISCUITS

These slightly sweet, slightly savoury, pleasantly short and delightfully buttery biscuits are flecked with *jeera* (cumin seeds). They are sold in chai shops all over Bombay for a few rupees each. Such temptation!

MAKES 10–12

~

75g unsalted butter, softened at room temperature

25g caster sugar

100g plain flour

½ tsp fine sea salt

1 tsp cumin seeds

1 tsp baking powder

1. Tip the butter and sugar into a large bowl and beat until light and fluffy.

2. Mix the flour, salt, cumin seeds and baking powder together, then tip into the creamed butter and sugar mixture. Mix to combine, gently bringing the dough together without overworking it. Form into a log shape, about 5cm in diameter, and wrap in cling film. Place in the fridge for 30 minutes.

3. Heat the oven to 200°C/Fan 180°C/Gas 6. Line a large baking sheet with baking parchment.

4. Remove the dough from the fridge, slice into discs, about 7–8mm thick, and lay on the lined baking sheet. Bake for 15–18 minutes, or until golden brown and cooked through.

5. Transfer the biscuits to a wire rack and leave to cool. They will keep in an airtight container for up to 2 days.

NANKHATAI

A buttery biscuit with a slightly savoury edge from the different flours, nankhatai is not unlike a shortbread. Pay a visit to Danesh at Paris Bakery for the best examples – packed with butter, sweet and crumbly.

Eaten still warm, these biscuits have a pleasant chewiness to them, becoming crumblier when left to cool completely.

MAKES 15

~

100g unsalted butter, softened at room temperature

100g granulated sugar

60g plain flour

60g chickpea (gram) flour

60g fine semolina

¾ tsp bicarbonate of soda

20g sunflower seeds or pistachio nuts

1. Heat the oven to 190°C/Fan 170°C/Gas 5. Line a baking tray with baking parchment.

2. Put the butter into a large bowl. Add the sugar and beat for 3 minutes, until light, smooth and creamy.

3. Add the flours, semolina and bicarbonate of soda and mix to combine, bringing the mixture together to form a dough; take care not to overwork it.

4. Divide the dough into 25g balls. Place each ball on the lined baking sheet and flatten very slightly, with a feather-light press of the fingers. Scatter a few sunflower seeds or pistachio nuts on top of each one, pressing them in lightly.

5. Bake for 18–20 minutes, rotating the tray halfway through cooking. The biscuits should be golden brown and cooked through.

6. Leave the biscuits on the tray for 10 minutes after baking to firm up, then transfer them to a wire rack to cool completely. They will keep in an airtight container for up to 2 days.

MASALA CHAI

There are many varieties of chai. The kind we make at Dishoom is the sort of spicy, sweet chai you will find at Bombay's innumerable *tapris* (street stalls), normally poured with great dexterity and skill from arm's length into a small, stout glass.

The powerful concoction of milk, sugar and caffeine is what keeps the city running. Were the tea supply suddenly to dry up, it's entirely possible that Bombay would simply grind to a halt. (It was rumoured in Bombay in the 1890s that Iranis were putting opium in their chai, such was its addictive nature. There was a fearsome activist called Sooderbai Powar, who agitated greatly against this alleged practice. Of course, the Iranis were far too astute to sell opium at the price of chai.)

Chai is also a staple of all Indian homes. It reminds Shamil of leisurely Sunday mornings with family. His father and grandfather used to love their chai. His aunt makes it with a few leaves of mint and a little lemongrass, which is how Parsis tend to brew it. Feel free to experiment, of course. (By the way, chai simply means "tea". For this reason you must never say "chai tea".)

SERVES 4

~

2 tbsp loose Assam or Darjeeling tea, or 3 English breakfast teabags

12 slices of fresh root ginger

1½ tsp black peppercorns

12 cardamom pods

2 cinnamon sticks

5 cloves

50g granulated white sugar

500ml whole milk

1. Put the tea, ginger and spices into a saucepan, pour on 1 litre boiling water and bring to the boil. Lower the heat and simmer until you can smell the spices, about 10 minutes.

2. Add the sugar and milk, turn up the heat and bring to the boil. Allow 10 minutes, stirring occasionally. (A skin will form, but this is strained off at the end.) Taste to see if the chai is to your liking; boil a little more if you wish for a stronger flavour. Patience will be rewarded!

3. Strain, discard the solids, and serve immediately.

Some of the many ways to enjoy chai

Irani chai: Uses condensed milk. Sweet and milky, it is best for dunking buttered bread and baked goods into.

Badshahi chai: A portion fit for a king, served in a much larger glass and using a higher proportion of milk.

Doodhpati chai: No water, just milk.

Noon chai: With an added pinch of salt.

Kali chai: Black (no milk).

Kitchen chai: Very strong, very sweet (drunk by the bucket-load by Dishoom chefs).

Khada chamuch: So sweet that the spoon stands up in the cup.

BRITANNIA & CO.

"This Irani restaurant is a lovely piece of vintage Bombay. It occupies
the ground floor of an elegant building, which dates from the early 1920s
and was designed by the Scottish architect George Wittet."

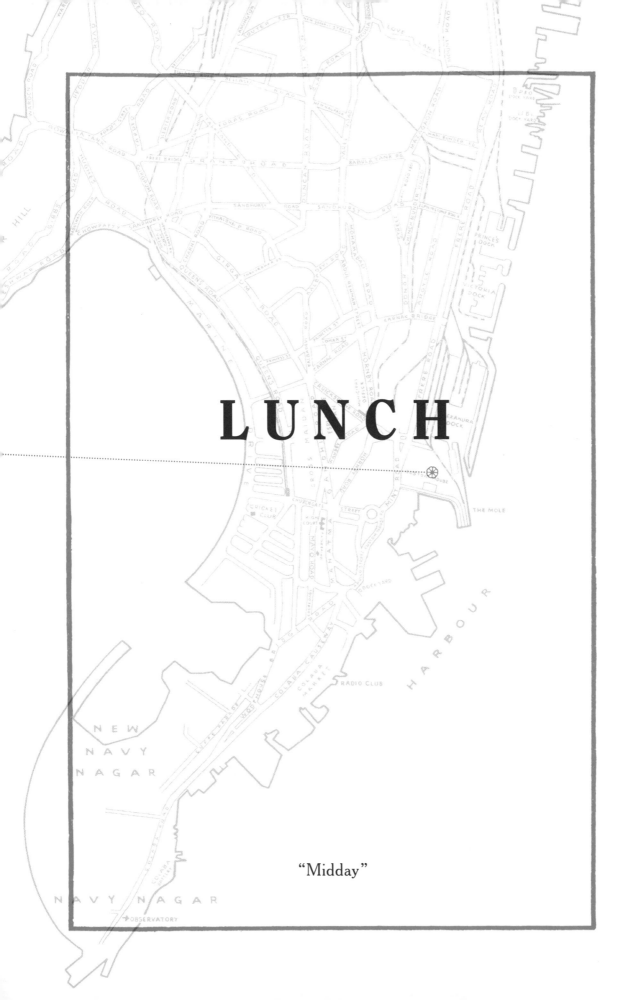

LUNCH

"Midday"

LUNCH AT BRITANNIA, THEN A WANDER AROUND BALLARD ESTATE, A BEAUTIFUL AND SLEEPY BACKWATER

BRITANNIA & CO. is a lovely piece of vintage Bombay. It occupies the ground floor of an elegant building, which dates from the early 1920s and was designed by the Scottish architect George Wittet. He also designed the Gateway of India, the imposing triumphal arch at Apollo Bunder in the Indo-Saracenic style, which was built to commemorate the (presumably triumphal) visit of King George V to this part of his empire in 1911. Unfortunately for King George, he only saw the rather less exciting small cardboard version of it, since the actual building was not completed until 1924.

Boman Kohinoor is the owner of Britannia & Co., and a man of legendary kindness. He shares his name with the famous diamond taken from India by the British to crown Queen Victoria the Empress of India. Certainly, don't leave Britannia without speaking to Mr Kohinoor. Many a conversation with him might go this way: "How old do you think I am?" he will ask. You might study him and perhaps feel slightly uncomfortable venturing a guess (he's clearly very old indeed). In turn, he will peer back at you through his milk-bottle-bottom thick glasses, with a hint of a smile about his lips. He gives you a clue. "I'm as old as this place." Eventually he relents: "I was born in 1923. The same year that Britannia opened."

He may also go on to tell you how his family came from the Yazd region in Iran in the early 1920s fleeing persecution, or how the British army requisitioned his restaurant in the Second World War, or how he went back to Iran in 1969 before returning to Bombay in 1977. It's hard to separate Britannia, the restaurant, from Mr Kohinoor, the man. They are the same thing.

Under Mr Kohinoor's watchful eye, Britannia is, in spite of (or perhaps because of) its graceful dilapidation, one of the loveliest of the surviving Irani cafés. Fans turn slowly under its high ceilings. Bentwood chairs from Europe creak pleasantly. Exposed wiring droops across flaking blue-green walls on which hang faded sepia portraits and an elegant clock. Smartly dressed waiters (moustachio'd and bow-tied) serve local office workers, lunching ladies and curious tourists with equal aplomb. Mr Kohinoor himself will take your order, just as he always has, his joy in serving you delicious food delightfully apparent.

You might smile at the life-size cardboard cut-outs of Prince William and Kate, who watch over the room without a trace of irony from their balcony vantage point. If you comment on them (and most likely even if you don't) Mr Kohinoor will proudly show you his collection of laminated letters from the Queen – well-thumbed evidence of his enduring fondness for the British monarchy.

Amongst the various signs on the exterior of the café ("Exotic Parsi and Iranian cuisine"; "Special Veg & Non-veg Foods"), there is one which sets out Britannia's motto: "There is no love greater than the love of eating." This (slightly paraphrased) Bernard Shaw maxim is set out around a logo of a rooster. It is most certainly true that at Britannia you will love to eat.

And what should you eat for lunch? (Britannia doesn't open in the mornings or evenings, except on Saturdays.) Your meal should involve a fragrant chicken berry pulao – a recipe created by Mr Kohinoor's wife when the family returned from Iran (presumably having packed the barberries required in the recipe). Also order the excellent Parsi speciality *salli boti* (a rich lamb curry topped with salli crisp-chips), which is typically mopped up with plenty of fresh chapati. You could also sample a local favourite, the confusingly named "Bombay duck" – not bird or beast, but a small, bony and slightly gelatinous, deep-fried fish. Admittedly this is an acquired taste. Dessert must be crème caramel and *mishti doi* (a Bengali-style

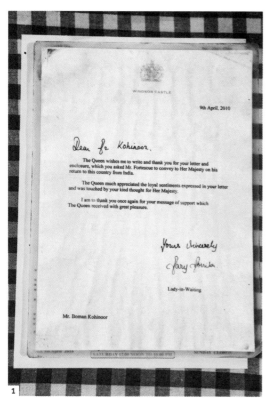

> "Under Mr Kohinoor's watchful eye, Britannia is, in spite of (or perhaps because of) its graceful dilapidation, one of the loveliest of the surviving Irani cafés."

set yoghurt-curd). And to drink? Tangy Sosyo, Pallonji's Parsi raspberry or fiery ginger soda (not for the faint of heart), or a light and refreshing fresh lime soda. "Nice and sweet, to beat the Bombay heat," as Mr Kohinoor likes to say.

Hunger sated, thirst slaked, belt loosened a couple of notches, you take your leave of Mr Kohinoor and Britannia. It is perfectly normal to already be planning to return. Of course, the great man is old enough that when you next return he might not be here. We will shed many tears when he eventually does pass. However, his delight in serving his customers is so tangible that when he does breathe his last he will surely look back over his life of loving service with joy and pride.

It may be high noon, but it is also high time to walk off that third chapati. If you have been paying attention, you might already be feeling intrigued by Ballard Estate's dreamy sleepiness, here in the middle of the crowded chaos of Bombay. Step out into the heat of the day and turn to your right, directly onto Sprott Road.

Ballard Estate was once just salty water. Between 1914 and 1918 (undeterred by momentous events in Europe) the Bombay Port Trust completed the reclamation of twenty-two acres from the sea. Sand and rock excavated for

1 Lovingly preserved correspondence from Queen Elizabeth II

2 Britannia, retaining much of its original character

3 Mr Boman Kohinoor, nonagenarian owner of Britannia

4 Chicken berry pulao, made to the recipe of the late Mrs Kohinoor

5 Life-size cardboard cut-outs of the Duke and Duchess of Cambridge

6 Smartly dressed and bow-tied Britannia waiter, Moosa

7 Elaborate ironwork above the doors of Britannia

the nearby Alexandra (now Indira) Dock were marshalled to make land. The new area was named in honour of Colonel Ballard, the first President of the Bombay Port Trust. When it was completed in 1918, the district would house the offices of the biggest and most successful shipping and commercial firms.

As you walk, you will see wide and leafy streets of handsome buildings, all built in the decade or two after the reclamation was completed. The streets running north to south were named after influential members of the Bombay Port Trust; from east to west, mere strides separate the coastal cities of Goa, Karwar, Mangalore, Cochin and Calicut. These streets are named for the busy daily trade that was taking place between these cities and the port of Bombay. The boats from each destination used to dock at the ends of the respective streets.

Today, the commanding heights of commerce and administration have moved elsewhere. Gradually the area has become a calm oasis, orderly tree-lined streets pleasantly ventilated by the breeze from the Arabian Sea. Once, there was a busy train station at Ballard Pier and boats that carried passengers up and down the west coast docked nearby. But the station closed in 1944 and the boats have moved elsewhere. The roads end abruptly at the high walls of the dockyards, forcing you to turn left, right, or back on yourself.

With Britannia behind you, amble up Sprott Road past Vakil House, a former printing press, and one of the few industrial buildings in this otherwise white-collar domain. Pause at the

Kaiser-I-Hind (Emperor of India) building, which housed the Bombay newspaper of the same name founded by Framjee Cowasjee Mehta, a prominent Parsi citizen and Indian nationalist. The paper was first published in both English and Gujarati in 1882, only four years after the British passed the Censorship Act, which was intended to curtail the freedom of the Indian press and prevent criticism of British rule. Kaiser-I-Hind – published as it was by eminent Bombayites in a local language – did well, and eventually became an important platform for the fledgling Indian Congress Party.

To your right you will see an octagonal single-story Art Deco island, slightly out of place within Ballard Estate's swell of lofty Edwardian neo-classicism. This is the Karfule petrol pump, and without a doubt it is the most charming petrol pump that you will ever have the pleasure of visiting. It owes its lovely and abiding eccentricity to its delightful and abiding owners, the Sequeira family, who have run the pump since its construction in 1938, and who have protected it rather doggedly over the years.

Be sure to visit and speak with the genial owner, Daniel, the grandson of the original owner. He might proudly explain the original features that he and his family have retained in defiance of

8 Decorated entrance to the Kaiser-I-Hind building
9 An assortment of papers from the Sequeira family archive
10 Karfule petrol pump's kindly owner, Daniel Sequeira

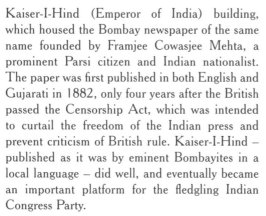

time (and, some would say, of logic). Admire the stylish terrazzo floor, the original Caltex signs and the elegant tower, which originally boasted a lovely Art Deco clock.

The Sequeiras' archive includes the original invoices from local architect G. B. Mhatre, who built the pump at a cost of 34,000 rupees, and documents indicating the selection of food served at the opening party on 3rd October 1938. The Sequeiras recently celebrated the petrol pump's eightieth birthday, recreating the menu and merriment of the original opening party.

ABOVE: Afshin Kohinoor, Mr Kohinoor's son

RIGHT: A selection of drinks available at Britannia

BRITANNIA & CO.

UNIQUE DRINKS

FRESH LIME SODA

ROSY RASPBERRY

SPICY GINGER

ICE CREAM SODA

N.A. BEER

CHOLE BHATURE

Take the humblest of ingredients: chickpeas, potatoes and, perhaps surprisingly, tea. Add spices, love and care, and you have *chole* – a simple and delicious vegetarian curry. It is best served with puffy bhature and raita, but plain boiled rice can replace the bread. It is also eaten for breakfast with puri (page 363).

The tea gives this dish a little welcome bitterness, from the tannins. You'll need to prepare the chickpeas at least 8 hours in advance in order to create a good, strong flavour. The trick is not to over-simmer the chickpeas or potato, otherwise they will release too much starch and thicken the sauce.

SERVES 2

~

400g tin chickpeas

3 English breakfast teabags

1 medium potato (120g), halved

35g tomato purée

1½ tsp chana masala

½ tsp ground cumin

¼ tsp fine sea salt

1 black cardamom pod

2 tbsp vegetable oil

1 bay leaf

1 cinnamon stick

75g onion-tomato masala (page 354)

¼ tsp garam masala (page 356)

1 tsp tamarind paste

1 tsp lime juice

FOR THE FRIED CHILLIES

1 tbsp vegetable oil

6 green chillies

A pinch of fine sea salt

TO SERVE

Red onion, diced

Coriander leaves, roughly torn

Ginger matchsticks

Lime wedges

Raita (page 124)

Bhature (page 369)

1. Tip the chickpeas and their liquid into a small saucepan and add an extra tinful of water. Place over a medium heat, add the teabags (don't let them burst) and bring to a gentle simmer. Cook for 5 minutes, then take off the heat. Cover and leave to stand for 8–24 hours.

2. Simmer the potato in a small pan of salted water until just tender. Drain and leave to cool.

3. Put the tomato purée, chana masala, cumin and salt into a small bowl and mix nicely; set aside. Using a pestle and mortar, give the cardamom pod a single, firm bash.

4. Warm a large saucepan over a medium-high heat and add the oil. Add the bay leaf, crushed cardamom pod and cinnamon stick to the pan and let them crackle for 1 minute, stirring often (be careful, it may spit a little).

5. Add the tomato purée mix, stir well for 1 minute, then turn the heat to low and add the onion-tomato masala. Sauté, stirring often, until you see the oil start to leave a paste around the edges, about 5–7 minutes.

6. Drain the chickpeas, reserving the cooking liquor; discard the teabags. Add the chickpeas to the saucepan along with 150ml of the liquor. Bring to a gentle simmer and add the garam masala, tamarind paste and lime juice. Simmer for 5 minutes, stirring regularly.

7. Dice the potato (into chickpea-sized pieces) and add to the pan. Stir gently, put the lid on and turn off the heat. Set aside to let the potato warm through.

8. For the fried chillies, warm the oil in a frying pan over a medium-high heat. Add the chillies and salt, and sauté for 2–3 minutes until soft and lightly charred.

9. Serve the chole in a deep bowl, topped with red onion, coriander and ginger, with the fried chillies, lime wedges and raita on the side, and bhature to scoop everything up.

RAJMA

This soothing and hearty dish of gently spiced kidney beans is a staple of the tiffin lunch-boxes that feed Bombay's white-collar workers, as part of the *dabba-walla* service. You'll see these white-capped gentlemen going about their deliveries all over Bombay. They find their way with unerring accuracy from Bombay's suburban homes to its offices, delivering around 150,000 home-cooked meals each day. The empty *dabbas* (containers) find their way home after lunch by the same service. Not all *dabba-wallas* can read, so they rely on a system of symbols, which makes it even more impressive that they almost never make a mistake. This is fortunate, since the *dabbas* convey food for different religious dietary requirements. (God forbid that a pure veg Hindu should receive the lovingly cooked lamb intended for a Muslim.)

The final garnish of fresh ginger, red onion, coriander and a squeeze of lime really makes this dish sing. Serve steamed rice and a bowl of raita (page 124) on the side.

SERVES 2–4

~

35ml vegetable oil

5g ginger paste (page 353)

5g garlic paste (page 353)

1 black cardamom pod

1 bay leaf

1 cinnamon stick

1 tsp ground cumin

¼ tsp deggi mirch chilli powder

15g tomato purée

1g fine sea salt

100g onion-tomato masala (page 354)

400g tin kidney beans

½ tsp garam masala (page 356)

50g tomatoes, chopped

A good handful of coriander leaves, chopped

3cm fresh root ginger, cut into matchsticks

25g butter

TO SERVE

Red onion, finely sliced

Ginger matchsticks

Coriander leaves, roughly torn

Lime wedges

1. Warm the oil in a medium saucepan over a medium heat. When hot, add the ginger and garlic pastes and sauté for 3–4 minutes, stirring almost constantly, until the garlic loses its raw smell.

2. Add the cardamom pod, bay leaf and cinnamon stick and cook for 1 minute. Add the ground cumin, chilli powder, tomato purée and salt, and cook for 3 minutes, or until you can see the oil start to separate around the edges.

3. Add the onion-tomato masala and bring to a simmer, stirring, then add the kidney beans, along with their liquid. Simmer for about 15 minutes, until the liquor has reduced and thickened.

4. Add the garam masala, tomatoes, chopped coriander and ginger matchsticks and simmer for 2–3 minutes. Stir in the butter.

5. Serve garnished with the red onion, ginger matchsticks and torn coriander, with lime wedges for squeezing on the side.

Note: To make this recipe vegan, leave out the butter at the end. You can swirl in a little oil from the onion-tomato masala instead, if you wish.

ALOO SABZI

Aloo (potato) *sabzi* (vegetable) is a vegetarian curry with plenty of heat, spice and freshness, finished with a tempering dose of butter, paneer and lots of lime juice.

We serve this curry in the traditional way with bedmi puri, and carrot and green chilli pickle, but it is delicious in its own right if you don't wish to serve the bread alongside. The recipe can easily be made vegan by leaving out the butter, yoghurt and paneer at the end.

SERVES 4–6

~

500g potatoes, peeled

2½ tsp ground coriander

1½ tsp deggi mirch chilli powder

1 tsp ground turmeric

1 tsp freshly ground black pepper

1½ tsp fine sea salt

50ml vegetable oil

1 tsp cumin seeds

⅓ tsp asafoetida

15g fresh root ginger, chopped

8g green chillies (2–3),
stems removed

120g drained tinned chickpeas
(½ x 400g tin)

1 tsp garam masala (page 356)

½ tsp dried fenugreek leaves,
finely crumbled

½ tsp amchur

20g coriander leaves, chopped

30g butter

150g paneer, cut into 1cm cubes

40ml lime juice

TO SERVE

Coriander leaves, shredded

Chopped red onion

Full-fat Greek yoghurt

Lime wedges

Carrot and green chilli pickle
(page 379)

Bedmi puri (page 370), optional

1. Boil the potatoes in salted water until just tender. Drain and allow to cool, then cut into small bite-sized pieces.

2. In a small bowl, mix together the ground coriander, chilli powder, turmeric, black pepper and salt. Set aside.

3. Place a large saucepan over a medium heat, add the oil and allow it to warm, then add the cumin seeds. Let them crackle for 20 seconds, then add the asafoetida and stir well. Toss in the chopped ginger and whole green chillies and stir again.

4. Add the dry spice mix and cook, stirring, for 1 minute, then pour in 700ml boiling water.

5. Add the cooked potatoes, crumbling about half of them in with your hands as you do so. Tip in the chickpeas, then turn the heat down to a lively simmer. Cook for 15 minutes, stirring regularly.

6. Add the garam masala, fenugreek, amchur and chopped coriander. Stir well and cook for a further 2 minutes.

7. Stir in the butter, paneer and lime juice, leave over the heat for 1 minute, then turn the heat off.

8. Serve the warm curry topped with coriander, chopped red onion and a spoonful of yoghurt. Accompany with lime wedges, carrot and green chilli pickle and bedmi puri if you like.

Note: If you are serving bedmi puri, prepare and roll out before you start the curry (to the end of step 4, page 370). Heat up the oil for deep-frying once the curry has finished simmering and deep-fry the stuffed puri just before serving.

MATTAR PANEER

This is a steadfast, humble and delicious vegetarian curry, as served in homes, cafés and roadside *dhabas* all over India. It has a rich tomato base, sweet peas and mild paneer cheese. Indian households generally have their own recipe.

The Hindi word for peas is *mattar* (pronounced mutter), which gives rise to the silly joke: "What did the peas say to one another? Nothing. They just muttered."

SERVES 2–4

~

300g onion-tomato masala (page 354)

¼ tsp fine sea salt

30g tomato purée

⅓ tsp granulated sugar

⅓ tsp garam masala (page 356)

¼ tsp ground cumin

100g frozen peas

200g paneer, cut into 2cm cubes

75ml double cream

TO SERVE

Coriander leaves, chopped

Kachumber (page 121)

1. Warm the onion-tomato masala in a medium saucepan over a medium heat. Add the salt, tomato purée, sugar, garam masala and cumin. Bring to a gentle simmer and cook for 10 minutes.

2. Add the frozen peas and 120ml water, bring back to a gentle simmer and cook for 5 minutes.

3. Add the paneer cubes and stir carefully, so that they don't break up. Allow to simmer gently for 10 minutes, stirring occasionally.

4. Add the cream, bring to a simmer and take off the heat. Serve garnished with chopped coriander, with a bowl of kachumber on the side.

KEEMA PAU

Keema (lamb mince) is well spiced, studded with green peas and usually served with *pau* (pillowy fresh bread buns), for much mopping. For us, this dish is synonymous with many places in Bombay: Olympia Coffee House and Café Paris on Colaba Causeway, and Radio Restaurant behind Crawford Market (supposedly where the local Muslim gangsters hang out). A good dish of this keema is guaranteed to transport us back to these places.

This dish relies on lamb mince with a decent level of fat (20% is ideal). There may seem to be a lot of ground coriander, but don't be tempted to use less. Its aromatic, slightly citrusy notes add brightness and depth, without being at all overpowering.

Eaten straight away, the keema has a lively freshness to it, due to the green paste of mint, coriander, chillies and spring onions. After a day in the fridge it has greater depth. Try both and see which you prefer.

SERVES 3–4

~

15g fresh root ginger

25g garlic (6–7 cloves)

20g spring onions (about 2), trimmed

20g coriander leaves, roughly chopped

10g mint leaves, roughly chopped

2 whole green chillies, plus an extra 10g roughly chopped

3 tbsp vegetable oil

1 onion, finely diced

3 tsp ground coriander

100g full-fat Greek yoghurt

450g lamb mince

1¼ tsp fine sea salt

2 bay leaves

⅓ tsp plain flour

50g frozen peas

TO SERVE

3–4 soft white bread buns, sliced in half

Butter, for spreading

A little chopped red onion

A few coriander leaves

3–4 lime wedges

1. Grate the ginger and garlic, using a microplane or the finest section of your grater, into a small bowl; set aside.

2. Blitz the spring onions, coriander, mint and 10g chopped green chilli together to make a paste, using a blender or mini food processor.

3. Heat the oil in a large saucepan over a medium heat. Add the onion and sauté gently for 5 minutes, stirring regularly, without browning. Add the grated ginger and garlic and cook for 2 minutes, stirring almost constantly. Add the ground coriander and cook for 2–3 minutes.

4. Turn the heat up, stir in the yoghurt and sauté for 3 minutes, by which point the yoghurt should start to separate. Turn the heat back down to medium, add the lamb mince, salt and bay leaves and mix well. Sauté, stirring regularly, until the moisture starts to leave the meat, then sprinkle the flour over the surface and stir well; this helps to lock in the moisture.

5. Add the green paste, turn the heat down low and simmer gently for 20 minutes.

6. Add the peas and whole green chillies and simmer over the lowest possible heat for a further 15 minutes, stirring occasionally. When the time is up, put the lid on, turn off the heat and allow the keema to stand for 10 minutes before serving.

7. Lightly toast and butter the cut sides of the bread buns.

8. Divide the keema between 3 or 4 bowls and garnish with the red onion and coriander. Serve with the toasted buns and lime wedges.

SALLI BOTI

This is a first-rate Parsi classic, the best example of which is served in the inimitable Britannia & Co. Tender chunks of lamb (goat, if you're in Bombay) are braised in a rich and flavoursome gravy then finished with crunchy salli crisp-chips. When served with a hot, buttered chapati and a bowl of kachumber, there are fewer more satisfying lunches. Ours is served with handkerchief-thin roomali roti.

SERVES 4–6

~

150ml vegetable oil

1 cinnamon stick

2 bay leaves

500g red onions, diced

1kg boneless leg of lamb, cut into 3cm pieces

50g garlic paste (page 353)

35g ginger paste (page 353)

2 tsp deggi mirch chilli powder

1 tsp ground turmeric

2 tsp fine sea salt

400g tin chopped tomatoes

40ml distilled white vinegar (pickling vinegar)

35g jaggery

1 tsp garam masala (page 356)

TO SERVE

Salli (page 173)

Chapatis (page 368)

Kachumber (page 121)

1. Warm a large saucepan or flameproof casserole dish over a medium-high heat and add the oil. Toss in the cinnamon stick and bay leaves and sauté for 1 minute; they should sizzle.

2. Add the red onions and cook until well caramelised, but still soft. This will take around 25 minutes, and needs to be done over a reasonably high heat, stirring very regularly, rather than "low and slow".

3. Add the lamb pieces and stir well. Turn the heat down a little and let them cook for 5 minutes, so the meat starts to release some moisture.

4. Stir in the garlic and ginger pastes and sauté for 4–5 minutes, being careful not to let the garlic burn (add a little water if you need to). Add the chilli powder, turmeric and salt and cook for 2 minutes.

5. Tip in the chopped tomatoes and cook until they have completely broken down and you see the oil separate from the sauce; this should take around 15 minutes. If the pan starts to become dry before the tomatoes have completely fallen apart, add a splash of water.

6. Top up with 150–200ml water, so that the lamb is just covered, and turn the heat down low. Put the lid on, at a slight angle so there is a gap to let some heat escape, and simmer gently for 1½ hours, or until the lamb is very tender, stirring occasionally. Top up with a little water if the lamb becomes exposed above the level of the liquid, but don't add more than you need to, as this will dilute the flavour.

7. Once the lamb is tender, add the vinegar, jaggery and garam masala and cook gently for a final 15 minutes. Serve garnished with a big handful of salli, with the bread and kachumber on the side.

CHANA CHAAT SALAD

This salad combines the crunch of seeds and sweet-sour pops of pomegranate and sultanas with more substantial couscous and chickpeas. Salads aren't commonly eaten in Bombay, where vegetables tend to be cooked into submission before they make it anywhere near your plate. However, this one makes a wonderful light lunch; it also works well as a side with the grills (pages 263–7 and 270–9).

SERVES 6 AS A SIDE

~

40g couscous

1 tsp olive oil

100g mixed sprouted grains

20g pumpkin seeds

2 tsp sesame seeds

400g tin chickpeas, drained and rinsed

1 medium tomato, deseeded and finely diced

40g raisins

70g pomegranate seeds (about ½ pomegranate)

A small handful of coriander leaves, finely chopped

Flaky sea salt

FOR THE DRESSING

1 small ripe avocado, halved, stoned and peeled (120g prepared weight)

80g coriander-mint dressing (page 378)

25ml lime juice

1. Put the couscous into a microwavable container (a large mug is perfect). Add 60ml boiling water and the olive oil and microwave on high for 1 minute. Leave to stand for 5 minutes then fluff up the couscous with a fork. (Alternatively, the couscous can be cooked in a small pan over a medium heat.) Once forked through, allow the couscous to cool.

2. Put the sprouted grains into a bowl and pour on boiling water to cover. Tip straight into a sieve to drain, and refresh under running cold water. Shake dry and set to one side.

3. Warm a dry frying pan over a high heat and add the pumpkin seeds. Toast for 2 minutes or until golden brown, shaking the pan to keep the seeds moving so they don't burn. Add the sesame seeds and toast for a further minute. Remove from the pan and set aside.

4. In a large bowl, combine the couscous, chickpeas, diced tomato, sprouted grains, raisins and pomegranate seeds. Season generously with flaky salt.

5. To make the dressing, blitz the ingredients, using a blender or mini food processor, to a smooth paste.

6. Add the dressing to the bowl along with the chopped coriander and three-quarters of the toasted seeds. Mix well then taste for seasoning, adding more salt if you wish. Garnish with the remaining toasted seeds to serve.

CHILLI POMELO SALAD

Hot, tangy, nutty, sweet. Fresh kale gives this salad plenty of bite and vigour, while the red chilli adds an addictive heat. Mint for freshness, juicy bursts of pomelo, the sweetness of dates and crunch of pistachios – all make it a little more interesting.

We serve this two ways: as a salad or side dish to share (as below), or with cooled, pulled murgh malai (page 273). It makes an exceptional lunch on a hot day.

SERVES 4 AS A SIDE

~

20g pistachio nuts

20g pumpkin seeds

1 pomelo or large pink grapefruit

80g kale, thick stalks removed, finely shredded

3 spring onions

1 red chilli

6 Medjool dates

10 large mint leaves

A small handful of coriander leaves

FOR THE DRESSING

3 tsp chilli drizzle (page 358)

1 tsp tamarind chutney (page 377)

20ml lime juice

A pinch of flaky sea salt

1. Crush the pistachios very lightly, using a pestle and mortar; a few gentle smacks should be fine. Warm a dry frying pan over a medium heat and add the pumpkin seeds. Toast for 2 minutes or until golden brown, shaking the pan to keep the seeds moving so they don't burn. Add to the pistachios and set to one side.

2. Cut the top and bottom off the pomelo or pink grapefruit. Using a small sharp knife, cut away the skin and all of the pith, then carefully cut between the membranes to release the segments. Set aside.

3. Wash the kale and spin dry (or pat with kitchen paper). Place in a large bowl.

4. Thinly slice the spring onions and red chilli on the diagonal, discarding the seeds from the chilli, then add to the bowl.

5. Pull the dates in half with your fingers, discard the stone, then slice each half into quarters and add to the bowl. (If your dates are very sticky, handle them with slightly wet fingers; the water will encourage the fruit not to stick to itself.)

6. Tear the mint and coriander leaves into the bowl, and add the reserved pomelo or grapefruit slices.

7. Mix the dressing ingredients together in a small bowl to combine.

8. Add three-quarters of the nuts and toasted seeds to the bowl, pour over the dressing and mix well; you might find it easiest to use your hands to make sure that everything is thoroughly coated. Scatter over the remaining nuts and seeds to serve.

PANEER
& MANGO SALAD

This salad marries sweetness and bitterness to excellent effect. It works best with a firm, slightly green mango, and bitter leaves, such as chicory, bull's blood and Treviso. Be generous when seasoning the paneer, since it can otherwise be bland. For a satisfying lunch, serve the salad with crispy sesame and onion seed naans.

You can swap the mango for pomelo or pink grapefruit segments, and the paneer for juicy, garlicky grilled prawns if you like.

SERVES 2

~

150g paneer

1 tbsp olive oil

1 medium mango, peeled and flesh cut from the stone (200g prepared weight)

60g assorted bitter salad leaves

60ml lime and chilli dressing (page 379)

20g crispy onions or shallots (see page 347)

Flaky sea salt and freshly ground black pepper

TO SERVE

Crispy sesame and onion seed naan (page 365)

1. Slice the paneer into long, thin slices, about 5mm thick. Add the olive oil and season generously with flaky salt and black pepper.

2. Slice the mango flesh into long strips.

3. Combine the paneer, mango and salad leaves in a bowl. Add the lime and chilli dressing and toss gently.

4. Transfer the salad to a serving bowl and sprinkle with the crispy onions or shallots. Serve with the crispy naan.

SLAW

Pomegranate seeds add a welcome pop of crunch and sweetness to this vibrant slaw. We use a mix of red and white cabbage – there's no real difference in flavour, but it does look rather pleasing. To serve up to six you only need half a cabbage, so do feel free to pick your favourite colour rather than buying both.

SERVES 6

~

½ red onion

¼ red cabbage

¼ white cabbage

½ red pepper

40g pomegranate seeds (just under ½ pomegranate), plus a few to garnish

8 mint leaves

25 coriander leaves, plus a few extra to garnish

3 tbsp mayonnaise

3 tsp tomato-chilli jam (page 59)

1. Slice the red onion into fine half-moon slivers and drop into a bowl of cold water.

2. Shred the cabbage as finely as you can, using either a sharp knife or a mandoline, and place in a large bowl. (Don't grate it, as this will make the slaw wet.)

3. Slice the red pepper into thin, long matchsticks, and add to the bowl, along with 2 tbsp pomegranate seeds.

4. Pile the mint leaves on top of one another, then roll up into a tiny cigar shape. Use your knife to thinly slice the "cigar", which will create ribbons. Add to the bowl.

5. Gently tear the coriander leaves into the bowl. Drain the red onions, pat them dry with kitchen paper and add these to the slaw too.

6. Add the mayonnaise and tomato-chilli jam and toss well to combine.

7. Serve the slaw garnished with a few pomegranate seeds and coriander leaves.

KACHUMBER

Kachumber is the closest thing we Indians have to a salad. It's a messy to-do of tomato, cucumber, onion and coriander. The salt helps the vegetables to release all their delicious flavours into the mix, while the lime juice lifts the whole affair.

SERVES 2

~

¼ red onion

1 large tomato (about 100g)

⅓ cucumber

A large pinch of fine sea salt

20 coriander leaves

Juice of ¼ lime

1. Slice the red onion into fine strips. Place in a small bowl and cover with cold water.

2. Halve the tomato, remove and discard the seeds, then slice the flesh into thin strips and place in a large bowl.

3. Slice the cucumber in half lengthways and carefully scoop out the seeds, using a teaspoon. Slice the cucumber into thin crescents and add to the tomato.

4. Drain the onion, pat dry with kitchen paper and add to the tomato and cucumber.

5. Add the salt, mix well and leave to stand for 5 minutes to allow the juices to mingle.

6. Shred half of the coriander leaves, keep half whole.

7. Add all the coriander to the salad, dress with lime juice, mix well and serve.

BOWL OF GREENS

This is a delicious, light side dish. The char from the grill adds interest to the fresh green vegetables, which get along very well with the flavours of chilli and lime.

Swap the melted butter for vegetable or coconut oil to make the dish vegan.

SERVES 4

~

300g broccoli (1 small head), cut into medium florets

150g mangetout

20g butter, melted

50g baby spinach

2 tbsp lime and chilli dressing (page 379)

1 tsp kabab masala (page 358)

1. Heat your grill to high and line a wide baking tray with foil.

2. Bring a large pan of lightly salted water to the boil. Add the broccoli florets, bring back to the boil and cook for 3 minutes. Remove with a slotted spoon and pat dry with kitchen paper.

3. Add the mangetout to the water, blanch for 1 minute then remove with a slotted spoon and pat dry.

4. Put the broccoli and mangetout into a bowl, add the melted butter and toss well to coat, then lay on the prepared baking tray. Grill the vegetables until lightly charred, about 5–7 minutes, turning once.

5. Put the grilled vegetables into a large bowl, add the baby spinach, lime and chilli dressing and the kabab masala and toss well to coat everything in the dressing. Serve immediately.

RAITA

This cooling yoghurt dish is a traditional accompaniment that goes well with almost any meal, but especially suits the biryanis (pages 232–9) and vegetarian curries (pages 100–5). For those who are sensitive to spice, this is a gift from the gods.

It's a little tricky to make a small amount of raita. However, it keeps very well in the fridge for a couple of days.

SERVES 8

~

250g full-fat Greek yoghurt

⅓ tsp fine sea salt

¼ tsp caster sugar

¼ red onion (25g), finely diced

40g deseeded cucumber, very finely diced

40g deseeded tomato, diced

6 coriander sprigs, finely chopped

8 mint leaves, finely chopped

2 or 3 pinches of cumin seeds

1. Put the yoghurt, 50ml cold water, the salt and sugar into a bowl or large measuring jug and mix nicely.

2. Add the onion, cucumber, tomato and herbs and stir until evenly combined. Cover and leave to stand for at least 20 minutes (ideally a couple of hours, in the fridge) in order to let the flavours infuse into the yoghurt.

3. Toast the cumin seeds in a hot, dry pan until they crackle. Crush the seeds, using a pestle and mortar, and sprinkle on top of the raita just before serving.

MEHER COLD DRINK HOUSE

"Head in the direction of Meher Cold Drink House, a tiny corner café in the heart of Fort. You will find Meher where Rustom Sidhwa Marg (formerly Gunbow Street) intersects with Parsi Bazaar Street."

AFTERNOON REFRESHMENTS

"3 o'clock"

AFTERNOON REFRESHMENTS AT MEHER COLD DRINK HOUSE, AND ANOTHER SLICE OF THE FORT DISTRICT

WITH THE HEAT of the day bearing down like a sultry hand on the back of your neck, you will most likely be ready for cool refreshment. Head in the direction of Meher Cold Drink House, a tiny corner café in the heart of Fort.

You'll find Meher where Rustom Sidhwa Marg (formerly Gunbow Street) intersects Parsi Bazaar Street. The inside walls are painted a pale and calming shade of blue, which contrasts with the brash Pepsi advertising. Ignore the call of the cold fizzy drink. Even though you may think you need one, you don't. Your choice is in fact very simple: salty or sweet. No fancy flavours here, just very good lassi, made the way it always has been. Take a seat on the hard fold-up benches, and sip. Enjoy the tang of cooling yoghurt and gaze out onto the street. Allow yourself a few quiet moments to watch the world go by, dreamily.

Meher Cold Drink House (est. 1939) counts as one of the landscape of Irani cafés that dot the city. Notice the board requesting patrons "Not to Smoke" and "Not to Spit" and the faded poster of "Prophets and Saints" at the cash counter, all classic little elements of an "Irani". Yet while the larger cafés are better known (and their gradual decline has been well discussed and documented), cold drink houses, like pharmacies – another business into which the Iranis ventured – aren't as much discussed. In fact, the family of the utterly charming Mr Dinshaw Irani, who owns Meher Cold Drink House, once ran a pharmacy right next door. Enterprising Iranis initially sold loose medicines over the counter at their cafés and provision stores, along with bread, eggs, cigarettes and other sundries. When regulations were tightened up in the middle of the last century, many set up full-scale pharmacies, almost always adjacent to their cafés.

You shouldn't need pills to revive you today. Your body should be now be cooled, your spirit refreshed and your mood somewhat sweetened,

perhaps like your lassi. Lick the creamy frill from your upper lip (or be relaxed and leave it in peace, until someone points it out) and hand your empty glass back across the counter.

As you exit Meher Cold Drink House, turn left in the direction of Sir Pherozeshah Mehta Road, which is an avenue as imposing as the gentleman after whom it is named. Sir Pherozeshah Mehta was a leading barrister (called to the bar in 1868 from Lincoln's Inn) and prominent Indian nationalist. He was one of the founding members of the Indian National Congress, which of course was later led by Mahatma Gandhi in the successful struggle for Indian independence.

In 1910, Mehta and Benjamin Horniman (whom you met earlier, in the second chapter) tried to buy a newspaper called the *Bombay Gazette*, intending to give a voice to Indian nationalists. Unsuccessful in this attempt, they went on instead to start the English-language *Bombay Chronicle* a few years later. Edited by Horniman, it quickly became an influential and trenchant nationalist newspaper and played a key role in breaking the news of the appalling Amritsar massacre in 1919 (see page 66). Quite apart from being a highly respected citizen, Mehta was always impeccably dressed and apparently always had his barber close by.

The buildings on Sir Pherozeshah Mehta Road are also towering presences with their solid stone structures. This is not the playful, colourful Art Deco you find elsewhere in Bombay, but a stronger no-nonsense style for the city's professional district. Building façades are punched with muscular bas-reliefs of worthy men and virtuous women farming the land or making important things with their hands. Large Art Deco lettering assumes prominence and importance, especially on the United India Life Assurance Building, whose name in stone wraps around the corner and

1

2

"This is not the playful, colourful Art Deco you find elsewhere in Bombay, but a stronger no-nonsense style for the city's professional district."

seems to hold up the roof. One of Bombay's best cornices, surely. Look for the statue of Lakshmi, the goddess of wealth and prosperity, watching over the business of the street atop her high lotus pedestal on the Lakshmi Insurance Building. No doubt the road's business people are reassured by her presence and perhaps mutter prayers to her as they go about generating wealth.

Soon after these Art Deco buildings were constructed on Pherozeshah Mehta Road in the 1930s and 40s, Iranis opened cafés on the ground floors of the corner buildings, offering commanding views of the stately avenue with your chai. Back then, you would have had your pick of Reserve Restaurant, Sailor Restaurant, Shahpur Restaurant, Café Royale or Café Mocambo.

Now walk north along the arcades on Dadabhai Naoroji Road. Crane your neck to look up at the lofty structures. Also enjoy the tiny street-side stalls set up within the shaded nooks and crannies, like the Bombay Pen Corner, which no longer sells pens, but has a beautiful sign and sells nice name plates and rubber stamps. After a few minutes, turn sharp left to find the New Empire cinema,

whose Art Deco gates will give you an inkling of the elegance of the interiors, apparently still there but no longer accessible to the public. Like the many other defunct single-screen cinemas in the area, New Empire started life as a theatre at the turn of the twentieth century. Indeed, this area was Bombay's foremost theatre district where you would come to be entertained by plays. Funniest and most popular of all were the *Parsi nataak* or Parsi theatre.

This tradition of Parsi theatre dates all the way back to 1850, when students from Elphinstone College formed a theatre company called The Elphinstonian Amateurs. Numerous other companies were formed and over the next century under British rule, theatre in Bombay flourished. Persian, Sanskrit and English classics would be performed in Gujarati, English, Urdu and Hindi. Productions also became lavish, with rich costumes and props, elaborate mechanical devices and increasingly baroque stage sets. While the plays were mostly financed and managed by Parsis, writers and actors were drawn from all of Bombay's various communities. The stage became a happily cosmopolitan and unifying place. Parsi theatre also played a key role in shaping Indian performing arts and had a significant influence on the evolution of Bollywood.

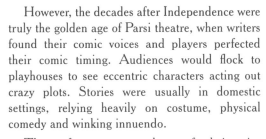

However, the decades after Independence were truly the golden age of Parsi theatre, when writers found their comic voices and players perfected their comic timing. Audiences would flock to playhouses to see eccentric characters acting out crazy plots. Stories were usually in domestic settings, relying heavily on costume, physical comedy and winking innuendo.

The performances were known for being rip-roaringly funny. One of Parsi theatre's most loved stock characters was Aspandyar, the male family servant and keeper of the family's secrets who was relentlessly henpecked by the bossy ladies of the house. He would invariably appear on stage dressed in baggy striped cotton shorts with a grubby madras-checked duster slung over his shoulder. An arch of his eyebrow paired with a well-chosen Gujarati cuss, or just a slightly indecent waggle of his leg might cause a whole audience to fall about with laughter. A very popular play was *Tehmul's Tangle* (based on a 1960s French farce) in which a hapless fellow juggles a trio of women with whom he is having affairs, all air hostesses and all arriving in town on the same weekend. Hilarity ensues.

Writers would also take serious classics and marinate them thoroughly in their ribald Gujarati Bombay humour. Shakespeare was a favourite. The solemn themes of the tragedies – hubris, betrayal and murder – would be joyfully laced with farce, cross-dressing and slapstick. *Othello*, *Romeo and Juliet*, and the *Merchant of Venice* were suddenly full of laughs, while *Hamlet No Omelette* was a free and funny interpretation of the tale of the

1 The impeccably groomed Sir Pherozeshah Mehta
2 The charming owner of Meher Cold Drink House, Mr Dinshaw Irani, holding a photo of his father, Mr Bomi Irani
3 Large Art Deco letters wrap around the United India Building
4 Goddess Lakshmi atop Lakshmi Insurance Building
5 Mehru Madon and Pheroze Antia in *Mehera ne Khatar*
6 The Art Deco gates of New Empire cinema

brooding Danish prince. Audiences lapped up the comedy, laughed until they cried and tumbled out of the playhouses sated and happy.

(If you are interested in reading more about Parsi theatre, pick up Meher Marfatia's book, *Laughter in the House*, which is enormous fun and, as you might imagine, full of funny photos.)

Before you end this walk, go back towards the main junction you came past earlier. This might be Bombay's grandest junction, with the onion-domed Bombay Municipal Corporation Building to your north and the glorious Victoria Terminus to your east. The station has officially been renamed Chhatrapati Shivaji Maharaj Terminus after the great seventeenth-century Marathi warrior king, but mostly it's still called VT.

VT and the Bombay Municipal Corporation Building were both built by the great British architect, Frederick William Stevens. The first thing that Stevens did when he learnt that he had received the commission to build the station was to

"To a passing Bombayite in 1888, it must have looked like a bizarre, immense, stone-built alien vessel of unimaginable scale, landed upon the dusty Indian earth."

7 Gothic arches inside the Victoria Terminus booking hall
8 People waiting in the vast Victoria Terminus

tour the European capitals for ten months to study their railway stations. Building works started in 1878, and took ten years and 1.6 million rupees to complete. Working with Bombay architects and engineers and assisted by students from the Sir J. J. School of Art, Stevens forged a style for the project which blended both Muslim and Hindu motifs with the Victorian Gothic Revival idiom. He created what is surely the pinnacle of Bombay Gothic. Indeed, as Sharada Dwivedi and Rahul Mehrotra write in their book *Bombay: The Cities Within*: "In time it came to be considered one of the finest stations in the world."

Stand and look at the exterior, ideally from right in front of the building facing the main dome. It is something to behold. The side wings extend forwards and embrace you, like a sort of Gothic Indian St. Peter's Basilica. There is a giant statue of progress personified, standing on top of the large central dome, carrying a flaming torch in her right hand and a wheel in her left. You can see magnificent domes, pointed arches, spires, turrets and gargoyles. It is elaborate, overstated and powerful. To the average passing Bombayite in 1888, it must have looked like a bizarre, immense, stone-built alien vessel of unimaginable scale,

landed upon the dusty Indian earth. It certainly spoke forcefully to the muscle and modernity of the British Empire.

The interiors are just as exuberant. You might wander inside in mute astonishment if you look up and around properly. You'll see grand Italianate marble columns, tall Gothic arches, polished blue stone, carved foliage, busts of grandees and sculptures of animals. There is too much to take in, even before you turn your attention to the human activity.

If you go during rush hour (and it's worth doing so, just to experience it) you'll be swept up with the crowds as they sweep through the hall. Each day over three million commuters pass through VT, arriving on the Bombay "locals" which burst at the seams with their super-dense crush-load. This term was invented to describe the difficult state of affairs that is five hundred and fifty commuters packed into a carriage designed for two hundred, which comes to about fifteen people per square metre. Commuting to work in Bombay is just not easy. By contrast, to take the local train outside the rush hour is a joy, with plenty of space and the wind in your face. You should certainly try and do this if you can.

ABOVE: The generous and welcoming family of Mr Dinshaw Irani

LEFT: Delicious sweet curd, served at Meher Cold Drink House

ABOVE: Bombay Pen Corner, which no longer sells pens

RIGHT: Train timetable inside Victoria Terminus

समय सारणी, छत्रपति शिवाजी टर्मिनस पर पहुचने वाली गाड़ीयाँ

अप गाड़ीयाँ	प्रारंभ	आगमन	प्लेट फार्म	दिन	क्र.	संख्या	अप गाड़ीयाँ नाम	प्रारंभ
	चेन्नई	03.45	16	दैनिक	19	12126	प्रगति एक्सप्रेस	पुणे
	भुबनेश्वर	03.55	17	दैनिक	20	12321	हावड़ा मेल (इलाहाबाद होकर)	हावड़ा
	पंढरपूर	04.10	15	शनि,रवि,सोम	21	11024	सह्याद्रि एक्सप्रेस	कोल्हापूर
	बीजापूर	04.10	15	मंग,बुध,गुरु,शुक्र	22	17032	हैदराबाद एक्सप्रेस	हैदराबाद
	कोपरगांव	04.10	15	दैनिक	23	11042	चेन्नई एक्सप्रेस	चेन्नई
स	केप	04. 0	14	दैनिक	24	11094	महानगरी एक्सप्रेस	वाराणसी
स	हैदराबाद	0 . 5	9	दैनिक	25	11008	दक्खन एक्सप्रेस	पुणे
होकर)	हावड़ा	05.2	15	दैनिक	26	16530	उद्यान एक्सप्रेस	बंगलूर
नांदेड होकर)	नागपूर	05.	08	दैनिक	27	12533	पुष्पक एक्सप्रेस	लखनऊ
प्रेस	मडगांव	05.50	15	दैनिक	28	51154	भुसावल सवारी	भुसावल
	कोल्हापूर	07.25	14	दैनिक	29	11030	कोयना एक्सप्रेस	कोल्हापूर
	सोलापूर	07.00	8	दैनिक	30	12128	इंटरसिटी एक्सप्रेस	पुणे
	सिकंदराबाद	07.10	15	दैनिक	31	16332	तिरुवनंतपुरम एक्सप्रेस	तिरुवनंतपुरम
	फिरोजपूर	07.35	17	दैनिक		16340	नागरकोइल एक्सप्रेस	नागरकोइल
	लातूर	08.05	11	दैनिक		16352	नागरकोइल एक्सप्रेस (तिरुपति होकर)	नागरकोइल
	गोंदीया	07.00	18	दैनिक	32	12860	गीतांजली एक्सप्रेस	हावड़ा
	औरंगाबाद	08.15	16	बुध	33	10104	मांडवी एक्सप्रेस	मडगांव
	पुणे	09.53	9	दैनिक	34	22106	इंद्रायणी एक्सप्रेस	पुणे
	पुणे	10.25	12	दैनिक	35	17618	तपोवन एक्सप्रेस	नांदेड
	मनमाड	10.45	16	दैनिक	36	12870	हावड़ा एक्सप्रेस	हावड़ा

अप गाड़ीयाँ	प्रारंभ	आगमन	प्लेट फार्म	दिन	क्र.	संख्या	अप गाड़ीयाँ नाम	प्रारंभ
स्प्रेस	आसनसोल	6: 5	16	मंगल	1	12134	एक्सप्रेस	मेंगलोर
क्स्प्रेस	छपरा	6:30	16	गुरु	2	12140	सेन्... प्रेस	नागपुर
प्रेस	अमरावती	6:25	12	दैनिक	3	12187	ग...स	जबलपुर
	नागपुर	: 5	18	दैनिक	4	11058	...प्रेस	अमृतसर
	हावड़ा	10:30	18	मंगल,बुध,गुरू,शनि	5	11306		सोलापुर
क्स.	गोरखपुर	12-15	18	रविवार	6			
	गोरखपुर	12-15	18	बुध	7			
					8			
					9			
					10			
					11			
					12			

FRESH LIME SODA

This citrus-salt-soda combination is unbeatable for quenching the thirst on a hot day (or for brightening up a rainy one). To quote Mr Kohinoor, "Fresh lime soda, nice and sweet, to beat the Bombay heat."

Feel free to use lemons in place of limes.

SERVES 1

~

A large pinch of flaky sea salt

25ml lime juice (freshly squeezed)

1 tbsp sugar syrup (see right)

Ice cubes

100ml soda water

TO GARNISH

Lime wedge

1. Crumble the salt into a tall glass. Add the lime juice, let it sit for a minute, then add the syrup and stir well.

2. Fill the glass with ice, then add the soda. We recommend you measure the soda to get the perfect salty-sweet balance. Stir and serve immediately, garnished with a lime wedge.

Sugar syrup: Put 200g granulated sugar and 200ml water into a saucepan over a medium heat and stir until the sugar has fully dissolved. Simmer for 1 minute then take off the heat and allow to cool. Store in a covered container in the fridge and use within a week. *Makes about 300ml*

SALTED LASSI

Lassis are the cool, refreshing yoghurt drinks found all over India. Meher Cold Drink House and Parsi Dairy serve the best versions in Bombay.

The quantities below are per person – if you're making more than one, scale up and blitz together. Lassis are reasonably thick, so it's best to drink them using a straw.

SERVES 1

~

135g full-fat Greek yoghurt

A large pinch of flaky sea salt

A small pinch of cumin seeds

Ice cubes (optional)

TO GARNISH

Mint sprig

1. Put all the ingredients into a blender, add 65ml cold water and blitz until light and frothy. If you prefer a cooler drink, pop in a couple of ice cubes before blending.

2. Pour the lassi into a tall glass, top with a sprig of mint and serve immediately.

Variations

For each of the following, omit the salt and cumin seeds.

Sweet lassi: Blitz the yoghurt and water with 50ml sugar syrup (page 138).

Mango lassi: Blitz the yoghurt and water with 70ml mango purée (fresh or tinned), 20ml sugar syrup (page 138) and a very small pinch of fennel seeds.

Rose & cardamom lassi: Blitz the yoghurt and water with 50ml rose syrup (page 332) and 1 lightly bashed green cardamom pod.

COLABA COLADA

A virgin piña colada dressed up for a balmy night out in Bombay, with a little chai syrup and coriander. This being a fresh, sweet and citrusy drink, it marries well with lighter dishes such as masala prawns (page 274), paneer and mango salad (page 116) or aloo tikki chaat (page 183). The addition of rum turns it into a wonderful tipple to share with friends (see below).

This quantity will fit comfortably in a standard jug blender. Don't be alarmed when the lime curdles the coconut cream.

SERVES 4

~

240ml pineapple juice (from a carton)

140ml coconut cream

60ml lime juice (freshly squeezed)

60ml chai syrup (see below)

24 coriander leaves

Ice cubes

TO GARNISH

A few dried coconut flakes

Lime slices (optional)

1. Put the pineapple juice, coconut cream, lime juice, chai syrup and coriander into your blender and pulse a few times to mix well. (Note that if the coconut cream has separated it will need to be poured into another vessel and stirred well to re-combine before adding to the mix.)

2. Add the same volume of ice as liquid in the blender. Blitz for 2 minutes or until completely smooth.

3. Pour straight into a tall glass and garnish with coconut flakes, and a slice of lime if you like.

Note: To turn this into a cocktail, add 100ml Santa Teresa or other white rum, and a splash of dark rum if you like, with the pineapple juice and coconut cream.

Chai syrup: To make this, first grind 10 cardamom pods, 8g cinnamon stick, 4 cloves and ½ nutmeg, grated, to a coarse powder, using a pestle and mortar (or spice grinder, but be careful not to grind too finely.) Add 6g chopped fresh root ginger and bash to a very coarse paste.

Put 750g granulated sugar into a large bowl and add ½ tsp vanilla bean paste or 1 tsp vanilla extract. Add the ginger spice paste and work everything together with your fingers. Cover with cling film and leave in a dry place overnight.

Pour 400ml hot water (cooled for 2 minutes after boiling) over the sugar mixture and stir well. Cover and leave to dissolve over 3–4 hours, stirring every now and then (or you can leave it overnight if that is easier).

Strain through muslin then pour into a sterilised bottle or jar. It will keep in a store-cupboard for up to 3 months. Chai syrup can also be used to pep up tea, coffee and milkshakes. *Makes 750ml*

WATERMELON SHARBAT

Sharbat is a soft drink with Persian origins and will quench your thirst. There is sweetness and flavour from the fruit juice, a little salt and sugar for rehydration, all lengthened nicely with soda water. A first-class summer refresher.

SERVES 1

~

A small pinch of flaky sea salt

25ml lime juice (freshly squeezed)

1 tbsp sugar syrup (page 138)

50ml watermelon purée (see note)

A sprig of mint

Ice cubes

100ml soda water

TO GARNISH

A small wedge of watermelon

1. Crumble the salt into a tall glass, add the lime juice and let it sit for 30 seconds.

2. Add the sugar syrup and watermelon purée.

3. Take the mint sprig, lay it across one palm and give it a short, sharp smack with your other hand. The brief pressure and heat from your hands will bring out the oils. Add to the glass.

4. Add as much ice as you can fit in the glass, then top up with soda. Stir and serve immediately, garnished with a small wedge of watermelon.

Note: To make the watermelon purée, remove the seeds from a slice of watermelon, then push the flesh through a sturdy sieve. You'll need about 1 heaped tablespoonful of watermelon flesh per drink.

Variation

Passion fruit sharbat: Replace the watermelon purée with passion fruit purée. Either use a good-quality brand, such as Boiron (which can be stored in the freezer after opening), or push fresh passion fruit pulp through a sieve, allowing 1 passion fruit per serving. Use coriander instead of mint, and garnish with a wedge of lime.

FALOODA

Sweet, extravagant and fun, this is a sort of Irani café version of a knickerbocker glory: a glass full of malai kulfi, vermicelli, rose syrup and sweet basil seeds. Apparently Kyani & Co. first dreamt up this unusual dessert-drink combination. Badshah, near Crawford Market, serves a famous one.

This can be enjoyed as a dessert or a drink. If you can't find basil seeds, use chia seeds; they're almost the same.

SERVES 4

~

25g white falooda noodles

1½ tsp basil seeds (tukmaria)

60ml condensed milk

190ml evaporated milk

35ml rose syrup (page 332)

4 malai kulfi (page 304)

TO GARNISH

20g pistachio nuts, lightly crushed

1. Break the falooda noodles into a few pieces each. Cook as per the pack instructions (usually boiling in water for 2–3 minutes); once cooked you should be able to cut the noodles with a spoon without too much trouble.

2. Soak the cooked noodles in a bowl of cold water for 10 minutes then drain well.

3. Put the basil seeds into a small bowl. Add 2 tbsp water and leave to soak for 15 minutes; the seeds should swell up. Drain well.

4. Mix together the condensed and evaporated milks.

5. To assemble, take four wide glasses. Place a heaped teaspoonful of noodles in each glass to cover the bottom and dot with a pinch of the basil seeds. Drizzle 1–2 tsp rose syrup into each glass, then top with 60ml of the milk mixture.

6. Remove the kulfis from their moulds, chop each one into bite-sized pieces and add to the glasses. Add a final flourish of noodles and basil seeds to each, just enough for decoration, then sprinkle with crushed pistachios and serve.

CHOWPATTY

"In a place as hectic as Bombay, the allure of Chowpatty is clear.
It is a place of relative calm, a place to idle in the breeze and in the sunset,
a pause from the relentless daily rhythms of the city."

SUNSET SNACKS

"5 o'clock"

A GENTLE STROLL ON CHOWPATTY
AT SUNSET, WITH PLENTIFUL SNACKS

IT IS ALMOST 5PM. You may be feeling pleasantly tired. The evening sea breeze hasn't yet picked up, although it is teasing you with its occasional promises to do so. The sun, having lost some of its ferocity, slinks contentedly towards the horizon. At this time of day Bombay relaxes and takes to the seafront to stretch its legs. There is plenty of shoreline to choose from (Bombay being washed by the Arabian Sea on three sides) but tonight, we're visiting Girgaum Chowpatty (generally known as just Chowpatty), at the top of Marine Drive.

Be sure to pause at the historic stone lamp post near the southern end of the beach and read the inscription: "Kennedy Sea-Face commenced 18th December, 1915. Completed 1920." The post marks the construction of the twenty-foot high sea wall that runs from Chowpatty down Marine Drive. Before this wall there was just a palm-fringed monsoon-battered stretch of seafront. Now the Drive is protected and is known as the Queen's Necklace, for the twinkling lights that wrap around the bay in a sensuous curve, like a string of pearls on a lover's neck. Most importantly, the city's breeze-eaters (in Hindi to go out to enjoy the breeze is to "eat" it), joggers and couples have space to enjoy the sunset.

It is also the only landmark that reminds the city of this stretch of road's first incarnation, the Kennedy Sea-Face. As is the custom in Bombay, the name of the road has changed several times in the hundred-odd years that this post has lingered here. Today the road bears the official post-colonial title of Netaji Subash Chandra Bose Road, though everyone knows it as Marine Drive. Such is the way with place names in Bombay. The names on your map, imposed by officialdom, have only sporadic correspondence with the names used by actual people. The worn grooves of usage take time to wear anew. VT (Victoria Terminus) will still be VT for decades to come, no doubt.

Now it is time to make your way on to the beach. Take off your shoes if you want. It's reasonably clean away from the food stalls, and there are few feelings

> "Here, you can partake in the serious business of idle pleasures. It has been like this for as long as we've known it, and no doubt much longer."

as fine as sand between the toes. Slow down your breathing as you allow the chorus of honking horns that has been your constant companion to fade into the background until it is reassuring, almost even relaxing.

In a place as hectic as Bombay, the allure of Chowpatty is clear. It is a place of relative calm, a place to idle in the breeze and in the sunset, a pause from the relentless daily rhythms of the city. Parents rest on blankets and contentedly watch the sea; teenagers sit closer together than their elders would allow; children chase each other around the sand, and beg their parents for sweet treats. A group of boys enthusiastically plays cricket, makeshift stumps unevenly standing in the sand. Old friends take their evening stroll, just as they've been doing for the past several decades.

Here, you can partake in the serious business of idle pleasures. It has been like this for as long as we've known it, and no doubt much longer. Shamil's grandmother used to bring him here a lot as a young boy, and he remembers the feeling of it being exactly the same as it is now. You will find yourself smiling without reservation.

Nanas and *nanis* (grandfathers/grandmothers) have been such dependable visitors to Chowpatty that in 1998 a portion of the beach was set aside as a garden for their use. Nana Nani Park, as the garden is delightfully called, is an evening destination for Bombay's senior citizens. You will find *nanas* and *nanis*, and *dadas* and *dadis* in their saris and sneakers doing the rounds of the garden or sitting chatting on the benches. Sometimes you will

hear the seniors laughing uproariously in the open, part of the Laughter Club tradition, supposedly another way to healthier living.

There is one major exception to all the calmness (and occasional bursts of laughter) on Chowpatty. If you are lucky enough to be here during Ganesh Chaturthi, in August or September, you'll come across joyfully noisy, overwhelming crowds. Great processions will bear huge statues of Lord Ganesh to the beach and will submerge them into the sea. Delightful mayhem!

Turning your mind to food (as you should), you'll notice that amongst all the idling, much purposeful snacking is taking place. This might be on home-cooked food from carefully packed *dabbas*, inevitably *thepla* and *shak* (slightly oily roti and spiced potatoes) for Gujaratis such as Shamil and Kavi – tastiest when cooked by their late grandmother. Others indulge in the offerings of the ramshackle cluster of street-food vendors at the southern end of the beach. Now that your mood is fine and mellow, head over there, take a look, and eat.

Wander amongst the stalls, perhaps pausing awhile to watch the vendors busily preparing their food and serving it to excited snackers. When you have decided what you'd like to eat, you can then savour it in the open air, surrounded by all kinds of Bombay life, the flavours of buttery pau bhaji or spicy bhel made doubly delicious by the view of the curving golden bay as the sun goes down. The food is cheap and the view is free. Sublime delight, available to all, for just a few rupees.

"The food is cheap and the view is free. Sublime delight, available to all, for just a few rupees."

So, walk the criss-cross paths between the stalls, and don't stop until you've seen and smelt everything: the falooda and golas with the too-colourful syrups, bhel puri in newspaper cones, pau bhaji, vada pau and dosas, pani puri, kulfis, candyfloss, chaats and *paan*. By the end, you'll be more than ready to eat, and you'll have been encouraged by so many cheerful vendors that you shouldn't hold back.

The choice is indeed great. As a visitor, be cautious with gola ices and perhaps even with pani puri, both of which rely on the water which is not always clean (you still have a lot to eat, and don't want your stomach giving up on you). Kavi fondly recalls having pani puri eating competitions as a child with his grandparents. If you ask him, he'll say this is why he loves pani puri so much.

You have to order a piping hot pau bhaji. This is Bombay's famous *pau* (oh-so-buttery bread rolls, whose recipe and name is derived from the Portuguese settlers' *pāo*), served with mashed, spiced mixed vegetables. The vegetables are cooked, then aggressively mashed up and laced with a cargo of yet more butter, all in front of you on a *tawa* (a large black heated metal disc). It is then

1 Monkey-nuts-walla
2 Mellow strolling along Chowpatty at sunset
3 Historic stone lamp post
4 Beach cricket at Chowpatty
5 Sharma Paanwala with lustrously waxed moustache

Chowpatty is also an excellent place to try some *paan*. These are the fragrant parcels you'll have seen being sold from shops and street stalls all over Bombay. A betel leaf is packed with grated coconut, gulkand (a preserve of rose petals), candied fennel seeds and dried fruits, all neatly folded up, popped in the mouth, and chewed vigorously. The red spatters across pavements and walls are the consequence of the traditional variety, which contains betel nut and sometimes tobacco and which needs to be spat out. Avoid these more pernicious components. You should only try the *meetha* (sweet) *paan*.

There's one stall in particular that has a fantastic keeper, Sharma Paanwala. He sports a long, lustrously waxed and well-groomed moustache. Visit him, place your order, and he'll assemble your neat parcel in seconds. From the speed at which his hands move while he twinkles his eyes

served up on a steel tray, the hot bread alongside. It's the most simple, most delicious snack. Eat it with your hands, scooping up the vegetables with your bread, sitting cross-legged on the sand next to the stalls, free of care, enjoying the sunset and the aforementioned sublime view.

> ## "If you're left feeling sociable and active, join in with one of the games on the beach away from the food stalls. Or start your own."

6 Mixed, spiced vegetables on a *tawa*, ready to be mashed

7 Teenagers idling amidst Chowpatty's food stalls

at you, it is obvious to you that he'd be able to do this blindfolded whilst reciting Sanskrit scriptures. Then, without hesitation or much warning, he deftly pops the *paan* into your mouth, which is somehow open and ready. It's an acquired taste: not just the food itself, but also being hand-fed in this way by a grown man who is not your mother. No matter. Embrace it. Ignore any urge to spit. Chew on the *paan* as it releases its delightful flavours and freshens your mouth. You may or may not agree that they are delightful flavours, but it's an experience either way.

Having chewed your *paan*, it's almost time to go. If you're left feeling sociable and active, join in one of the games on the beach away from the food stalls. Or start your own. When we last visited Chowpatty with our team for Bombay Bootcamp, a chef suggested we play a game of *kabaddi*. An interesting sport, *kabaddi* is taken very seriously in India and played competitively. It involves two teams of seven – athletically raiding, tagging and leaping around, all within tight boundaries and all while repeating the word *kabaddi* within a single breath. Lines were drawn. Teams were picked. After five minutes crowds had gathered to watch us and everyone was wearing unreservedly happy smiles. If *kabaddi* is not your thing, there is plenty of beach cricket (this is India after all), football and sometimes volleyball. The boys who play the games are always welcoming of extra players.

Finally, be sure to admire the way the last of the sunlight reflects off the buildings of Nariman Point, briefly and beautifully trapped in golden interstices. Watching the sunset at Chowpatty will leave you feeling both mellow and refreshed. May this be long-lasting. If you're sitting down on the sand, stand up. Slap your legs back to life. Hold on to your waistline – it's almost dinnertime.

ABOVE: A cooler full of malai kulfi

LEFT: Business is brisk for the kulfi-wallas at Chowpatty

ABOVE: Piping hot bhaji, ready to be coupled with buttered pau

RIGHT: Snacking on the sands

PAU BHAJI

Pau bhaji was originally conceived as a filling lunch for Bombay's textile workers. It takes the cheapest of vegetables (perhaps odds and ends, perhaps a little past their best) and turns them into a flavoursome, buttery mash – the *bhaji*. The *pau* – toasted Bombay bread buns – are used to shovel up the delicious mix.

We've given a more authentic method for those who want to try the true *pau-bhaji-walla* experience, and a simpler version (see note). Be generous with the butter, as it is key to the deliciousness.

SERVES 4
~

350g floury potatoes, peeled

35ml vegetable oil

300g Spanish white onions, finely diced

400g chopped tomatoes (flavoursome ripe fresh, or good-quality tinned)

10g tomato purée

1¼ tsp deggi mirch chilli powder

1¼ tsp ground cumin

1 tsp ground turmeric

3 tsp pav bhaji masala

60g butter, plus extra to serve if required

Fine sea salt

FOR THE SOFT VEGETABLE BASE

3 large cauliflower florets, diced

1 small green pepper, finely diced

50g green beans, finely chopped

60g carrots, finely diced

50g frozen or fresh peas

½ tsp fine sea salt

TO SERVE

4 soft white bread buns, halved toasted and buttered

Coriander leaves

Chopped red onion

Lime wedges

1. Roughly chop the potatoes and boil in salted water until just tender, then drain.

2. Meanwhile, prepare the soft vegetable base. For the authentic method: warm a wide, heavy-based frying pan over a medium heat, add all the ingredients with 300ml boiling water and simmer, mashing as the mix starts to become tender. Keep mashing and simmering, adding more water whenever the mixture dries, until you have a soft, loose paste. (For a quick version, see note.)

3. Place a wide, heavy saucepan over a medium-high heat and add the oil. Add the onions and sauté until dark golden brown, stirring very regularly, about 15 minutes. Add the tomatoes and tomato purée and sauté until the oil separates, about another 10 minutes, stirring regularly. Add all the spices and 1 tsp salt and cook, stirring frequently, for 5 minutes.

4. Add the butter, potatoes and mashed vegetables to the onion and tomato mix and stir to combine. Add a splash of water, if required, to keep the mixture a nice, loose consistency, and put a lid on the pan. Cook over a medium heat, lifting the lid regularly to mash the mixture with a potato masher, until everything is well combined. This should take about 10 minutes (be careful of the steam when you mash).

5. Divide the pau bhaji between 4 wide bowls and serve with the buttered, toasted buns and garnishes on the side. For a really rich finish, you can add a dollop of butter before serving.

Note: To prepare the soft vegetable base using the quick method, bring 300ml water to the boil in a pan, add the salt and all the vegetables and boil until tender. Drain, saving some of the water. Using a stick blender or hand masher, work the veg to a loose paste, adding as much of the water as you need.

BHEL

There are *bhel-wallas* on many corners in Bombay, deftly mixing little newspaper cones of bhel on demand: a light almost-salad of puffed rice, sev, chopped onions, tomatoes, chilli and chutney. Every *bhel-walla* has his own version: an extra chutney here, slivers of green mango there. We add ruby-red pomegranate seeds for colour and flavour.

Mamra is puffed rice, and fine sev is a very thin type of chickpea noodle. Make sure you buy a good-quality (slightly more expensive) Bombay mix, as it will have a higher proportion of nuts and other delicious bits.

The components can be prepared in advance, but must be mixed just before serving to keep everything crisp. Eat immediately to avoid it getting soggy.

SERVES 4

~

FOR THE FRESH MIX

2g chopped green chilli (about ½ medium chilli)

10g coriander leaves, chopped

10g fresh root ginger, very finely chopped

50g red onion, finely diced

50g tomato, finely diced

25g pomegranate seeds (less than ½ pomegranate)

FOR THE DRY MIX

40g Bombay mix

15g mamra (see above)

15g fine sev (see above)

FOR THE DRESSING

40g tamarind chutney (page 377)

20g coriander-mint chutney (page 378)

10g lime juice

A pinch of fine sea salt

TO FINISH

Coriander leaves, shredded

1. For the fresh mix, toss all the ingredients together in a large bowl and set aside.

2. For the dry mix, mix the ingredients together in a small bowl and put to one side.

3. For the dressing, stir the chutneys, lime juice and salt together in a bowl until evenly combined.

4. Just before serving, add the dry mix to the fresh mix and pour on the dressing. Toss well to coat everything in the sticky dressing. Serve immediately, scattered with shredded coriander.

BUTTER-BHUTTA

Blackened, buttered *bhutta* (corn-on-the-cob), with plenty of lime and masala. This is a classic of Chowpatty, where it's cooked in a *bhatti* (a mud-lined bucket) filled with charcoal. The grill is balanced on top, so the flames can lick the corn.

This is delicious cooked under the grill, and even better on a barbecue. (Extra points for a barbecue on the beach. Make your own *bhatti* for complete credibility.)

SERVES 2–4

~

2 corn-on-the-cobs, trimmed of all leaves

1 tsp fine sea salt

30g butter, melted

TO SERVE

¼ tsp deggi mirch chilli powder

1 tsp flaky sea salt

4 lime wedges

1. Preheat your grill to high or heat up the barbecue.

2. Bring a pan of water to the boil. Add the corn cobs and salt and bring back to the boil. Cook for 3 minutes, then drain and pat dry with kitchen paper.

3. Using a cleaver or heavy-duty knife, carefully chop each corn cob in two.

4. Coat the corn in melted butter, using a pastry brush. Grill until the corn is quite charred all over, turning and basting with the melted butter every 2–3 minutes. Try to gradually build up the colour rather than burn the corn.

5. While the corn is grilling, mix together the chilli powder and sea salt.

6. To finish, dip a lime wedge in the chilli-salt mix and rub all over the surface of one piece of corn. Repeat with the other pieces of corn and lime wedges.

7. Serve the corn with the remaining chilli-salt mix and spice-dipped lime wedges. Provide lots of napkins.

LAMB SAMOSAS

The most famous of all the Indian snacks. There are two types of samosa: Punjabi-style, which tend to be larger and wrapped in a thick pastry similar to shortcrust; and the smaller, lighter Gujarati-style made with fine filo pastry. At Dishoom we serve the latter, although both types are delicious and we have eaten more in our lifetime than we care to count.

We have given two folding methods (illustrated overleaf); whichever you use, you must always fold tightly and neatly, so as not to leave gaps or holes. For the spring roll wrappers, find an Indian brand like Taj.

MAKES 24

~

1 packet frozen spring roll wrappers (each about 25cm square)

2 tsp plain flour

Vegetable oil for deep-frying

FOR THE FILLING

140g frozen peas

20ml sunflower oil

½ tsp cumin seeds

175g red onion, diced

2g garlic paste (page 353)

3g ginger paste (page 353)

10–15g green chilli (3–4), very finely chopped

½ tsp deggi mirch chilli powder

½ tsp ground cumin

⅓ tsp ground turmeric

⅓ tsp ground black pepper

8g fine sea salt

350g very lean lamb mince

1 tbsp lime juice

10g coriander leaves, chopped

1½ tsp garam masala (page 356)

⅓ tsp ground cinnamon

TO SERVE

Lime wedges

1. Remove the spring roll wrappers from the freezer and set them aside to defrost while you prepare the filling.

2. For the filling, put the peas into a bowl, pour on boiling water to cover and leave for 5 seconds then drain well.

3. Warm the oil in a medium saucepan over a medium heat. Add the cumin seeds and let them crackle for 30 seconds.

4. Turn the heat down, add the red onion and cook until translucent, about 5 minutes; don't let it colour. Add the garlic and ginger pastes and the green chilli and sauté for 3 minutes. Stir in the chilli powder, ground cumin, turmeric, black pepper and salt and sauté for 2 minutes.

5. Add the lamb mince, turn the heat up a little and sauté for 5 minutes, stirring almost constantly. The mince should be very lightly browned throughout.

6. Turn the heat down, add the lime juice, cover and cook for 15 minutes, stirring regularly. The mixture should be quite dry; if necessary, cook with the lid off for a few minutes to drive off excess liquid.

7. Add the peas, chopped coriander, garam masala and cinnamon. Mix nicely and allow to cool completely before forming the samosas.

8. Mix the flour with enough cold water (1–2 tbsp) to make a "glue" (it should be thick enough to coat things but thin enough to easily spread).

9. Fold the samosas to enclose the filling, following one of the two methods shown overleaf.

10. To deep-fry the samosas, heat the oil in a deep-fryer or other suitable deep, heavy-based pan to 160°C. Deep-fry in batches for 4–5 minutes, flipping the samosas over occasionally, until the pastry is dark golden brown. Drain well on kitchen paper before serving, with lime wedges.

SAMOSA FOLDING: METHOD 1

Place a samosa wrapper on a flat surface. Take a tablespoonful of mixture and squeeze it with your hands to try and keep it together. Place in the bottom left-hand corner of the wrapper, leaving enough room to be able to fold that corner over.

Fold the corner by bringing the bottom left point over the filling.

Take the corner into the centre of the pastry.

Fold the left side over the right to create a rectangle.

5

Fold the bottom right-hand corner up.

6

Now fold the triangle up. You should have a samosa shape with an open flap.

7

Paint the open flap with the flour "glue".

8

Fold the flap over to enclose the filling and seal.

SAMOSA FOLDING: METHOD 2

1

Cut the samosa wrappers in half to create rectangles and lay one horizontally on the work surface.

2

Take the top right-hand corner and fold it diagonally downwards so that the right-hand corner now overlaps the bottom of the strip. Press down very gently, just to make a crease and keep it in place, rather than to seal. You will have created a diagonal line across the pastry.

3

Now fold the left-hand pastry over that diagonal line to bring the bottom edges in line with each other and create a cone.

4

Make a circle shape with your thumb and forefinger, then carefully pick the pastry up so that you're nesting the cone in the circle.

5

Spoon the samosa filling into the filo cone and push the filling down with your fingers so that it isn't quite all the way to the top.

6

You should now have a filled cone with a large flap of pastry. Fold the pastry tightly over the samosa, following its shape.

7

Paint the last fold with the flour "glue".

8

Fold the flap over the filling to enclose and tightly shut.

VEGETABLE SAMOSAS

These are formed and cooked in the same way as the lamb samosas on page 166. One of the key elements of this filling is not to let the red onion brown; it needs to be translucent and sweet. The potatoes and carrots should be diced to around the same size as the peas.

SERVES 24

~

1 packet frozen spring roll wrappers (each about 25cm square)

2 tsp plain flour

Vegetable oil for deep-frying

FOR THE FILLING

340g potatoes, peeled

100g carrots, peeled

100g frozen peas

30ml vegetable oil

½ tsp cumin seeds

100g red onion, diced

3g garlic paste (page 353)

2g ginger paste (page 353)

10g green chilli (2–3), very finely chopped

½ tsp deggi mirch chilli powder

¼ tsp ground cumin

¼ tsp ground turmeric

¼ tsp ground black pepper

¼ tsp amchur

7g fine sea salt

20ml lime juice

1 tsp ground cinnamon

½ tsp garam masala (page 356)

10g coriander leaves, chopped

1. For the filling, bring a pan of salted water to the boil. Cut the potatoes and carrots into 1cm dice. Add to the boiling water and cook for 3–4 minutes, until just tender. Add the peas, count to 10, then drain. Place the vegetables in a bowl of cold water for 5 minutes to cool quickly, then drain again.

2. Warm the oil in a medium saucepan over a medium heat. Add the cumin seeds and let them crackle for 30 seconds. Turn the heat down, add the red onion and cook until translucent, about 5 minutes; don't let it colour. Add the garlic and ginger pastes and the chopped green chilli and sauté for 3 minutes.

3. Add the chilli powder, ground cumin, turmeric, pepper, amchur and salt. Stir well and sauté for 2 minutes. Add the lime juice, cinnamon, garam masala and chopped coriander, and stir well.

4. Add the potatoes, carrots and peas to the pan, stir well to combine, then take off the heat. Allow to cool, then chill before making the samosas – the mixture is easier to work with when it is fridge-cold.

5. Mix the flour with enough cold water (1–2 tbsp) to make a "glue" (it should be thick enough to coat things but thin enough to easily spread).

6. Fold the samosas to enclose the filling, following one of the two methods shown on pages 168–71.

7. To deep-fry the samosas, heat the oil in a deep-fryer or other suitable deep, heavy-based pan to 160°C. Deep-fry in batches for 4–5 minutes, flipping the samosas over occasionally, until the pastry is dark golden brown. Drain well on kitchen paper before serving.

Illustrated on page 167

SALLI

These delicious, crispy potato matchstick-fries are a popular snack, typically dressed with a sprinkling of "magic" masala (page 357) and several squeezes of lime.

They are also used for adding crunch to keema per eedu (page 42), salli boti (page 110), and almost any curry that has a rich gravy. Plain salli can be bought from most Indian grocers; here's a recipe if you wish to make them at home.

SERVES 2–4

~

250g potatoes (2 medium), peeled

Vegetable oil for deep-frying

Fine sea salt (optional)

1. Slice the potatoes into discs, as thinly as you can, using a mandoline, if you have one. (If not, your sharpest knife, a careful hand and some patience will do.) Slice these discs into 1–2mm wide matchsticks and place in a colander or sieve.

2. Rinse the potato matchsticks well under cold water, to get rid of residual starch, then tip onto a clean tea towel to dry. Pat with some kitchen paper to dry them further.

3. Heat the oil in a deep-fryer or other suitable deep, heavy-based pan to 160°C. There's a reasonable chance that the holes in your fryer basket (if you have one) will be too big for the salli; if this is the case, simply use a wide slotted spoon.

4. Fry the potato matchsticks in batches, moving them around in the oil so they don't stick together, allowing 2–3 minutes per batch. The aim is to get them crispy, without taking on too much colour. Once crisp, remove them from the oil and place on kitchen paper to drain. Allow to cool for 10 minutes, during which time, if they are fried properly, the salli will get a little crisper.

5. If your salli haven't crisped, or you wish to make them extra crispy, scatter them on a baking tray lined with kitchen paper and place in a preheated oven at 110°C/ Fan 100°C/Gas ¼ for 30 minutes.

6. Season the salli with a little fine sea salt, if you like.

VADA PAU

In his book, *Maximum City* (an essential and spicy read about Bombay), Suketu Mehta talks about vada pau: "Whose city is Bombay? Bombay is the vada pav eaters' city, Mama of the Rajan Company had said to me. It is the lunch of the chawl dwellers, the cart pullers, the street urchins; the clerks, the cops, and the gangsters." Quite right.

Bombayites have endless arguments about which vendor sells the best ones. In our view it is the Ashok Vada Pav stall near Kirti College in Dadar, almost an hour's drive (in traffic) from south Bombay. They serve their *vadas* (potato patties) spicy and hot, straight from the fryer. The heat and the chilli combine to give you an addictive hit which burns your mouth, made even better with hot chai. There's always a queue of people in the street, waiting for the next round.

If you're staying in south Bombay but can't or won't make a two-hour round trip for a small sandwich, the more convenient stall on the pavement outside the Central Telegraph Office at Flora Fountain does a reasonably good version.

It's a simple dish, a bit like a chip butty, but obviously much better. There are quite a few components to a vada pau, but once the prep is done, they are very quick to fry and serve. Perfect for brunch, lunch or a satisfying party snack, they are best eaten as soon after cooking as they won't burn your mouth. Don't let a cooked vada pau sit around… and, honestly, why would you?

The potato mix can be prepared in advance and stored for up to 24 hours in the fridge. The patties are actually a little easier to batter if they've been allowed to firm up in the fridge a while. The batter mix can be prepared in advance and stored in the fridge for up to 24 hours.

Illustrated overleaf

MAKES 6

~

FOR THE POTATO MIX

500g floury potatoes, peeled

10g garlic (about 2 cloves), grated

5g fresh root ginger

1 tsp fine sea salt

30ml vegetable oil

12 fresh curry leaves (or 3 tsp dried)

2 tsp black mustard seeds

½ tsp ground turmeric

½ tsp chaat masala

½ tsp ground coriander

15g coriander leaves, chopped

FOR THE BATTER MIX

80g chickpea (gram) flour

½ tsp deggi mirch chilli powder

½ tsp ground turmeric

½ tsp baking powder

½ garlic clove

A large pinch of fine sea salt

FOR THE FRIED CHILLIES

Vegetable oil for deep-frying

A handful of green chillies

TO ASSEMBLE AND SERVE

6 pau bread buns or soft white bread buns

1 quantity tamarind drizzle (page 358)

1 quantity ghati masala (page 357)

6 tsp coriander-mint chutney (page 378)

1. For the potato mix, cut the potatoes into even-sized chunks, add to a pan of boiling salted water and simmer until tender. Drain in a colander and allow to steam-dry for 2 minutes. Tip the potatoes into a bowl and mash coarsely with a fork (you don't want a completely smooth mash, but neither do you want big lumps).

2. Pound the garlic, ginger and salt to a paste, using a pestle and mortar.

3. Heat a small saucepan over a medium-high heat and add the oil. Add the curry leaves and mustard seeds and allow to crackle for 30 seconds. Turn the heat down, add the garlic and ginger paste and stir until lightly browned – this should take 2–3 minutes; don't let it burn. Add the ground spices and cook for 2 minutes.

4. Add the fried garlic and spice mix to the potatoes with the chopped coriander and mix to combine. Let it cool a little, then divide the mixture into 6 portions (each 80g). Roll each into a ball then flatten into a fat patty.

5. For the batter, mix the flour, spices and baking powder together in a bowl. Using a knife, crush the garlic with the salt to a paste on a board. Pour 80ml water into the dry ingredients, add the garlic paste and mix to a batter.

6. Heat the oil in a deep-fryer or other suitable deep, heavy-based pan to 180°C. Cut a small slit in each chilli using a sharp knife; this helps to limit their popping as they are fried. Lower the chillies into the hot oil and fry for 30 seconds; take care, as the oil can splash when they go in. Remove the chillies and drain on kitchen paper. Allow to cool a little then sprinkle with sea salt.

7. Split the bread buns, keeping one edge intact. On the bottom half, sprinkle 1 tsp tamarind drizzle and 2 or 3 big pinches of ghati masala.

8. You'll need to cook the potato patties in 2 or 3 batches. Dip them into the batter to coat completely, then remove with a spoon and lower into the hot oil. Deep-fry until golden brown, about 3 minutes, then remove and drain on kitchen paper while you fry the rest.

9. To assemble, place a fried patty in each bun. Top with 1 tsp coriander-mint chutney and a lick of tamarind drizzle then sandwich together. Add a few fried chillies to each plate for nibbling, and provide a dish of extra ghati masala for dipping.

OKRA FRIES

Shamil grew up resisting okra – he never got past the slimy texture. However, Naved's recipe has since convinced him and many other lifelong okra-avoiders. These little snacks are crispy, light and deliciously addictive. They are even better when dipped into a chutney. The bowl will be empty before you know it.

SERVES 4

~

175g okra

4g garlic paste (page 353)

4g ginger paste (page 353)

¼ tsp deggi mirch chilli powder

Vegetable oil for deep-frying

15g chickpea (gram) flour

10g cornflour

½ tsp "magic" masala (page 357)

TO SERVE

Chilli, coriander-mint and/or tamarind chutney (pages 377–8)

1. Wash the okra under cold water and pat completely dry with kitchen paper. Take off and discard the top of each okra, leaving the tail intact. Slice in half lengthways if young and small; quarter the okra lengthways if large.

2. Mix together the garlic and ginger pastes, chilli powder and 4 tsp water. Add the okra halves and mix well to ensure they are well coated.

3. Heat the oil in a deep-fryer or other suitable deep, heavy-based pan to 180°C.

4. Mix the two flours together. Sprinkle over the okra and toss very gently to coat.

5. Fry the okra in the hot oil, in batches if necessary, until golden and crispy, about 4–5 minutes. Drain on kitchen paper, sprinkle with "magic" masala and serve immediately, with your choice of chutneys(s).

DAHI BHALLA CHAAT

Although it's originally from the north of India, *chaat* has been cheerfully adopted in Bombay. The term actually denotes a wide range of street snacks (generally vegetarian) that make liberal use of chutneys, yoghurt and dressings. Although small, they pack plenty of flavour: spicy, sweet, sour, salty, all in one. The plentiful toppings add delicious texture. There are truly few better ways to start a meal or sate a mild hunger pang.

This recipe is based on *dahi* (yoghurt) and *bhalla* (deep-fried daal dumplings). There are several components, but they're easy to prepare and quick to assemble.

SERVES 4–6

~

FOR THE BHALLA

200g split (white) urad daal

5g fine sea salt

2g coriander leaves, chopped

1g black peppercorns, crushed

5g fresh root ginger,
very finely chopped

Vegetable oil for deep-frying

**FOR THE SWEET YOGHURT
TOPPING**

200g full-fat Greek yoghurt

30g caster sugar

FOR THE TAMARIND DRIZZLE

60ml tamarind chutney
(page 377)

50ml chilli drizzle (page 358),
strained

**FOR THE GREEN CHUTNEY
TOPPING**

½ quantity coriander-mint
chutney (page 378)

1 tbsp vegetable oil

TO ASSEMBLE

A few pinches of fine sea salt

½ tsp deggi mirch chilli powder

½ tsp cumin seeds, toasted
and crushed

8–10 papdi (optional), see note

1. For the bhalla, tip the daal into a large bowl and cover generously with cold water. Leave to soak for 12 hours.

2. Drain the soaked daal and tip into a blender. Add 190ml cold water and blitz to a very smooth, very thick and stiff batter. Transfer to a bowl, add the salt, chopped coriander, black pepper and ginger and mix well. Cover and leave the batter to rest at room temperature for 1 hour, or for up to 8 hours in the fridge.

3. You'll need to fry the bhalla in batches. Heat the oil in a deep-fryer or other suitable deep, heavy-based pan to 160°C. Add dessertspoonfuls of batter and fry gently for 15 minutes until golden brown and cooked right through (with no wet dough in the centre). Remove and drain on kitchen paper while you fry the rest.

4. Fill a large bowl with very cold water. Add the fried bhalla and tap them to submerge. Cover the bowl with cling film and place in the fridge for 12–24 hours. If you'd like to speed up this stage, soak the bhalla in iced water in the fridge for 6 hours. (They're slightly better if soaked for longer.)

5. For the sweet yoghurt, mix the yoghurt and sugar with 2 tbsp water. For the tamarind drizzle, mix the tamarind chutney and chilli drizzle together. For the green chutney, mix the coriander-mint chutney and oil with 1 tbsp water.

6. Remove the bhalla from the fridge just before serving. Lift out of the bowl, squeeze out excess water and tear each bhalla into 2 or 3 pieces.

7. Distribute the torn bhalla over the base of a large serving dish. Sprinkle with the salt and most of the chilli powder and toasted cumin. Break half of the papdi over the top.

8. Cover generously with the sweet yoghurt topping (you should be able to make out the shapes of the bhalla, but they should otherwise be covered).

20g raisins, soaked in water for 30 minutes, then drained

30g pomegranate seeds (less than ½ pomegranate)

10 coriander leaves

2 tsp fine sev

9. Scatter over the raisins and pomegranate seeds, then swirl over some tamarind drizzle and the green chutney topping. Sprinkle with a little more chilli powder and toasted cumin, to create a nice pattern. Garnish with the coriander leaves and remaining papdi, if using, breaking them up slightly. Sprinkle with fine sev and serve.

Note: Papdis are fried discs of dough, available from good specialist Indian grocers.

ALOO TIKKI CHAAT

Little patties made of *aloo* (potato), formed into *tikki* (pieces) and layered with various *chaat* toppings. The fried chickpeas add delicious pop and crunch. Some of the toppings are the same as for dahi bhalla chaat (page 180), which is helpful to know if you are planning on making both!

SERVES 6

~

FOR THE ALOO TIKKI

500g floury potatoes, skin on

1 tsp fine sea salt

12g cornflour

⅓ tsp ground white pepper

125g ghee, for frying

FOR THE CRISPY CHICKPEAS

20g cornflour

20g strong white bread flour

A large pinch of fine sea salt

½ tsp deggi mirch chilli powder

120g drained tinned chickpeas
(½ x 400g tin)

Vegetable oil for deep-frying

FOR THE SWEET YOGHURT TOPPING

200g full-fat Greek yoghurt

30g caster sugar

TO ASSEMBLE AND SERVE

1 quantity tamarind drizzle
(page 358)

4–6 tsp coriander-mint chutney
(page 378)

½ tsp cumin seeds, toasted
and crushed

½ tsp deggi mirch chilli powder

5g coriander leaves

30g pomegranate seeds
(less than ½ pomegranate)

1. For the aloo tikki, boil the potatoes in salted water until tender. Drain and leave until cool enough to handle, then grate into a bowl, discarding the skins as you go. Add the salt, cornflour and white pepper and mix well to combine. Form into 6 patties (each 80g), and set aside.

2. For the crispy chickpeas, in a large bowl, mix the cornflour, bread flour, salt and chilli powder together, then add 50ml cold water and mix to a batter. Add the chickpeas and mix well.

3. Heat the oil in a deep-fryer or other suitable deep, heavy-based pan to 180°C. Have some kitchen paper ready to drain the chickpeas once fried. Using a slotted spoon, carefully lower some of the chickpeas into the hot oil. Fry for 2 minutes, then remove and drain on kitchen paper. Repeat with the remaining chickpeas.

4. To make the sweet yoghurt topping, mix the yoghurt and sugar with 2 tbsp water.

5. To fry the aloo tikki, heat the ghee in a large frying pan over a medium-high heat. Add the potato patties and cook for 2–3 minutes on each side, pressing down on the top of the patty to slightly burst the edges so they become very crispy.

6. To assemble, place the aloo tikki on a deep serving plate or individual plates and top generously with the sweet yoghurt topping. Scatter over the crispy chickpeas and trickle with tamarind drizzle. Delicately dollop small amounts of coriander-mint chutney around the plate(s). Sprinkle toasted cumin and chilli powder over the surface and garnish with coriander and pomegranate seeds to serve.

CHILLI CHEESE TOAST

This sounds very Western, but it's very Indian too. Indians eat this when in need of a little comfort. It is particularly delicious with a cold Kingfisher at Leopold's in Colaba.

In Bombay your chilli cheese toast would invariably be made with Amul, the ubiquitous Indian dairy brand. Their famous hand-drawn ads feature the Amul "moppet" (a national icon) accompanied by clever, topical puns. For us Indians, Amul tastes like home. We use mature Cheddar instead of processed Amul cheese, but if you can get hold of the real thing, it will make this dish taste more authentic.

SERVES 1

~

60–120g mature Cheddar

1–2 large, thick slices of white bloomer, sourdough or brioche (depending on size of slice)

2 spring onions, chopped

1 green chilli, very finely chopped

Coarsely ground black pepper

1. Grate the cheese and let it come up to room temperature; it needs to be quite soft and workable.

2. Heat the oven to 230°C/Fan 220°C/Gas 8 and place a baking tray inside to warm.

3. Toast the bread until very lightly browned on both sides. Set aside to cool slightly while you prepare the remaining ingredients.

4. Put the cheese, spring onions and green chilli into a bowl, add plenty of black pepper and mix well. Using the back of a spoon (or your fingers), work the cheese into a paste by pressing it firmly into the side of the bowl.

5. Spread the cheese mix evenly on top of the toast and press down, using the back of the spoon to create a firm, even layer that goes all the way to the edges of the toast. Place the toast on the baking tray in the oven for 6–8 minutes, or until the cheese topping is deep golden brown and bubbling.

KALA GHODA

"Weave through the cars parked all over the square to admire the statue
of a fine black horse. This is not the original which gave the area its name.
Once, the proud, bearded, be-medalled Edward VII sat astride his steed.
Bombayites, favouring the steed over the man, came to call the area
Kala Ghoda, literally 'black horse'."

FIRST
DINNER

"7 o'clock"

FIRST DINNER AT TRISHNA, FOLLOWED BY A BRIEF EXPLORATION OF KALA GHODA

YOUR FIRST STOP of the evening will take you to the bustling precinct of Kala Ghoda, located just to the north of Colaba and east of Oval Maidan. Begin at the junction of MG Road and B Bharucha Road (formerly called Esplanade Road and Military Square Lane), so you can first wander down the narrow back streets populated (a touch incongruously) with cafés, the odd deli, an art gallery or two, and obscure boutiques. Browse and enjoy it, of course. It is somewhat removed from the Bombay we have seen today: if you squint and with a bit of effort, you could imagine yourself in an entirely different place.

As night falls, the daytime population of slightly tired and lightly sweaty office workers will be winding their way through the streets to get back on the densely packed and heavily sweaty local train, which will convey them reliably back to their homes in the northern suburbs of Bombay. Bombay sandwich-wallas pack up their stalls to sleep before another impatient day of trading tomorrow. Tourists trickle out of the Jehangir Art Gallery. Some of them find their way confidently on foot, others, less sure of themselves, look worried until they find their way into one of the small Bombay taxis.

Meanwhile, trendily dressed young people (the sort who might be described as "modern" by their *auntie-jis*) filter in to fill up the cafés and bars, where they sip cold-brewed coffee and share their hot gossip. They air-kiss and chatter. Reflections are checked in shop windows. Like them, Kala Ghoda smartens up a bit for the evening.

Now, for the first (brace yourself) of tonight's three dinners, you should make your way to Trishna, an old favourite of many. Mahesh Lunch Home, in nearby Fort, vies to be known as Bombay's favourite seafood spot, but we've always gone back to Trishna.

> "The main event is the famous 'butter pepper garlic crab'. If you lust after these ingredients individually, you will appreciate the helpful transparency of the dish's name."

The interior is dimly lit, but nonetheless welcoming. You will be seated in one of two rooms, one pleasant and rather unremarkable, the other happily deliberate in its marine-themed design. The dishes you are about to eat should (hopefully) owe their existence to the sea, and the room will no doubt remind you of this in case you forget.

Questions of décor aside, turn your attention to where it should be – on the food. Though the koliwada (pieces of fish or seafood cooked in a spicy batter) is excellent, and should be sampled, the main event is the famous "butter pepper garlic crab". If you lust after all these ingredients individually, you will appreciate the helpful transparency of the dish's name. Having chosen your spiny beast from the selection offered by the enthusiastic waiters, you wave it goodbye and patiently await its demise and subsequent preparation. It will return so thoroughly immersed in butter, pepper and garlic that you wouldn't raise an eyebrow if it started speaking French. Take up your cracker, pick up your pick, and set to work. Don't be afraid to crunch away with gusto. Everyone else will be doing the same. You mustn't be put off, however, if you are not a fan of dismantling whole crustaceans. It is certainly possible, if less satisfying, to ask for the crab neatly pre-shelled. Make the choice according to your levels of energy, enthusiasm or squeamishness.

"With your first dinner complete you should now probably take a few moments to stretch your legs."

Either way, the end result is delicious. You'll want to dive in with both hands, scooping up the soft chunks of fresh white crab meat before they leak any more butter-pepper-garlic goodness onto the plate. Wash each rich mouthful down with (another?) icy-cold Kingfisher or even a glass of very cold local wine. Trishna may lack the ramshackle charm of an Irani café, and certainly lacks the street-side immediacy of munching on meaty snacks on Mohammed Ali Road, but eating crab at Trishna is something that will not fail to make your heart feel tight with happiness. (A feeling no doubt enhanced by the protestations of your arteries.)

With your first dinner complete you should now probably take a few moments to stretch your legs. Weave through the cars parked all over the square to admire the statue of a fine black horse. This is not the original which gave the area its name. Once, the proud, bearded, be-medalled Edward VII sat astride his steed. Bombayites, favouring the steed over the man, came to call the area Kala Ghoda, literally "black horse", with a casual disregard for the poor old monarch, who may understandably have felt a little dejected. Nowadays the old king continues

to live quietly, and perhaps more happily, in the Byculla Zoo, relocated as part of an enthusiastic post-Independence purge of colonial relics. The new black horse, looking slightly smug at having thrown off its rider, was introduced only recently by the Kala Ghoda Association, the group behind the Kala Ghoda Arts Festival, which takes place every year in February.

Also in Kala Ghoda is the once iconic Rhythm House that used to house Bombay's oldest music seller, which very sadly shut up shop in 2016. Its closure was much fretted over and mourned. Bombayites of a certain age have fond memories of spending hours there rifling through the racks, or earnestly debating a single purchase with friends, or perhaps appropriating one of the listening booths for a secret tryst. The Curmally family, who ran the shop lovingly for over seventy years, are friends of ours. Though they must have seen more of Bombay's musical history pass through their hands than anyone else, Mehmood told us (with great regret) that they never archived so much as a flyer.

To the northeast of the square is the site of the Wayside Inn, the (now closed) Irani café where the great and revered Babasaheb Ambedkar

sat at table no. 4 and wrote vast swathes of the notes that would become the Indian Constitution. Dr Ambedkar was born an "untouchable" in the Hindu caste system (the very lowest of the low), in a small town a few hundred kilometres south of Bombay. In spite of all his circumstances, he travelled to study at Columbia in New York, at the LSE in London, accumulated four separate doctorates and was called to the bar at Gray's Inn. He eventually rose to be India's first Law Minister. He was a tireless campaigner throughout his career against the brutal injustices of the caste system. He was surely one of India's most inspiring sons and worth spending a moment pondering his life.

To the south of the square, you can't miss the strikingly modern (for south Bombay) curved façade of the Jehangir Art Gallery, Bombay's iconic contemporary art gallery. The city's foremost modern artists such as M. F. Husain, S. H. Raza and V. S. Gaitonde – together the Bombay Progressives – emerged around the time the gallery was built in the 1960s in the post-Independence flush of possibility.

Café Samovar was the small, ramshackle café attached to the gallery that served some of these artists, as well as film stars, star-struck students

1 The curvy cantilevered porch of Jehangir Art Gallery
2 Prized seafood at Trishna
3 A smiling waiter presents the famous butter pepper garlic crab
4 Photo of Watson's Hotel taken in 1871
5 The remaining signage of Rhythm House

and oblivious tourists alike. It was a delightfully unexpected thing to happen across, a tiny, welcoming refuge tucked away in the shadow of this decidedly modern and well-to-do gallery. Run by the lovely Usha Khanna, it survived a decades-long tussle over its right to continue existing there. For fifty years the café kept gallery-goers and locals alike topped up with samosas, pakoras, dahi vadas and parathas. Eventually, the trustees of the gallery – who wanted more space – had their way, and now, sadly, this humble café is no more.

To the northwest of the square, you will note an alarmingly dilapidated building that looks on the point of collapse. This is a sad fate of what was once the majestic Esplanade Hotel (now called Esplanade Mansions). The hotel, popularly known as Watson's Hotel, opened in 1871 and was Bombay's first grand hotel.

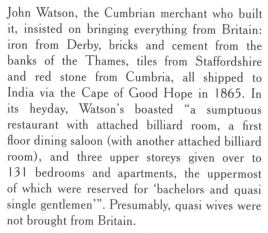

John Watson, the Cumbrian merchant who built it, insisted on bringing everything from Britain: iron from Derby, bricks and cement from the banks of the Thames, tiles from Staffordshire and red stone from Cumbria, all shipped to India via the Cape of Good Hope in 1865. In its heyday, Watson's boasted "a sumptuous restaurant with attached billiard room, a first floor dining saloon (with another attached billiard room), and three upper storeys given over to 131 bedrooms and apartments, the uppermost of which were reserved for 'bachelors and quasi single gentlemen'". Presumably, quasi wives were not brought from Britain.

In stark contrast to Watson's, the nearby David Sassoon Library has been beautifully maintained. It dates from 1870 and takes its name from the Baghdadi Jewish merchant prince and philanthropist who made his fortune in Bombay trading opium, oil and cotton and whose family sponsored the original Kala Ghoda statue. If you should happen to visit in the daytime, walk confidently past the front desk and go up to the first floor, taking a moment to admire the

6 The façade of Esplanade Mansions, formerly Watson's Hotel

7 "Bombay Fornicators" on the verandah of the David Sassoon Library

8 The David Sassoon Library and Reading Room

striking green stained-glass windows (which are the reason the windows in Dishoom Edinburgh are also green stained).

Find your way out from the reading room onto the verandah, which is furnished with an ample number of "Bombay Fornicators" – a style of chair that invites you to adopt an odd, almost supine position with your legs propped up on its extended arms. Nowadays the original purpose has quite likely fallen out of favour (at least here), and so on any given afternoon at the David Sassoon Library you'll see a number of well-dressed old gentlemen, heads flung contentedly back, legs akimbo, dozing peacefully on its shady verandah.

ABOVE: A beautiful sign-written shield sits at the entrance to the David Sassoon Library

RIGHT: A statue of David Sassoon

BUTTER GARLIC CRAB

Mahesh Lunch Home serves an excellent version of this dish, although Trishna's is more famous. Ours is somewhat lighter than the Bombay equivalent, and gets along very well with the fresh herbs and green chilli. It's a simple recipe, but very indulgent – one for a special occasion. We invented it for Diwali one year.

For ease, the recipe below uses shelled crab meat, but you can start with a whole crab, if you prefer: a 1–1.2kg crab is perfect for two (see note).

SERVES 2 AS A MAIN DISH, OR 4 AS A SMALL STARTER

~

75g butter

25g garlic (6–7 cloves), finely chopped

1 tsp freshly ground black pepper

10g fresh root ginger, finely chopped

1–2 green chillies, finely chopped

4 spring onions, trimmed and chopped

300g crab meat (white or a mix or white and brown)

3 dill sprigs, leaves only, chopped

1 tbsp chopped coriander leaves

1 tbsp lime juice

TO SERVE

Coriander leaves

Spring onion, green part, sliced

Lemon wedges

4 soft white bread buns, halved, toasted and buttered

1. Place a medium frying pan over a medium heat. Add the butter and let it melt, then add the chopped garlic and fry until light golden brown, about 8 minutes.

2. Add the black pepper, ginger, chilli and spring onions, turn the heat up to high and sauté for 1 minute.

3. Add the crab meat with 2 tbsp water and sauté for 2–3 minutes. Add all of the remaining ingredients and sauté for 1 minute.

4. Serve immediately, garnished with coriander leaves and spring onion. Accompany with lemon wedges for squeezing and buttered, toasted buns.

Note: If using a whole cooked crab, twist and pull the legs from the body. Push the body up to release it from the main crab shell and remove the feathery gills (dead man's fingers) from the body. Split the claws into two and crack them, then split the body into 4 pieces. Remove and discard any loose shell fragments before adding to the pan at step 3, and add 100ml water instead of 2 tbsp. Cook over a high heat for 3–4 minutes.

PRAWN KOLIWADA

Long before Bombay ballooned into a city of twenty million, the Kolis – a small fishing community – called the original seven swampy islands their home.

Originating from this community, the koliwada recipe involves dipping pieces of fish or seafood into spicy batter and deep-frying them. We use prawns but you can substitute other types of seafood – chunks of tilapia, cod or hake will all work very nicely. Due to the lengthy marinating, the prawns (or other fish) must be very fresh, or freshly defrosted.

SERVES 4 AS A SMALL STARTER OR SNACK

~

20g rice flour

20g chickpea (gram) flour

2½ tsp deggi mirch chilli powder

1½ tsp garam masala (page 356)

1½ tsp ground cumin

⅔ tsp ground turmeric

⅔ tsp fine sea salt

7g ginger paste (page 353)

10g garlic paste (page 353)

2 tbsp fresh curry leaves, very finely chopped

40ml lime juice

300g raw king prawns

Vegetable oil for deep-frying

TO SERVE

Lime wedges

Tamarind chutney (page 377) and/or coriander-mint chutney (page 378)

1. Mix the flours, spices and salt together in a bowl.

2. Add the ginger and garlic pastes, chopped curry leaves and lime juice and mix to a smooth, thick paste.

3. Pat the prawns as dry as you can using kitchen paper. Spread the spice paste over them and massage well to ensure they are evenly coated. Cover and leave to marinate in the fridge for 6–24 hours.

4. Heat the oil in a deep-fryer or other suitable deep, heavy-based pan to 180°C. Deep-fry the prawns, in batches if necessary, for 2–3 minutes, until deep golden brown and cooked through.

5. Serve with lime wedges for squeezing and tamarind and/or coriander-mint chutney for dipping.

Note: The prawns can be cooked in a generous amount of oil in a frying pan rather than deep-fried if you prefer, though deep-frying gives a slightly better, more evenly cooked result.

SOFT-SHELL CRAB MASALA

Soft-shell crabs are not native to Bombay; this dish is Naved's invention. If you can't find them, the recipe works well with white crab meat, mussels, clams or large tiger prawns – skip the deep-frying and simply heat these in the cooked masala.

You can serve the dish with rice or bread, if you prefer (see note). A buttery malabar paratha (page 372) will do very nicely.

SERVES 4

~

FOR THE MARINADE

12g garlic paste (page 353)

10g ginger paste (page 353)

20ml lime juice

½ tsp fine sea salt

¼ tsp ground turmeric

FOR THE CRAB MASALA

6 soft-shell crabs

170ml vegetable oil

500g Spanish white onions, finely diced

12 fresh curry leaves

25g garlic (6–7 cloves), chopped

25g fresh root ginger, chopped

1 tsp deggi mirch chilli powder

1 tsp ground coriander

½ tsp ground turmeric

1 tsp fine sea salt

250g tomatoes, chopped

Vegetable oil for deep-frying

1–2 green chillies, sliced into strips

150ml coconut milk

10g tamarind chutney (page 377)

40ml lime juice

1 tsp garam masala (page 356)

1. Mix the marinade ingredients together in a large bowl. Pat the crabs dry with kitchen paper then, using a large, sharp knife, cut them in half, straight down the body. Toss in the marinade to coat. Cover and refrigerate while you prepare the masala.

2. Pour 90ml of the oil into a large saucepan and warm over a medium-high heat. Have a bowl of cold water ready by the hob. Add the onions to the oil and sauté until very dark golden brown; this should take about 25 minutes and produce a dark paste. If it starts to catch on the base of the pan, add a small splash of water. Set to one side.

3. Pour the remaining 80ml oil into a frying pan and warm over a medium heat. Add the curry leaves and let them crackle for 30 seconds. Add the garlic and ginger and fry for 4–5 minutes, until light golden brown.

4. Add the chilli powder, ground coriander, turmeric and salt and fry, stirring constantly, for 6–7 minutes. Add 1 tbsp water if the mix gets a little claggy.

5. Add the tomatoes and cook for 12–15 minutes, or until they've disintegrated. Add 1–2 tbsp water if the mixture dries up before the tomatoes are fully broken down.

6. Add the browned onions, sliced chilli and coconut milk to the frying pan, stir well and simmer for 5 minutes then add the tamarind chutney, lime juice and garam masala. Turn the heat down very low (or even off) while you cook the crabs.

7. Heat the oil in a deep-fryer or other suitable deep, heavy-based pan to 160°C.

8. Give the crabs a little shake then carefully lower them into the hot oil and deep-fry for 3–4 minutes until crispy, golden and cooked. Take care when they enter the oil, as they can spit. If the legs start to burn, your oil is too hot.

Coriander leaves

Ginger matchsticks

Lime wedges

9. Lift the soft-shell crabs out of the oil and drain well. Add them to the masala and toss to coat thoroughly. Serve garnished with coriander and ginger, with lime wedges on the side.

Note: If you are serving this dish with bread, cook over a slightly higher heat, until the coconut milk is totally cooked through. This will result in slightly more sauce, which can then be mopped up with the bread.

PRAWN MOILEE

This is Naved's special dish at Dishoom Covent Garden. It's a light, fragrant and utterly delicious south-Indian-style curry, packed with juicy prawns and tempered with coconut milk. Although it looks impressive, it is actually very easy to make, so you can serve it either as a week-night supper or as an indulgent dinner. We serve it with *idiyappam*, the white, lacy noodle pancakes, also known as stringhoppers. If you can't get these, it goes just as well with steamed rice.

SERVES 4

~

6 green chillies

55ml vegetable oil

2 tsp mustard seeds

30 fresh curry leaves

300g Spanish white onions, sliced (a little chunky is good)

15g garlic paste (page 353)

15g ginger paste (page 353)

2 tsp fine sea salt

1 tsp freshly ground black pepper

1¼ tsp ground turmeric

25g fresh root ginger, cut into matchsticks

400ml coconut milk

250ml coconut cream

24 large prawns

300g medium tomatoes, cut into small bite-sized wedges

TO SERVE

Lemon wedges

1. Remove and discard the stalks from the chillies, then slice each one into 3 or 4 long strips. Set to one side.

2. Place a large saucepan over a medium heat. Add 40ml of the oil, let it warm for a few seconds, then add the mustard seeds and 20 curry leaves. Let them crackle for a few seconds.

3. Add the onions and sauté lightly for 12–14 minutes, until soft but not coloured.

4. Add the garlic and ginger pastes, salt, black pepper and turmeric and sauté for 3 minutes, stirring regularly. Add the sliced chillies and ginger matchsticks and cook for 3 minutes.

5. Pour in the coconut milk and cream and simmer for 20 minutes, stirring occasionally.

6. While the curry is simmering, place a small frying pan over a medium-high heat and add the remaining 1 tbsp oil. Toss in the rest of the curry leaves and fry for 1 minute, until crisp. Drain on kitchen paper and set aside.

7. Add the prawns and tomatoes to the sauce and simmer gently for a further 5–6 minutes, until the prawns are cooked; do not overcook or they will be tough.

8. Serve scattered with the fried curry leaves, with lemon wedges on the side.

Note: If you'd like to prepare the dish in advance, make the sauce (up to and including step 5), chill and refrigerate, then reheat and continue from step 6 just before serving.

MUTTON PEPPER FRY

Pepper fry hails from Kerala, in the south of India, where it is traditionally made with beef. It's a sort of dry meat curry with a thick sauce and an addictive heat from the dried chillies and liberal use of black pepper. We like to use mutton, as its strong flavour stands up to the spices well; if you can't get hold of it, use lamb. It is best served with parathas, either freshly prepared (see page 372) or ready-made south-Indian-style paratha, which you can buy frozen from good Indian grocers.

SERVES 4

~

500g boneless mutton or lamb leg steaks, cut into 4cm pieces

Fine sea salt

FOR THE MARINADE

20g ginger paste (page 353)

20g garlic paste (page 353)

1 tsp ground turmeric

1 tbsp vegetable oil

FOR THE SPICE MASALA

3 dried red chillies

1 small cinnamon stick

18g coriander seeds

10g black peppercorns

1 tsp fennel seeds

1 clove

4 fresh curry leaves

FOR THE CURRY

60ml vegetable oil

½ tsp mustard seeds

8 fresh curry leaves

3 dried red chillies

200g red onions, finely diced

15g ginger paste (page 353)

15g garlic paste (page 353)

1 tsp deggi mirch chilli powder

½ tsp ground turmeric

3g long pepper powder

10g freshly ground black pepper

200g tomatoes (fresh or tinned)

2 tsp chopped coriander leaves

1. For the marinade, mix the ingredients together in a large bowl, adding 1 tsp salt. Add the mutton pieces and turn them to coat all over. Cover and leave to marinate in a cool place for 2 hours, while you prepare the spice masala and curry base.

2. For the spice masala, put the ingredients into a dry, heavy-based frying pan then place over a medium heat, so the spices gradually warm with the pan. Gently toast for 1–2 minutes, until you just start to smell the spices. Tip out onto a plate and allow to cool completely, then grind to a fine powder, using a pestle and mortar.

3. For the curry, warm a heavy-based saucepan over a medium-high heat and add the oil. Add the mustard seeds, curry leaves and dried red chillies and let them sizzle for 1 minute, or until the mustard seeds start to pop, whichever is the shorter time.

4. Add the red onions and sauté over a medium-high heat, stirring frequently, until dark brown, 20–25 minutes.

5. Stir in the ginger and garlic pastes and continue to sauté for 3–4 minutes, until the garlic is very lightly browned, stirring almost continuously so that it doesn't burn.

6. Add the chilli powder, turmeric, 1½ tsp salt, all the pepper and 15g of the spice masala. (Keep the rest in a jar for another use.) Cook for 2 minutes, then add 50ml water and stir well to create a thick, pliable paste. Turn the heat right down and cook for a further 10 minutes, stirring regularly, until the oil separates from the spices.

7. Chop the tomatoes, add to the curry and cook over a medium heat for 20–25 minutes. Add a small splash of water whenever the pan starts to dry. The tomatoes need to completely disintegrate and build up a good colour.

8. Add the marinated mutton to the sauce along with 150–200ml water. Bring to a simmer and simmer gently for about 2 hours; the meat should be tender but not breaking down. Top up with a little water now and then, if you need to.

TO SERVE

1 tbsp vegetable oil

6 fresh curry leaves

Coriander sprigs

Lemon wedges

Parathas

9. When the curry is almost ready, heat the oil in a small frying pan over a medium-high heat, add the curry leaves and fry for 1 minute until crisp.

10. Stir the chopped coriander through the curry. Serve in deep bowls dotted with the fried curry leaves, with coriander on the side, lemon wedges for squeezing and plenty of parathas to mop up the rich sauce.

CHICKEN RUBY

Ruby Murray was a 1950s Irish pop singer, whose name became Cockney rhyming slang for curry. This is our take on butter chicken, which was invented at the famous Moti Mahal in Delhi. Apparently, the cook first made this dish for his staff using leftover tandoori chicken in a makhani sauce. The owner then put it on the menu, and it soon became their most popular dish.

SERVES 4

~

700g skinless, boneless chicken thighs

20g unsalted butter, melted

1 quantity makhani sauce (page 360)

50ml double cream

FOR THE MARINADE

10g fresh root ginger, chopped

20g garlic (5–6 cloves), chopped

5g fine sea salt

1 tsp deggi mirch chilli powder

1½ tsp ground cumin

½ tsp garam masala (page 356)

2 tsp lime juice

2 tsp vegetable oil

75g full-fat Greek yoghurt

TO GARNISH

Ginger matchsticks

Coriander leaves, chopped

1 tbsp pomegranate seeds

1. For the marinade, blitz the ingredients together in a blender to a smooth paste. Transfer to a bowl.

2. Cut the chicken into 4cm chunks. Add to the marinade and turn to coat. Cover and leave to marinate in the fridge for 6–24 hours.

3. Heat the grill to medium-high. Place the marinated chicken on a rack in the grill pan, brush with the melted butter and grill for 8–10 minutes, until cooked through and nicely charred.

4. Warm a large saucepan over a medium-low heat. Add the makhani sauce, cream and grilled chicken and simmer very gently for 10 minutes.

5. Serve the curry garnished with ginger matchsticks, chopped coriander and pomegranate seeds, with a bowl of steamed rice on the side.

PHALDARI KOFTA

Filled with paneer, cashews, dried fruit and other delicious things, these vegetable dumplings are a lovely celebratory dish we make for Diwali. The effort that goes into them is what makes the dish special. They are a pleasure to make for four, but would be quite a task to make for four hundred! Here they are served with a bowl of greens (page 123) and kachumber (page 121).

SERVES 4 GENEROUSLY

~

FOR THE KOFTAS

130g potato (1 medium-large)

175g fine green beans

250g cauliflower

175g carrots, peeled

100g paneer

30g breadcrumbs

2 tbsp maida or strong white bread flour

1 tsp ground cumin

½ tsp freshly ground black pepper

½ tsp garam masala (page 356)

1 tsp fine sea salt

FOR THE FILLING

30g cashew nuts

A pinch of saffron strands

55g paneer

10g fresh root ginger

30g mature Cheddar, grated

20g dried cranberries or raisins, chopped

8g green chillies (2–3), finely chopped

Juice of 1 lime

½ tsp fine sea salt

1. For the koftas, cut the potato in half and boil in salted water until just tender.

2. In the meantime, using a food processor, blitz the green beans, cauliflower and carrots to a "grated" texture. (If you don't have a food processor, grate the cauliflower and carrots and finely chop the beans, or use a stick blender to blitz them to a paste.)

3. Leave the blitzed vegetables to stand for 5 minutes then tip them onto a clean tea towel, wrap well and squeeze out as much moisture as you can. Transfer the vegetables to a large bowl.

4. Drain the potato and leave until cool enough to handle, then grate into the bowl of vegetables. Grate the paneer into the bowl, too. Add the breadcrumbs, flour, spices and salt and mix well. Now work the mixture with your hands to form a thick, malleable paste.

5. For the filling, warm a frying pan over a medium-high heat. Add the cashews and toast until golden brown, then tip onto a plate and leave to cool. Turn off the heat and scatter the saffron in the still-warm pan; allow it to toast in the residual heat.

6. Grate the paneer into a bowl. Grate the ginger on top, using a microplane. Using your fingers, crumble the saffron over the top. Add all the remaining ingredients, except the toasted cashews, and mix nicely.

7. Using a pestle and mortar, bash the cashews until they are broken into small pieces (not ground). Add to the filling and stir well, then use the back of your spoon to squish the mixture against the side of the bowl.

8. To assemble and cook, tip the flour onto a plate. Weigh the filling out into 8g portions, using your hands to squash each into a ball as you go. (It needs a little force, and doesn't need to be very neat.) Weigh out 35g portions of the kofta mix.

Continued overleaf

2 tbsp maida or strong white bread flour

Vegetable oil for deep-frying

1 quantity makhani sauce (page 360)

TO SERVE

1 tbsp pomegranate seeds

A few coriander leaves

9. Take a portion of kofta mix and flatten it against your palm, making a disc (pic 1). Make a well in the centre and use your hand to create a cup shape (pic 2). Place a ball of filling in the hollow (pic 3). Carefully mould the kofta mixture around the filling to form a neat ball (pic 4). Roll the ball in the flour to coat, then set aside while you assemble the remaining koftas.

10. Heat the oil in a deep-fryer or other suitable deep, heavy-based pan to 160°C. Fry the koftas in the hot oil in batches until deep golden brown; this should take 7–8 minutes. As the vegetables cook, they will start to lose their shape a bit; this is when they are ready.

11. Warm the makhani sauce in a large frying pan. When it reaches simmering point, add the dumplings, stir to ensure that they're coated, and simmer for 3 minutes. Serve immediately, scattered with the pomegranate seeds and coriander leaves.

HOUSE BLACK DAAL

This creamy black daal – our version of a *daal makhani* – is perhaps Dishoom's signature dish. It hasn't changed in all the years we've been cooking it and it's still the first thing Naved checks on entering any of our kitchens, where each batch is lovingly cooked over 24 hours. In smaller quantities, it requires 4–5 hours of your attention, but your efforts will be richly rewarded and you'll make it time and again.

Cooking daal isn't necessarily about exact timings but it is about knowing what to look for at each stage. It is vital to cook the daal grains completely at step 2, and to be vigilant during step 5. It takes quite a long time for the "sauce" to thicken and become creamy – you must watch the pan closely to ensure it doesn't stick and you must stir the pot frequently.

SERVES 8–10

~

300g whole (black) urad daal

12g garlic paste (page 353)

10g ginger paste (page 353)

70g tomato purée

8g fine sea salt

⅔ tsp deggi mirch chilli powder

⅓ tsp garam masala (page 356)

90g unsalted butter

90ml double cream

TO SERVE

Chapatis (page 368)

1. Put the daal into a large bowl, cover with water and whisk for 10 seconds. Let the daal settle, then pour out the water. Repeat 3 or 4 times, until the water is clear.

2. Tip the daal into a large saucepan and pour in at least 4 litres cold water. Bring to the boil and cook steadily for 2–3 hours. Skim off any impurities that rise to the surface, and add more boiling water as required to keep the grains well covered. The daal grains need to become completely soft, with the skins coming away from the white grain. When pressed, the white part should be creamy, rather than crumbly. When cooked, turn off the heat and allow the pan to sit for 15 minutes.

3. In a bowl, mix the garlic and ginger pastes, tomato purée, salt, chilli powder and garam masala to a paste.

4. Carefully pour off the daal cooking water then pour on enough freshly boiled water to cover the daal by 3–4cm. Bring to the boil over a medium-high heat and add the aromatic paste and butter. Cook rapidly for 30 minutes, stirring regularly to prevent the mixture from sticking.

5. Lower the heat and simmer for 1–1½ hours, stirring very regularly to prevent it from sticking and adding a little boiling water if the liquid level gets near the level of the grains. Eventually, it will become thick and creamy. The creaminess must come from the grains disintegrating into the liquid and enriching it, not from the water being allowed to evaporate leaving only the grains behind.

6. Add the cream and cook for a further 15 minutes. Serve with chapatis or other Indian breads.

Note: When reheating any leftover daal (well, one can but hope!), you may need to add a little more liquid; use cream or cream and water, rather than water alone.

MOHAMMED ALI ROAD & SURROUNDS

"It's probably best for you to ease your way in via the area of Bohri Mohalla before diving into the thick of it on Mohammed Ali Road. Begin at the northern end of Mutton Street, the backbone of the famous 'Chor Bazaar', or thieves' market."

SECOND DINNER

"8 o'clock"

SECOND DINNER IN AND AROUND THE CROWDED MOHAMMED ALI ROAD

IT'S NOW TIME TO EXPLORE the delights and demands of Mohammed Ali Road and its surrounding streets. Ready your senses, for they are about to be assaulted. All the more so if you are visiting during the holy month of Ramadan.

This area is crowded at most times, but the hungry peoples that descend during Ramadan fill it past bursting. The sun sets, the devoutly longed-for call of the muezzin sounds out across the rooftops and the streets are flooded with life. There are people everywhere, intently focused on eating after a long day of fasting and prayer. Many wear traditional Bohri dress: the men in white *kurtas* and *sayas* (overcoats) and white and gold *topis* (caps), the women in pastel-coloured cloak-like *ridas*. People cluster in tight groups around the food stalls, which are all turning out dishes with haste. In amongst the people ambles the odd goat or two, bleating good-naturedly and nibbling at stray scraps of food. Beggars ask for goodwill in the form of food or rupees, both more forthcoming than usual during this holy time.

There are stalls selling brightly coloured everything. In the midst of the melee, plucky men on rickety bicycles, sometimes carrying passengers, steer their way through the densely packed bodies without falling off. When he was working in Bombay, Naved loved visiting Mohammed Ali Road to break his fast during Ramadan. When you visit you'll see why.

It's probably best for you to ease your way in via the area of Bohri Mohalla before diving into the thick of it on Mohammed Ali Road. Begin at the northern end of Mutton Street, the backbone of the famous "Chor Bazaar", or thieves' market. Although these shops-cum-treasure-troves will be closing up for business in the early evening, during the day you can browse a fascinating collection of antiques, jumbled objects in precarious stacks, old photos, copies of Eve's Weekly from 1957, typewriters, tobacco tins, motorcycle parts, rusty padlocks and more or less anything else you can

"When he was working in Bombay, Naved loved visiting Mohammed Ali Road to break his fast during Ramadan. When you visit you'll see why."

conceive of. Some shops are devoted to a specific thing, clocks or gramophones, say, whereas others seem to trade cheerfully and optimistically in anything they come across. (The things most wares have in common is that they are old, of dubious origin, and generally in need of a decent clean.)

At the end of Mutton Street, turn left and left again to find Saifee Jubilee Street, where you will make your way to the latest incarnation of a small eatery called Surti Bara Handi. *Bara handi* translates literally as "twelve pots", and the name contains a tantalising promise: twelve pots, each nursing a different, delicious curry, which has been simmering gently for many hours. Nayeem Surti is the gracious and well-spoken owner. His grandfather brought these recipes – and the unique *bara handi* style of cooking – from Surat in Gujarat to Bombay several decades ago. It is said that his grandfather received the restaurant as a reward for becoming a *hafiz* – someone who has memorised the whole of the Koran.

As a result of a major redevelopment project in the area, Surti Bara Handi was recently obliged to relocate. For a while Nayeem had to stand outside the old shop and send confused customers to his new location, but word has now spread. Although the shop is new, the set-up is familiar: several pots (each emanating the most delicious scent) sunken into a counter facing the street, with one of Nayeem's uncles perched on a platform, lovingly tending to the contents of each pot with a long ladle. (These days there are usually nine pots,

"This is heavy, hearty, put-hairs-on-your-chest cooking, without doubt, but also some of the most delicious that you can find in Bombay."

not twelve, as they only serve *bheja* (brain), *khiri* (udder) and tongue during Ramadan.)

Take a seat inside at one of the Formica-topped booths or out on the plastic picnic furniture in the street. You may want to ask for a paper napkin to mop your brow as there is no chance of air conditioning. Try the nihari, or perhaps the paya. In common with most of the restaurants in this Muslim area, the selection is unabashedly meaty, and no part of the animal is overlooked: the slow, gentle cooking allows fat, marrow and flesh to render down into the deeply flavoursome gravies, leaving the bones to be cracked, sucked, and set aside. All dishes can be further enriched with a generous slick of *nalli* (bone marrow). This is heavy, hearty, put-hairs-on-your-chest cooking, without doubt, but also some of the most delicious that you can find in Bombay.

Before your next stop, you should pause for something sweet, honouring the local Bohri *thaal* tradition, which sees several diners sharing from one large plate, alternating a savoury dish with a sweet one. Around the corner from Surti Bara

1 Attentive servers of Surti Bara Handi
2 Assorted bric-a-brac at Chor Bazaar
3 Traffic seldom eases on Mohammed Ali Road
4 The sunken pots at Surti Bara Handi
5 Rich and unctuous curries of Nayeem Surti

Handi you will find Taj Ice Creams, one of the last purveyors of hand-churned ice cream in Bombay. Remarkably, this business was founded in 1887, a time when ice was the preserve of the wealthy and electricity was rumoured miracle. Despite those obstacles – and despite, or perhaps thanks to, the heat and humidity that Bombay endures for much of the year – it thrived. It is now run by the founder's great-grandson Hatim and great-great-grandson Aamir, who still bear the helpful surname of Icecreamwala. (Traditionally, the suffix *-wala* or *-walla* denotes the trade of the owner. So Icecreamwala translates as "one who makes ice cream".) Be sure to sample the Alphonso mango and *sitafal* (custard apple) flavours. Savour the density, flavour and texture that attests to the dexterous hand that stirred the ice cream.

Now back to savoury. Just down the street you should stop at Indian Hotel. (Do not attempt to spend the night here; in India the word "hotel" is often used as a term for a place to eat.) Look for the *tawa* (large, sizzling hot plate) piled with fried snacks. The most delicious are the chicken baida roti (thinly rolled dough with chicken mince and a beaten egg placed on top, then folded over and shallow-fried) and the bheja rolls (spiced lamb brain rolled with the thin dough and similarly shallow-fried). I've never met anyone who has tried the chicken baida roti here and hasn't loved it. The bheja rolls are admittedly a slightly more acquired taste, but consider having them anyway. The texture of brain is not unlike scrambled eggs, although creamier and tastier, and the effect is like a rich, spicy egg roll.

You will now follow this street to its end, where you hit the main drag of Mohammed Ali Road, reputed to be Bombay's most congested street. Pause and marvel at the sheer volume of traffic flying fast and slow in both directions, several vehicles deep, accompanied by a chorus of horns honked with devotion. There are designated places to cross, but they are less useful than you might hope. Say a quick prayer to your most reliable god, watch for a gap, and navigate confidently and quickly to the central reservation. Repeat to the other side. Strong eye contact with drivers and "slow down" gestures with your hand can also be of help. (If in doubt, walk closely behind a confident looking local.)

Follow the crowds southwards. Walk past the white dome of the Raudat Tahera, the mausoleum of spiritual leaders of the Bohri community on your right. Walk past the Shalimar restaurant, where the biryani is extremely good. Make your way to the famous Noor Mohammedi to sample their very delicious shammi kababs – chicken and chickpeas, ground very fine and then spiced, formed into a small patty and fried. (It's said that this softer-than-soft and delicate dish was invented to feed a toothless nawab.) Pause to admire the sketch that M. F. Husain gave to the restaurant. Given how prolifically his work appears in Bombay's restaurants, we can safely assume that he liked eating, and that he regularly paid for his food in pencil and paper.

"By this point, your stomach should be begging for a breather, but we have a last stop to make."

By this point, your stomach should be begging for a breather, but we have a last stop to make. Continue south on Mohammed Ali Road, making your way through the increasingly crowded pavements, as pedestrians and hawkers and stalls spill out onto the road to compete with the relentless traffic. You are heading for the large, brightly lit mosque ahead, which marks where we leave Mohammed Ali Road behind and dive into the super-dense crush-load crowd on Ibrahim Merchant Road.

Our final stop is the Burhanpur Jalebi Center to eat surely the best jalebis in Bombay (and perhaps even known to man). These are made not with flour, but with *mawa* (curd) as per the family's original recipe from their shop in Burhanpur in Madhya Pradesh. The thin curls of *mawa* are piped into scalding hot oil where they sizzle companionably and quickly take on the chestnut-brown colour of an exemplary gulab jamun (rather than the day-glo orange normally associated with jalebis). Eat them quickly, just before they're cool enough. (Blow; bite; wince; blow; bite.) You may well think you're full beyond bursting but against your better judgement you're going to eat at least two.

It's time to stop eating, at least for now. From here, it's only a few minutes' walk to Masjid station, where you can hop onto the Bombay local train (pleasantly empty at this hour) and take the short ride back to Victoria Terminus. It's relatively easy to figure out which train to use, and to buy a ticket from the counter. The ride is best enjoyed by standing next to the open doorway, with the wind ruffling your hair. If you've eaten perhaps a little too much, this will feel good.

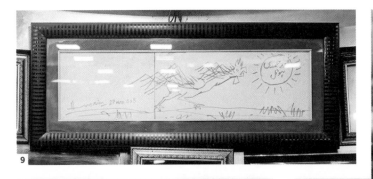

An important note on this area

We must close this chapter with a small word of warning: the places that we have described may well no longer exist when you come to visit, as the area around Mohammed Ali Road is currently undergoing a dramatic reconstruction.

The much-talked-about Bhendi Bazaar Redevelopment Project consists of turning hundreds of dilapidated and overcrowded residential and commercial buildings, three-quarters of which are reputed to be dangerous and unfit for human habitation, into seventeen shiny new skyscrapers. It is the largest urban redevelopment that India has ever seen, and, in typical Bombay fashion, progress has been slow and fraught with problems. (If ever a city loved a good, long property dispute, it's Bombay.)

6   Hand-churned ice cream from Taj Ice Creams
7   Aamir H. Icecreamwala and Hatim S. Icecreamwala, proprietors of Taj Ice Creams
8   Delicious baida roti from Indian Hotel
9   Noor Mohammedi proudly display their sketch by M.F. Husain
10 Cooling jalebis
11 Wandering goat nibbling on a photograph
12 Burhanpur Jalebi Center, purveyors of Bombay's best jalebis

13 Passing men and women in typical Bohri dress
14 Bombayites take the local train
15 Inside Masjid train station

"It's time to stop eating. From here, it's only a few minutes' walk to Masjid station, where you can hop onto the Bombay local train (pleasantly empty at this hour) and take the short ride back to Victoria Terminus."

However, while it might sound like a lusty developers' dream, this is not the familiar story of beleaguered locals versus property magnates. The project was initiated by a ninety-eight-year-old man, the respected spiritual leader of the local community of Dawoodi Bohra Muslims (a thousand-year-old Shia sect whose ancestors are believed to be immigrants from the Yemen). His vision was that this community should unite its efforts (and, more unusually, drum up the finances) to completely demolish and regenerate the area, except its holy sites, which must remain untouched. Remarkably, they appear to be succeeding. Each time we visit, the area has changed a little more.

We can't help but mourn the future absence of an area so dense and so romantic with character and history – something that no skyscraper will be able to replicate.

ABOVE: Gulam Mustafa Hafiz Ismail Surti who handles operations at Surti Bara Handi

RIGHT: A quiet moment at a shop counter on an otherwise busy evening

ON BIRYANI

The story goes that Asaf-ud-Dowlah (Nawab of Awadh, and considered the architect of Lucknow) once caught a whiff of a wonderful aroma emanating from his workers' quarters. The cooks were stewing rice and meat in large pots to feed the army of labourers who were working on the construction of the Asafi Imambara. The Nawab then demanded that his cook prepare him this delicious dish to try for himself. The royal cook obliged, adding more fancy ingredients like saffron, pepper and cardamom, along with the best meat and rice. This is said to be the origin of what we now think of as biryani.

Our biryanis are cooked using the traditional method known as *dum* cooking. Meat, rice and whatever spices could be garnered were placed in a copper pot. The pot was then sealed tightly with dough and left on the embers, so that the ingredients would cook in their own juices.

The lists of ingredients and methods for the biryanis that follow may, at first glance, seem long and complex. However, the recipes are reasonably simple once you've mastered the preparation of the rice. It is helpful to break things down and think of a biryani as being comprised of three parts: a flavoursome base containing the meat or vegetables and a sauce or marinade; next, some par-cooked, seasoned rice; and finally a topping of saffron water and a little butter and cream – a golden touch before the biryani is sealed for baking.

Crispy brown fried onions are essential to the flavour of the biryanis, providing pockets of savour and sweetness throughout the dish. You might also like to serve raita (page 124) and kachumber (page 121).

You must take good care with these recipes to achieve well-cooked meat without drying out the rice. Choose your cooking vessel carefully too, as it is essential to the success of the dish. You will need a deep, medium saucepan, about 20cm diameter, with a heavy base; or a casserole dish (ideally, cast-iron) with a tight-fitting lid. We've recommended a foil seal, held in place by the lid, but you may prefer a traditional dough seal (see below).

Crispy fried onions: Thinly and evenly slice 400g Spanish white onions (about 2) into half-moons. Heat 250ml vegetable oil in a saucepan over a medium heat. Add the onion slices and fry until deep golden brown, about 15 minutes, stirring regularly to ensure even cooking. Drain on kitchen paper.

Saffron water: Warm a dry frying pan over a low heat. Turn off the heat and add a very large pinch of saffron strands to the pan. Allow to toast in the cooling pan for 3 minutes, then transfer to a bowl. Let the saffron cool, then pound to a powder using a pestle and mortar (ideally, kept specifically for saffron). Add 1 tbsp boiling water and set aside until needed.

To create a dough seal: Mix 200g plain flour with 1 tsp fine salt and add just enough hand-hot water to form a smooth, elastic dough (about 100ml). When ready to seal your biryani for the oven, roll the dough into a thin sausage shape, long enough to cover the rim of the cooking pot entirely. Press the dough onto the rim, then add the lid and press firmly to form an airtight seal. Do make sure you've added absolutely everything else in the recipe before you do this!

CHICKEN BERRY BRITANNIA

This chicken biryani is our homage to Britannia's chicken berry pulao, using cranberries in place of the more authentic Persian barberries, which are tricky to find. (Despite much cajoling, Mr Kohinoor has never shared his wife's famous recipe.) It is prepared in the *kacchi* style, originating from Hyderabad, in which marinated raw meat goes into the pot, to be cooked at the same time as the rice.

SERVES 4–6

~

FOR THE RICE

300g basmati rice

2 tsp fine sea salt

Juice of ½ lime

FOR THE BASE

500g skinless, boneless chicken thighs, each cut into 3 pieces

20g ginger paste (page 353)

25g garlic paste (page 353)

1½ tsp deggi mirch chilli powder

2 tsp fine sea salt

2 tsp ground cumin

1½ tsp garam masala (page 356)

2 tbsp lime juice

100g full-fat Greek yoghurt

30ml vegetable oil

3 green chillies, each cut into 4 long strips

3cm fresh root ginger, cut into fine matchsticks

1 quantity crispy fried onions (page 230)

6 large mint leaves, chopped

5g coriander leaves, chopped

FOR THE TOPPING

20g unsalted butter

3 tbsp double cream

1 quantity saffron water (page 230)

35g dried cranberries

1. Firstly, soak the rice. To do this, put the rice into a large bowl and cover generously with water. Using your fingers, gently move the rice around in the water to remove the starch, being careful not to break up the grains. Allow the rice to settle, then pour off the water. Repeat twice with fresh water, then cover again with fresh water and leave to soak for 45 minutes.

2. For the base, place the chicken in a bowl. Mix all the remaining ingredients together, add to the chicken and turn to coat. Cover and place in the fridge to marinate until you are ready to assemble the dish.

3. Heat the oven to 200°C/Fan 180°C/Gas 6. Drain the rice when the soaking time is up. Pour 2 litres boiling water into a large pan and add the salt and lime juice.

4. Transfer the chicken and marinade to your biryani cooking pot (see page 230) and place over a low heat to warm through while you cook the rice.

5. Tip the drained rice into the boiling water and stir well. Boil for 4–5 minutes until the rice is three-quarters cooked. You can tell when the rice has reached this stage by taking a grain between your forefinger and thumb, and pressing down on it with your nail; it should still be slightly firm and break into 5 or 6 pieces. Drain the rice; you don't need to shake it dry as a little extra moisture helps during cooking. Place it in the biryani pot, on top of the chicken.

6. In a small pan, or in the microwave, warm the butter and cream until the butter melts. Mix together, then trickle over the rice, followed by the saffron water. Scatter the cranberries over the top.

7. Cover tightly with two layers of foil. Place over a high heat for 2–3 minutes, until the foil puffs up and you see a little steam start to escape. Put the lid on, transfer to the oven and bake for 35–40 minutes. Let the biryani stand, still covered, for 10 minutes before serving.

AWADHI LAMB BIRYANI

This biryani is prepared in the *pakki* style, in which the lamb is cooked before going into the pot, resulting in tender meat and a delicious, rich gravy that infuses the rice as the biryani bakes. The method has two stages: making a base stew with the lamb, which you can do ahead (see note), before assembling the biryani.

If you wish to make an even grander dish, use a mix of lamb cuts on the bone, such as ribs, sliced shank and saddle.

SERVES 4–6

~

FOR THE BASE

40ml vegetable oil

1 small red onion, sliced

3 cardamom pods

2 bay leaves

1 cinnamon stick

600g boneless lamb leg, cut into 3–4cm chunks

15g ginger paste (page 353)

25g garlic paste (page 353)

¾ tsp fine sea salt

¾ tsp yellow chilli powder (or ½ tsp deggi mirch)

½ tsp ground turmeric

½ tsp garam masala (page 356)

60g full-fat Greek yoghurt

200ml lamb stock (page 359)

A pinch of ground cardamom

A pinch of ground mace

3cm fresh root ginger, cut into matchsticks

Juice of ½ lime

1 tsp rose water

1 tsp kewda water (page 348)

1 tbsp double cream

3 green chillies, sliced into 3–4 long strips

6 large mint leaves, shredded into ribbons

25 coriander leaves

1 quantity crispy fried onions (page 230)

1. For the base, warm the oil in a large saucepan over a medium-high heat. Add the red onion and cook, stirring regularly, until dark golden brown, about 20 minutes. Add a splash of water if it starts to dry up or catch.

2. Add the cardamom pods, bay leaves and cinnamon stick and let them crackle for 1 minute.

3. Add the lamb and cook for 3–4 minutes, until lightly browned on all sides, stirring very regularly so that it doesn't stick.

4. Add the ginger and garlic pastes to the pan and sauté for 4 minutes, stirring almost constantly. Add the salt, chilli powder, turmeric and garam masala and sauté for a further minute.

5. Stir in the yoghurt and sauté until the oil begins to separate around the edges of the pan; this should take about 5–6 minutes.

6. Turn the heat down to medium and aim to keep the lamb at a moderate simmer. Add the stock and simmer, without a lid, for 50–60 minutes, until the lamb is tender but not falling apart.

7. While the lamb is simmering, soak the rice. To do this, put the rice into a large bowl and cover generously with water. Using your fingers, gently move the rice around in the water to remove the starch, being careful not to break up the grains. Allow the rice to settle, then pour off the water. Repeat twice with fresh water, then cover the rice again with fresh water and leave to soak for 45 minutes.

8. Remove the lamb pieces and spices from the cooking liquor with a slotted spoon. Discard the bay leaves and cinnamon and set the lamb to one side. Pour the cooking liquor into a measuring jug; you need 120ml for the finished dish. If there is more than this, return the liquor to the pan and boil to reduce over a high heat until you have the right amount.

FOR THE RICE

300g basmati rice

2 tsp fine sea salt

Juice of ½ lime

FOR THE TOPPING

30g butter

3 tbsp double cream

1 quantity saffron water
(page 230)

9. Heat the oven to 200°C/Fan 180°C/Gas 6. Place the lamb in your biryani cooking pot (see page 230). Add the 120ml cooking liquor, along with the ground cardamom, mace, ginger matchsticks, lime juice, rose water, kewda water, cream, sliced green chillies, mint, coriander leaves and crispy fried onions. Stir well.

10. Drain the rice when the soaking time is up. Pour 2 litres boiling water into a large pan and add the 2 tsp salt and lime juice. Boil for 4–5 minutes until the rice is three-quarters cooked. You can tell when the rice has reached this stage by taking a grain between your forefinger and thumb, and pressing down on it with your nail; it should still be slightly firm and break into around 5 or 6 pieces. Drain the rice; you don't need to shake it completely dry as a little extra moisture helps during cooking. Place it in the biryani pot, on top of the lamb.

11. In a small pan, or in the microwave, warm the butter and cream until the butter melts. Mix together, then trickle over the rice, followed by the saffron water.

12. Cover tightly with two layers of foil. Place over a high heat for 2–3 minutes, until the foil puffs up and you see a little steam start to escape. Put the lid on, transfer to the oven and bake for 20 minutes. Allow the biryani to stand, still covered, for 10 minutes before serving.

Note: You can prepare the base ahead to the end of step 6, then allow it to cool and refrigerate. Continue from step 7 when you are ready to assemble and cook the final dish.

Illustrated overleaf

JACKFRUIT BIRYANI

Jackfruit is an unusual ingredient with a meaty texture appreciated by vegetarians and non-vegetarians alike. In India it is used (unripe and savoury) in curries and biryanis, or simply eaten ripe and sweet from a street-side seller. A whole jackfruit is enormous and hard to come by, so tinned jackfruit is used here for convenience. Buy tender, young (unripe) jackfruit in a light brine, not the fruit tinned in syrup.

SERVES 4

~

FOR THE RICE

300g basmati rice

2 tsp fine sea salt

Juice of ½ lime

FOR THE JACKFRUIT

2 x 400g tins jackfruit (about 450g total drained weight)

10g garlic paste (page 353)

10g ginger paste (page 353)

½ tsp fine sea salt

¼ tsp ground turmeric

½ tsp deggi mirch chilli powder

Vegetable oil for deep-frying

FOR THE BIRYANI BASE

150g baby new potatoes

1 quantity crispy fried onions (page 230)

10g garlic paste (page 353)

10g ginger paste (page 353)

1 tsp fine sea salt

1 tsp deggi mirch chilli powder

1½ tsp ground cumin

¼ tsp garam masala (page 356)

20ml lime juice

150g full-fat Greek yoghurt

2 green chillies, sliced into strips

3cm fresh root ginger, cut into fine matchsticks

6 mint leaves, roughly chopped

25 coriander leaves

1. Firstly, soak the rice. To do this, put the rice into a large bowl and cover generously with water. Using your fingers, gently move the rice around in the water to remove the starch, being careful not to break up the grains. Allow the rice to settle, then pour off the water. Repeat twice with fresh water, then cover again with fresh water and leave to soak for 45 minutes.

2. To prepare the jackfruit, pat dry with kitchen paper and cut larger pieces in half. In a large bowl, combine the garlic and ginger pastes with the salt, turmeric, chilli powder and 1 tbsp water. Add the jackfruit, turn to coat and leave to marinate for 30 minutes.

3. Cut the potatoes into bite-sized pieces, add to a pan of boiling salted water and cook until almost tender. Drain and pat dry; set aside.

4. Heat the oil in a deep-fryer or other suitable deep, heavy-based pan to 170°C. Heat the oven to 200°C/ Fan 180°C/Gas 6.

5. Deep-fry the marinated jackfruit in the hot oil, in two batches if necessary, until golden brown and crispy all over; this will take about 10 minutes. Drain on kitchen paper. Add the boiled new potatoes to the oil and fry for 5 minutes. Drain on kitchen paper.

6. Combine all of the biryani base ingredients, including the fried potatoes, in your biryani cooking pot (see page 230). Add the jackfruit and stir to combine. Set aside.

7. Drain the rice when the soaking time is up. Pour 2 litres boiling water into a large pan and add the 2 tsp salt and lime juice. Tip the rice into the pan and stir well. Boil for 4–5 minutes until the rice is three-quarters cooked. You can tell that the rice is at this stage by taking a grain between your forefinger and thumb, and pressing down on it with your nail; it should still be slightly firm and break into around 5 or 6 pieces. Drain the rice; you don't need to shake it completely dry, as a little extra moisture helps during cooking. Place it in the biryani pot, on top of the jackfruit.

FOR THE TOPPING

30g sultanas

30g butter

3 tbsp double cream

1 quantity saffron water
(page 230)

8. Scatter the sultanas on top of the rice. In a small pan, or in the microwave, warm the butter and cream until the butter melts. Mix together, then trickle over the rice, followed by the saffron water.

9. Cover tightly with two layers of foil. Place over a high heat for 2–3 minutes, until the foil puffs up and you see a little steam start to escape. Put the lid on, transfer to the oven and bake for 20 minutes. Allow the biryani to stand, still covered, for 10 minutes before serving.

Note: To make this vegan, swap the Greek yoghurt for live coconut yoghurt, use extra-virgin coconut oil instead of butter and omit the cream.

NIHARI

Nihari was originally conceived as an extremely nourishing breakfast. It is a rich and hearty lamb stew which used to be given to labourers to keep their strength up over a long day. The name comes from the Urdu *nihar*, meaning early morning. Nowadays it is more commonly eaten at dinner, and often enjoyed at religious celebrations like Eid al-Adha, the Muslim festival that marks the end of the annual pilgrimage to Mecca. Meat from the animals sacrificed during the festival is usually given to the less privileged, so that even the poorest families can eat well.

SERVES 4–6

~

170ml mustard oil

700g Spanish white onions, sliced

2 lamb shanks, each cut into 2 or 3 thick rounds across the bone

4–6 lamb shoulder chops

500g boneless lamb leg, cut into 4cm chunks

60g garlic paste (page 353)

30g ginger paste (page 353)

4 tsp deggi mirch chilli powder

4 tsp ground turmeric

10g fine sea salt

200g full-fat Greek yoghurt

1.2 litres lamb stock (page 359)

A large pinch of saffron strands, steeped in 15ml boiling water

1 tbsp lime juice

1½ tsp rose water

1 tsp kewda water (page 348)

2 tsp garam masala (page 356)

¼ tsp ground cardamom

A large pinch of ground mace

1 tbsp chickpea (gram) flour

FOR THE POTLI

1 tsp dried rose petals

1 tsp black peppercorns

4 cloves

2 bay leaves

5 green cardamom pods

1. Place a large, wide saucepan over a medium-high heat and add the mustard oil. Add a quarter of the onions and sauté for 15–20 minutes or until dark golden brown, stirring regularly. Add a splash of water if they start to catch.

2. For the potli (spice bundle), put the ingredients in a piece of muslin and tie with kitchen string.

3. Add all of the lamb meat to the onions and sauté until lightly seared, about 3–4 minutes. Turn the heat down to medium.

4. Combine the garlic and ginger pastes and dilute with 100ml water, then add to the mix. Stir well and sauté for 5 minutes, then add the potli.

5. Scatter the remaining onions over the meat to form a layer, then sprinkle the chilli powder, turmeric and salt over the surface; do not stir. Lower the heat to a simmer, put the lid on and let the onions start to steam. After 5 minutes, stir and replace the lid. Let the onions cook, covered, for 45 minutes, stirring regularly. The steam from the onions should be enough to prevent burning, though you can add a little stock (from the quantity listed) if needed.

6. When the onions have disintegrated, add the yoghurt and cook until the oil separates, then add the lamb stock. Simmer gently for 1 hour, stirring occasionally. The lamb should be completely tender.

7. Turn off the heat and transfer the lamb to a plate with a slotted spoon, leaving most of the onions behind. Remove and discard the potli. Pass the sauce through a sieve into a large bowl or jug, pressing down firmly on the solids in the sieve, to extract as much flavour as possible; discard the residue. Allow the sauce to settle for about 15 minutes, then skim off the fat and place it in a small bowl; reserve this.

1 cinnamon stick, in pieces

1 tsp fennel seeds

1g pathar ke phool or black stone flower (optional)

2g paan ki jad or betal flower root (optional)

TO SERVE

Mint leaves

Coriander leaves

Ginger matchsticks

Lime wedges

Green chilli, finely sliced

Crispy fried onions (page 347)

Crispy sesame and onion seed naan (page 365)

8. Pour the sauce back into the pan and bring to the boil over a high heat. Simmer rapidly for 10 minutes, skimming off any impurities from the surface.

9. Add the saffron water, lime juice, rose water, kewda water, garam masala, ground cardamom and mace, stir well, then turn the heat right down.

10. Warm a small saucepan over a medium-high heat and add 2 tbsp of the reserved fat. Sprinkle in the chickpea flour and cook, stirring, for 2 minutes to make a thin roux. Allow to cool for 1 minute, then whisk into the stock over the heat and cook, whisking for a few minutes to thicken it slightly. (Be careful as it can steam and splash.)

11. Return the lamb to the gravy and heat through gently, then transfer to a warmed serving dish. Serve with the plate of garnishes on the side and warm sesame and onion seed naan.

Illustrated overleaf

PAYA

Nihari and paya could be from the same family. Both are eaten for breakfast as well as dinner in India. Paya is a nourishing, robust dish of lamb's trotters in a rich soup. Our version is slightly spicier and includes lamb shanks. We serve it with *taftaan*, a soft, leavened bread similar to Turkish *pide*, but fluffy, pillowy naan is good too. The trotters must be fully trimmed and cleaned before boiling; a good butcher should do this for you, and a South Asian butcher will know paya well.

SERVES 4–6

~

8 lamb's trotters, hair singed off and cleaned

1 cinnamon stick

1 tsp fennel seeds

2 tsp coriander seeds

1 bay leaf

50g whole garlic (12–14 cloves), plus 7g (1–2 cloves) chopped

160ml vegetable oil

250g Spanish white onions, finely sliced

2 cloves

1 tsp black peppercorns

½ tsp cumin seeds

8 green cardamom pods

150g red onions, roughly chopped

50g fresh root ginger, chopped

30g garlic paste (page 353)

2 large lamb shanks, each cut into 2 or 3 thick rounds across the bone

3 tsp deggi mirch chilli powder

5 tsp ground coriander

½ tsp ground turmeric

2 tsp fine sea salt

100g full-fat Greek yoghurt

½ tsp garam masala (page 356)

2 tsp lime juice

1. Place the lamb's trotters in a large pan, cover with boiling water and allow to sit for 5 minutes, then drain.

2. Bash the cinnamon stick into pieces, using a pestle and mortar. Tie the fennel and coriander seeds, bay leaf and half of the bashed cinnamon stick in a piece of muslin with kitchen string to make a potli (spice bundle).

3. Place the drained lamb's trotters back in the pan and add the potli and chopped garlic. Pour in enough boiling water to cover comfortably. Bring to a simmer over a medium heat and simmer for 1½ hours, or until the trotters are very tender but not falling apart.

4. Meanwhile, warm 60ml of the oil in a saucepan over a medium heat. Add the white onions and cook, stirring regularly, until soft and dark brown, about 30 minutes. If they start to catch, add a splash of water. Transfer to a blender or mini food processor and blitz to a paste.

5. Once cooked, lift the trotters out onto a plate. Strain the stock through a sieve into a bowl; discard the residue.

6. Using a spice grinder or pestle and mortar, crush 1 clove, ½ tsp black peppercorns, ¼ tsp cumin seeds, 4 green cardamom pods and half of the remaining cinnamon to a fine powder. Using a blender or mini food processor, blitz the spice powder with the red onions, whole garlic cloves and chopped ginger to a fine paste; set aside.

7. Heat the remaining 100ml oil in a large pan over a medium-high heat. Add the last of the cinnamon and whole spices and let sizzle for 10 seconds, then lower the heat to medium and add the garlic paste. Sauté for 3 minutes until golden brown, stirring almost constantly.

8. Add the lamb shanks and sauté for 3 minutes, then add the spiced red onion paste. Sauté, stirring regularly, for 15–20 minutes until the paste is properly cooked and releases its oil. If the paste starts to stick before it is ready, turn the heat down a little and keep scraping the bottom of the pan; it will stop sticking once it releases a little oil.

Ginger matchsticks

Mint leaves, shredded

Coriander leaves, chopped

Green chillies, sliced

Crispy fried onions (page 347)

Taftaan, pide or soft white bread rolls

9. Add the chilli powder, ground coriander, turmeric and salt and cook for 10 minutes. Add a splash of water (about 2 tbsp) when the mixture starts to stick to prevent it burning.

10. Add the yoghurt and cook until the oil thoroughly separates, about 10 minutes. Add the browned onion paste and cook for 3 minutes.

11. Add 600–700ml of the reserved lamb trotter stock (enough to cover the shank pieces) and simmer until completely tender, about 1½ hours.

12. Add the cooked trotters and another 400ml stock to the pan and simmer for 15 minutes. Add the garam masala and lime juice, stir well and take off the heat.

13. To serve, divide the trotters and shank meat between serving bowls. Pour in plenty of gravy and scatter with some of the garnish ingredients. Serve the remaining garnish and bread on the side.

HALEEM

Haleem is a thick, savoury porridge, made of cracked wheat, daal, lamb and spices, cooked over several hours and pounded to a smooth consistency. It is one of the more challenging recipes in this book, requiring unusual ingredients and some patience. With good care, these will be richly rewarded.

This is a richer, creamier version of the haleem shared on the streets of Bombay during Muharram. Naved learnt the recipe while working with the esteemed chef Imtiaz Qureshi in Bombay. Chef Imtiaz was awarded one of the highest civilian honours in India, the Padma Shri, for his contribution to the culinary arts.

SERVES 6

~

18g split (white) urad daal

20g cracked wheat (bulgur)

10g pearl barley

50g white rice

750g boneless lamb leg

600ml milk

50g garlic paste (page 353)

35g ginger paste (page 353)

10g green chillies (2–3), chopped

75g butter

2 tsp fine sea salt

10g coriander leaves

10g mint leaves, chopped

125ml double cream

½ tsp ground cardamom

¼ tsp ground mace

FOR THE POTLI

1 tsp dried rose petals

1 tsp black peppercorns

4 cloves

2 bay leaves

5 green cardamom pods

1 cinnamon stick, in pieces

1 tsp fennel seeds

1g pathar ke phool or black stone flower (optional)

2g paan ki jad or betal flower root (optional)

1. Tip the urad daal, cracked wheat and pearl barley into a bowl. Cover with cold water, mix well, let it settle, then pour off the water. Cover generously with fresh cold water and soak for 3 hours.

2. For the potli (spice bundle), put all the ingredients in a piece of muslin and tie with kitchen string.

3. Tip the rice into small bowl and cover with cold water. Move the rice around in the water to wash it, then drain. Repeat twice more.

4. Tip the soaked grains and rice into a small saucepan and add 750ml boiling water. Bring to a simmer over a medium heat. Cook, stirring regularly, until very tender, about 40 minutes. The grains should break up and form a thick porridge. Add a splash more boiling water if it gets too thick towards the end of cooking.

5. Meanwhile, cut the lamb into 2–3cm cubes and place in another pan. Cover with boiling water, leave for 3 minutes, then drain. Return the meat to the pan and add the potli, milk, ginger and garlic pastes and green chillies. Simmer over a medium-low heat until completely tender, about 1½ hours.

6. Add the grain mixture to the meat and simmer, stirring often, until the meat starts to fall apart, 30–45 minutes. Add a little water during cooking if it becomes very thick. Remove and discard the potli.

7. Transfer half of the haleem to a blender and pulse until fairly smooth. With the remaining half, use a spoon to crush the pieces of meat up a little in the pan.

8. Return the smooth haleem to the pan. Add 60g of the butter with the salt, coriander and mint. Stir well and simmer for 25–30 minutes, stirring very regularly to stop it from burning. The mix will start to form a thick, almost dough-like consistency and darken slightly.

TO SERVE

2 tbsp saffron water (page 230)

Crispy fried onions (page 347)

Ginger matchsticks

Coriander leaves

Mint leaves, shredded

Green chillies, sliced

Lemon wedges

Crispy sesame and onion seed naan (page 365)

9. When the mixture starts to come away from the edges of the pan, cook for a further 5 minutes.

10. Pour in the cream and allow to simmer for 10 minutes until it reaches a thick porridge-like consistency. Add the remaining 15g butter, ground cardamom and mace and stir well.

11. To serve, spoon the haleem into warmed bowls and drizzle 1 tsp saffron water over each portion. Top with the crispy onions, ginger matchsticks, coriander, mint and chillies. Serve with the lemon wedges and naan.

BADEMIYA

"A big boss of Colaba. It began as a small counter on Tulloch Road in 1946, as the world was watching the final episodes of India's struggle for independence."

THIRD
DINNER

"9 o'clock"

YET ANOTHER BITE TO EAT, AT BADEMIYA, AND A TOUR OF COLABA BY NIGHT

COLABA IS THE FIRST PLACE that many tourists new to the city will head for, un-thumbed guidebook in hand. Beautiful buildings and famous landmarks sit amongst an economy boosted by tourist money and by the time-honoured expectation that visitors can, with persistence, be sold any old junk. You can hardly move without someone trying to negotiate a price with you for giant balloons of many colours, or postcards faded from having never been bought, or offering to take your photo by the Gateway of India for a fee.

The stately Taj hotel overlooks the Gateway and the bay beyond. Fashionable, expensive restaurants rub shoulders with the bland international imports of Subway and McDonald's. However, in the way of this city, there is colour and eccentricity to be found in Colaba if you know where to look.

Bademiya is a big boss of Colaba. It began as a small counter on Tulloch Road in 1946, as the world was watching the final episodes of India's struggle for independence. It has completely overgrown its original little patch on the pavement and now covers all the pavements and the ground floor of a large and dilapidated old gallery. Each night it even extends over the road itself, overwhelming it with crowds. Bombayites in cars ease their way gently through the throng of Bombayites on foot, all of them here for the famous sheekh kababs, chicken tikka and roomali rotis.

Enjoy seeing the warm car bonnets spread with newspaper serving as useful tables each night. Watch and smell skewers of meat smoke and sizzle and spit on the open flaming grill, right there on the pavement. Marvel at the unruffled chef tossing and stretching dough in the air, pulling it over the hot round dome. We timed his performance once – a fresh roti every thirty seconds over long stretches of time with the relaxed expression of someone strolling at Nariman Point at dusk. Order a juicy mutton sheekh kabab, or be adventurous and try the bheja fry – spicy goat's brain – with the texture of very soft, rich scrambled eggs. Late night delight!

> "Enjoy seeing the warm car bonnets spread with newspaper serving as useful tables each night."

Stand on the street in the midst of the hubbub, and notice that all of your senses are engaged in savouring Colaba by night.

Bademiya is a good story of the promise of Bombay. It was opened by Mohammed Yaseen, a young migrant to the city arriving in the 1940s from what is now Pakistan. Yaseen started out by supplying meat to hotels in the city but his local spiritual guide, Hazrat Fida Mohammed Adam Chisti, perhaps seeing talent in him, gave him a gift of 20 rupees and encouraged him to open a small sheekh kabab counter in Colaba. The business grew gradually but steadily, thanks in large part to the patronage of the naval staff that were based in the area.

By the time of the sensational trial of the dashing Commander Nanavati in 1959 (the respected naval officer shot his wife's lover three times, then handed himself in to the police), those of Bombay's citizens involved with the case, from the governor to the sailor, were probably all taking their late-night food breaks at Bademiya. (If you have time, look up the fascinating New Yorker article on Commander Nanavati from the November 1960 issue. A more recent book, *In Hot Blood* by Bachi Karkaria, is also very good.)

Having *dabaoed* (pressed down) your kababs, your subsequent stroll might take you along Lansdowne Road to the old Sailors' Home at the junction around Regal Cinema. Built in 1876 by F. W. Stevens (who also designed the great Victoria Terminus), the building was converted into the Maharashtra Police Headquarters after Independence. But back in the day, the Sailors' Home was where seamen in the city,

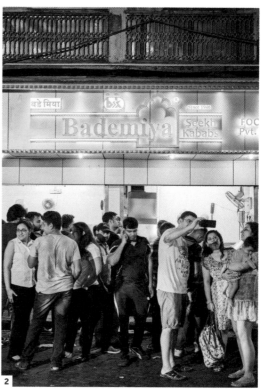

"It is certainly true that Irani cafés have stoically stayed open serving their customers through Bombay's history and through its calamities: riots, floods, bomb blasts."

generally considered a nuisance by the Bombay authorities, were kept out of trouble. The stir-crazy mariners took full advantage of their shore leave in the tropical palm-fringed port city, with its exotic temptations. They drank with gusto in the grog-shops and taverns, whored in the Duncan Road brothels and picked fights wherever they went. Inebriated and looking for trouble, they became a problem that was much too public. The new Sailors' Home was intended to corral them and to perhaps let them be inebriated in a contained space.

Walk down the busy (and actually quite pleasant) Colaba Causeway towards Leopold's, an Irani café of sorts, owned by the entrepreneurs Farhang and Farzadh Jehani. This is the Colaba of the backpacker, the hippie, the Arab and African tourists, and they say, of the drug dealers and smugglers. It is all cheerfully fictionalised in the Bombay backpackers' favourite novel, *Shantaram*, a yarn of the author's own amazing derring-do in the city. Apparently a heroin addict

convicted of armed robbery back in Australia, he escaped prison, came to India and then sat (a lot) in a glamorously seedy Leopold Café with other attractive ne'er-do-wells amongst the slowly-spinning ceiling fans, bentwood chairs and old portraits. He also worked in Bollywood, started a medical centre for slum dwellers, was imprisoned again in a notorious local jail, and escaped to become a player in the Bombay mafia. All part of a decent mid-life gap year experience, apparently.

Colaba in the 1980s certainly was a gathering place for the stateless Afghanis running a successful drug trade, Iranians and Iraqis escaping the Iran-Iraq war, and other various flotsam and jetsam washed up from the ocean or the airport. Gang wars between the Afghanis and Iranians, and then the Iranians and Iraqis, occasionally broke out on the streets. Some ended at the Colaba Police Station right opposite Leopold's.

One set of visitors from over the sea were totally unwelcome. They arrived on 26 November 2008 in speedboats and docked on the waterfront not far from the Gateway of India. Leopold's, the Taj hotel and a Jewish community centre were the three targets attacked in Colaba. The shootouts lasted four days. Elsewhere in Bombay they also attacked Victoria Terminus and the Oberoi hotel.

In total, there were 164 deaths in the attacks. Leopold's was one of the earliest targets. The terrorists killed eight people in minutes before moving on to the next location. The owners were in the loft of the restaurant, and survived. In the next twenty-four hours, after assisting the wounded, they had a meeting with their staff and decided to open Leopold's the next day in spite of the trauma and the still very real danger.

1 A car bonnet serving as a dining table
2 Crowds queuing for Bademiya's famed kababs
3 Uniformed waiters buzz amid cars and tables
4 Commander Nanavati and his English wife, Sylvia
5 Leopold Café
6 Maharashtra Police Headquarters

It is certainly true that Irani cafés have stoically stayed open serving their customers through Bombay's history and through its calamities: riots, floods, bomb blasts. Leopold's itself might have evolved from a provision store and café to what is now really a beer bar with international food, but one has to give it respect for serving people from anywhere at more or less any hour of the day through thick and thin. Even now, despite the tourists, we always enjoy eating plates of chilli cheese toast and drinking ice-cold Kingfishers at Leo's.

We cannot let you leave Colaba without telling you about the far-out rock music and club scene that thrived here in the 1960s and 1970s. From Leopold's, turn left on Arthur Bunder Road, which was once home to two legendary night-clubs – Slip-Disc, and then Voodoo. Slip-Disc

opened in 1971 and Bombay's rockers danced and tranced through the night on its imported light-up dance floor in their bell-bottoms.

In 1972, a pair of British musicians, Robert Plant and Jimmy Page, were drifting through Bombay. Looking for a good night out, they had been directed to Blow-Up, the club in the Taj hotel. Finding it not rock'n'roll enough for their taste, they wandered around the corner, and turned up at the much grungier Slip-Disc. At first the security man, having looked them up and down, told them that no hippies were allowed. Fortunately, someone did recognise them and they went in. Apparently, Plant breathed in the warm comforting fug of marijuana smoke, settled back into a chair and sighed "back to sanity at last". The ensuing impromptu Led Zeppelin gig is

7   Original poster advertising The Reaction's
    first concert in 1966
8   The Jets' farewell gig in 1966
9   Dishoom's "Slip-Disc" vinyl LP from 2015
10 The Combustibles (Lionel Taylor, the late
    Bobby Furtado, Nissim Ezekiel, George
    Taylor and Everett Perry) in Bombay, 1970

thirty minutes of legend in Bombay's rock-culture
history. The Slip-Disc club was immortalised in
every Indian rocker's imagination. Oh, to have
actually been there in 1972! Please indulge our
little enthusiasms; get hold of a copy of Sidharth
Bhatia's excellent book, *India Psychedelic*, and
enjoy his lovingly written account of this short cul-
de-sac of music history, full of the most colourful
and fantastic characters. (When we released our
own vinyl LP of 1960s Bombay-London music to
celebrate the launch of Dishoom Carnaby in 2015,
we named it *Slip-Disc*, after the club.)

In the 1990s Slip-Disc became Voodoo,
a popular gay club. Here the bohemian and
not-bohemian of Bombay could relax and be
themselves, in a place of refuge where Bombay's
more conservative expectations could be forgotten

"You might well want to walk off all that goat brain, beer, trancing and dancing."

for a while. Sadly, Voodoo closed down in 2012
after a raid led by the notoriously party-pooping,
hockey-stick-wielding Assistant Commissioner of
Police, Vasant Dhoble. (You'll meet him in the
final chapter, when it will be high time for a tipple.)

You might well want to walk off all that goat
brain, beer, trancing and dancing. Having now
made your acquaintance with the grills and kababs
of Bademiya, you're almost finished with your
food tour. Next stop will be pudding on Marine
Drive, followed by a welcome nightcap at the Taj.

ABOVE: Sheekh kababs roasted on Bademiya's open charcoal grill

LEFT: Pictures and posters in Leopold Café, along with bullet holes from the terrorist attack

ON GRILLING

It is said that the technique of grilling kababs on a skewer was first invented by soldiers on the march, who used their swords to skewer meat then cook it over the open fire. They would simply grill plain meat sprinkled with salt and perhaps some spices. Palace kitchens then added a lot of spices to their grills, to make them fit for the royal table.

Marinades: With a few exceptions, we marinate meat and fish for 24 hours before grilling. This is important not only for getting the flavour into whatever you are marinating, but also for improving the texture. Some of our marinades have two stages. This is less complicated than you might think; it is just a way to layer flavour and improve tenderness. The ingredients and the fridge do the work.

Skewers: For kababs, grilling is easier if you use flat or square metal skewers. The metal conducts heat and the shape helps the meat stay in place when you turn them over, instead of spinning around on the stick. If you are using wooden skewers, you'll need to pre-soak them in warm water for 30 minutes or so before using, to prevent them burning under the grill.

Cooking: Charring is part of grilling and key to the flavour of these dishes, though it takes a little care with a domestic grill. Domestic grills vary, but it can work well to grill on a rack under a very high heat, but with some distance from the heat source. For example, you might position the grill rack on the second notch down rather than right below the heat. This should give enough heat to create some colour, but the distance should mean that the meat won't overcook. Of course the best way to cook these dishes at home is on the barbecue, if you can.

LAMB SHEEKH KABAB

A sheekh kabab is formed from spiced lamb mince, wrapped around a skewer, then grilled. To create our mince for this recipe we blend a mixture of 80% lean lamb leg and 20% fresh lamb suet to give the best balance of fat for optimum succulence. If you can manage this at home, we strongly recommend it.

If you're unable to buy lamb suet and your lamb mince is quite lean, processed cheese slices are a secret trick that will add a welcome richness. For the most succulent kababs, finely chop the cheese, mix with your lamb mince and then pass through the fine setting of a hand mincer.

SERVES 4

~

2 tsp coriander seeds

2 tsp cumin seeds

10g coriander stalks

10g green chillies (2–3)

50g red onion, roughly chopped

500g lamb mince (20% fat)

2 processed cheese slices, finely chopped (optional)

1½ tsp fine sea salt

25g garlic paste (page 353)

15g ginger paste (page 353)

1 tsp freshly ground black pepper

2½ tsp garam masala (page 356)

TO SERVE

Mint leaves, chopped

Red onion slices

Lime wedges

1. Warm a dry frying pan over a medium heat. Add the coriander and cumin seeds and toast for 2 minutes, shaking the pan regularly. You should be able to smell the spices. Tip them out onto a plate and allow to cool, then crush to a powder, using a pestle and mortar or spice grinder.

2. Using a blender or mini food processor, briefly blitz the coriander stalks, green chillies and red onion to a coarse paste (do not make it fine).

3. If you have a mincer, pass the lamb (with the cheese, if using) through it for especially juicy kababs.

4. Put the lamb mince and salt into a large bowl and mix well to ensure they are thoroughly combined. Add the coriander, chilli and onion mix, along with the crushed toasted seeds, garlic and ginger pastes, black pepper and garam masala. Mix vigorously for 2–3 minutes (using a stand mixer if you have one). You should see tiny white strands forming in the meat, which indicates that it is ready. Cover and refrigerate for 30–60 minutes. (If you are using wooden skewers, soak them now.)

5. Portion the kabab mix into 10 balls, each weighing 60g. Push a kabab stick through the centre of each, then press the mixture into a thin sausage shape around the skewer, using your hands. The prepared kababs can be covered and stored in the fridge for 3–4 hours if you're not grilling them immediately.

6. Heat the grill to medium-high. Grill the kababs for 4–6 minutes, turning regularly, until nicely browned and cooked through, but still soft and tender inside. Let the kababs rest for 2 minutes, then transfer them to plates and garnish with chopped mint and red onion. Serve at once, with lime wedges.

LAMB BOTI KABAB

Boti simply means a small slice of meat, and this dish of tender chunks of lamb has a healthy kick from the spicy marinade. It works brilliantly on a barbecue.

SERVES 4–6

~

500g boneless lamb leg steaks (3–4)

FOR THE MARINADE

100g full-fat Greek yoghurt

20g papaya paste

10g ginger paste (page 353)

25g garlic paste (page 353)

3 tsp deggi mirch chilli powder

1 tsp fine sea salt

1 tbsp lime juice

25ml vegetable oil

1½ tsp garam masala (page 356)

A pinch of caraway seeds, crumbled between two fingers

1¼ tsp ground cumin

TO GRILL

1½ tsp kabab masala (page 358)

25g unsalted butter, melted

20ml lime juice

TO SERVE

Mint leaves, shredded

Kachumber (page 121)

Lime wedges

1. Place a sieve over a bowl and line with muslin. Pour the yoghurt into the muslin cloth and leave it to strain for at least 3 hours (see note).

2. In the meantime, trim the lamb of any fat and cut into 3cm chunks. Pat as dry as you can with kitchen paper. Place in a bowl, add the papaya paste and toss the lamb chunks to coat. Cover and leave to stand for 30 minutes.

3. In a large bowl, mix the strained yoghurt together with the remaining marinade ingredients.

4. When the 30 minutes is up, tip the lamb into a sieve to drain off the liquid and give the sieve a shake to remove excess moisture. Mix the meat into the yoghurt marinade, cover and refrigerate for 24 hours.

5. Take the lamb out of the fridge 30 minutes before cooking. (If you are using wooden skewers, soak them now.) Heat the grill to medium-high.

6. Thread the meat onto your skewers, taking care not to pack it on too tightly.

7. Grill the kababs for 6–8 minutes, turning regularly, until slightly charred and cooked through but not overdone. Sprinkle with the kabab masala, butter and lime juice, turning the kababs to coat all over. Finish with a sprinkling of shredded mint. Serve immediately, with kachumber and lime wedges for squeezing.

Note: Straining the yoghurt for 3 hours reduces the water content so that the marinade sticks to the meat; it's even better if you can manage to strain it overnight in the fridge.

SPICY LAMB CHOPS

Succulent and richly flavoured, these chops are delicious. The first marinade helps to tenderise the meat, while the second creates deep and complex flavours as the chops are steeped in jaggery and lime over 24 hours. The combination of sweet and sour creates a wonderful harmony.

The recipe works best with thick, meaty lamb chops. Mutton works, as does goat if you can get it. Thicker chops mean you can grill for a while longer and build up some colour, and chops from the shoulder end can be particularly successful.

SERVES 4 AS A STARTER

~

8 meaty lamb cutlets

FOR THE FIRST MARINADE

10g garlic paste (page 353)

5g ginger paste (page 353)

1 tsp malt vinegar

⅓ tsp fine sea salt

6g papaya paste (optional)

FOR THE SECOND MARINADE

2½ tsp cumin seeds

1 tsp coriander seeds

1 clove

1 scant tbsp HP Sauce

25g coriander stalks

1½ tsp garam masala (page 356)

25g garlic paste (page 353)

35g ginger paste (page 353)

⅓ tsp crushed black peppercorns

8g jaggery

35ml lime juice

5g red chilli, roughly chopped

5g green chilli, roughly chopped

5g fine sea salt

2 tsp vegetable oil

TO GRILL AND SERVE

25g unsalted butter, melted

Mint or coriander leaves

1 tbsp pomegranate seeds
(optional)

1. Place the lamb chops in a shallow dish. For the first marinade, mix all the ingredients together in a small bowl. Rub the marinade into the chops, cover and refrigerate for 2 hours.

2. While the chops are in the fridge, prepare the second marinade. Warm a heavy-based frying pan over a medium heat. Add the cumin and coriander seeds along with the clove and toast for 2 minutes, shaking the pan to stop them from burning. Tip them straight into your mortar and pestle and leave to cool.

3. Blitz all of the other marinade ingredients to a paste, using a blender or mini food processor.

4. Grind the cooled toasted spices to a coarse powder and add it to the paste.

5. When the first marinade time is up, take the chops out of the fridge and coat them with the second marinade. Cover and refrigerate for 24 hours.

6. Heat the grill to high and take the chops out of the fridge. Toss them again to ensure an even coating of marinade. Place on a foil-lined baking tray and brush with melted butter.

7. Grill the chops for 2–3 minutes, until they start to sizzle. Turn them over, brush with melted butter and grill for a further 2–3 minutes. Repeat until nicely caramelised.

8. Allow the chops to rest for 3 minutes before serving, scattered with mint or coriander and pomegranate seeds, if you like.

LAMB RAAN

A wonderful dish of tender, slow-cooked *raan* (leg) of lamb, pulled into silky shreds and combined with a deliciously savoury masala. Apparently, it has a heritage going back to Alexander the Great's battles in India. We serve it as a centrepiece, complemented with other dishes.

We suggest using a half leg of lamb (top end) as this fits into most casserole dishes, but the recipe is flexible, and will work with any cut of lamb leg on the bone – from four lamb shanks to a whole leg. You can also make a seriously tasty Christmas raan, using a large turkey leg (remove the skin before shredding the meat in step 6). If you don't have a suitable pot, you can cook the raan in a deep baking dish, tightly covered with a double layer of foil. Be generous with the final seasoning: the meat should be savoury and nicely spiced, with lots of lime to bring the dish together.

If you are fortunate enough to have any leftovers, pile into soft pillowy bread buns and garnish with slaw (page 118), gherkins, baby spinach and fried green chillies to make our popular lamb raan bun.

SERVES 4–6

~

½ leg of lamb on the bone, 1.2–1.4kg

2 tsp fine sea salt

1¾ tsp deggi mirch chilli powder

35g garlic (8–9 cloves)

30g fresh root ginger

1 bay leaf

4 cloves

16 black peppercorns

2 cinnamon sticks

6 green cardamom pods

3 black cardamom pods

75ml malt vinegar

TO ASSEMBLE

40g unsalted butter

2 tsp kabab masala (page 358)

25ml lime juice, or more to taste

1. Place the lamb in a dish. Mix the salt and chilli powder together and rub the mixture all over the lamb. Leave to marinate in the fridge for 30 minutes.

2. Grate the garlic and ginger using a microplane, or grind to a fine paste using a pestle and mortar. When the 30 minutes is up, rub the garlic and ginger paste all over the lamb. Cover and refrigerate for 12–24 hours.

3. Take the lamb out of the fridge 5 hours before you want to eat and leave it at room temperature for 30 minutes. Heat the oven to 180°C/Fan 160°C/Gas 4.

4. Place the lamb joint in a deep casserole pot (that has a lid). Add the bay leaf, spices and vinegar and pour in enough water to come at least halfway up the meat (around 300ml). Put the lid on and place the pot in the oven. Roast for 4 hours, turning the joint over every hour and topping up the water if the level goes below one-third of the way up the lamb.

5. Once cooked, remove the lamb from the oven and leave it to rest in its cooking liquor for 20–30 minutes. Preheat the grill to high.

6. Pour the cooking liquor through a sieve into a measuring jug; discard the residue in the sieve. Working in the dish, pull the meat from the bone; set the bone aside. Shred the meat using two forks or your hands. Add 120ml of the reserved cooking liquor, the butter and 2 tsp kabab masala. Mix, taste, and add a little more cooking liquor, lime juice or kabab masala as you wish.

TO SERVE

Lime wedges

Extra kabab masala

Fried green chillies (optional)

7. Scatter the meat on an ovenproof tray and place it under the hot grill for 4–5 minutes, to create a few crispy bits on top. Place the reserved bone in a serving dish and pile the meat on and around it, so that it resembles a joint.

8. Bring the lamb raan to the table in the dish. Have lime wedges and a dish of extra kabab masala on the table for guests to add more if they wish. You might like to serve a bowl of fried green chillies, too.

CHICKEN TIKKA

Chicken tikka masala is supposedly Britain's favourite dish. If it's yours, then you may be disappointed: this dish is not it.

Tikka simply means piece, or chunk – so this is chicken pieces, marinated then grilled. The marinade is based on sweet vinegar, not yoghurt – and there's not a drop of food colouring in sight.

It makes a nice starter, or delicious lunch in a chapati roll (page 281).

SERVES 4 AS A STARTER

~

500g boneless chicken thighs, with skin

FOR THE MARINADE

30g fresh root ginger

10g garlic (2–3 cloves)

10g green chillies (2–3)

30ml rice vinegar

1 tsp deggi mirch chilli powder

1 tsp ground turmeric

1½ tsp fine sea salt

2 tsp granulated sugar

1 tbsp vegetable oil

TO GRILL AND SERVE

25g unsalted butter, melted

Lime wedges

1. Cut each chicken thigh into 3 pieces and pat dry with kitchen paper. Place in a large bowl.

2. For the marinade, blitz the ingredients together in a blender or mini food processor to a smooth paste.

3. Spoon the marinade over the chicken pieces and turn them to coat. Cover and leave to marinate in the fridge for 6–24 hours.

4. Take the marinated chicken out of the fridge 20 minutes before cooking. (If you are using wooden skewers, soak them now.)

5. Heat the grill to high. Thread the marinated chicken onto skewers, leaving enough space between the pieces for the heat to penetrate. Grill for 12–15 minutes, turning and basting regularly with the melted butter, until deep golden brown with some charring. Check that the chicken pieces are cooked through.

6. Let the cooked chicken rest for 5 minutes before serving, with lime wedges for squeezing.

MURGH MALAI

With the exception of paneer, cheese does not play a role in traditional Indian recipes. But somewhere, a canny chef must have come up with the idea of using it for a rich marinade, instead of the usual yoghurt. This version also includes coriander stems and green chillies, though it is relatively mild. Chicken thigh meat is used in preference to breast, because it is softer in texture and will carry more of the flavours of the dish.

Murgh malai can be cooled and shredded into our chilli pomelo salad (page 115) for a refreshing, sustaining lunch.

SERVES 4 –6

~

500g boneless, skinless chicken thighs

FOR THE FIRST MARINADE

12g garlic paste (page 353)

10g ginger paste (page 353)

½ tsp fine sea salt

2 tbsp malt vinegar

FOR THE SECOND MARINADE

90g mature Cheddar, grated

2 tbsp full-fat Greek yoghurt

50ml double cream

½ medium egg, beaten

1½ tsp fine sea salt

15g cornflour

2 green chillies, deseeded and finely chopped

20g coriander stalks, very finely chopped

TO FINISH AND SERVE

20g unsalted butter

A few pinches of kabab masala (page 358)

A generous squeeze of lime juice

Coriander leaves

Lime wedges

1. Cut each chicken thigh into 3 pieces and pat dry with kitchen paper. Place in a large bowl.

2. For the first marinade, mix the ingredients together in a small bowl. Spoon over the chicken and turn to coat. Cover and place in the fridge while you prepare the second marinade, though if you can, leave it for up to 2 hours.

3. Blitz the grated cheese, yoghurt, cream, egg, salt and cornflour together in a blender or food processor to a smooth paste. Add the chopped chillies and coriander stalks and mix nicely.

4. Take the chicken out of the fridge, pour the second marinade over it and mix well. Cover and return to the fridge to marinate for 6–24 hours.

5. Remove the marinated chicken from the fridge about 20 minutes before cooking. (If you are using wooden skewers, soak them now.)

6. Thread the chicken onto skewers, leaving enough space between the pieces for the heat to penetrate. Grill for 12–15 minutes, turning regularly, until deep golden brown with some charring. Check that the chicken pieces are cooked through.

7. Sprinkle the cooked chicken with the butter, kabab masala and lime juice, turning the skewers to coat all over. Finish with a sprinkling of coriander leaves and serve with lime wedges.

MASALA PRAWNS

Bombay is surrounded by the sea. Accordingly, ever since people have lived here, they've always eaten a lot of fish. At Sassoon Dock, the raucous fish market in south Bombay, you can find sea creatures of every shape, size and flavour, laid out in baskets, on tarpaulins, or piled in vast heaps on the floor. (If you visit, consider wearing an old pair of shoes that you are happy to throw away afterwards.)

Buy the largest prawns you can find. If they are very large, you will be able to turn them over during cooking, to get a crispy edge on both sides without overcooking the flesh. You'll need to make the marinade in advance so that it can drain in the fridge for a few hours, otherwise it will be too wet.

SERVES 4 AS A SMALL STARTER OR SNACK

~

300g peeled raw king prawns (tail shells on), deveined

2 tsp chickpea (gram) flour

FOR THE MARINADE

20g coriander stalks

12g garlic paste (page 353)

4g fresh root ginger, chopped

7g green chillies (1–2)

¼ tsp coarsely ground black pepper

1 tsp lime juice

25g red onion

½ tsp fine sea salt

10g spring onion

1 small tomato (60g), halved and deseeded

1 tbsp vegetable oil

TO GRILL AND SERVE

30g unsalted butter, melted

Coriander sprigs

Lime wedges

1. Place a sieve over a bowl and line with muslin. Blitz all the marinade ingredients in a blender to a smooth paste. Tip into the muslin-lined sieve, cover with cling film and leave to strain in the fridge for 6–12 hours.

2. Pat the prawns dry – as dry as you can – with kitchen paper and place in a bowl.

3. Warm a dry frying pan over a medium heat. Add the chickpea flour and toast for 2–3 minutes, keeping it moving. You'll notice a strong aroma when it is ready. Tip onto a plate and allow to cool.

4. Remove the marinade from the fridge and discard any liquid that has collected in the bowl.

5. Add the toasted chickpea flour to the prawns and toss to combine, then add the marinade and mix well. Cover and refrigerate for 2–3 hours.

6. When you are ready to cook, heat the grill to high. Line a baking sheet with foil, and lay the prawns on the foil. Baste them with melted butter and grill for 3–4 minutes until lightly charred. Do not turn them over, unless they are very large.

7. Serve the prawns scattered with coriander, with lime wedges on the side for squeezing.

MACCHI TIKKA

This is a mild and subtle fish dish (in Hindi *macchi* simply means fish). We recommend using a firm, flat white fish, which will be easier to handle. Tilapia fillets are perfect; sole and plaice also work well. You can use a thicker, chunkier fish like cod or monkfish, but you'll need to turn them very carefully during cooking for a good result, as the chunks can fall off the skewer as you grill them.

The oil used to fry the garlic isn't used in the rest of the recipe. You may want to keep it, though, as it will be delicious to cook something else with.

SERVES 4

~

4 fillets of firm, flat white fish, 150g each

FOR THE FIRST MARINADE

3g garlic paste (page 353)

2g ginger paste (page 353)

20ml lime juice

¼ tsp fine sea salt

FOR THE SECOND MARINADE

75ml vegetable oil

15g garlic (3–4 cloves), finely chopped

6g chickpea (gram) flour

60g full-fat Greek yoghurt

⅓ tsp fine sea salt

⅓ tsp ground turmeric

½ tsp deggi mirch chilli powder

1 tsp lime juice

¼ tsp garam masala (page 356)

3g ginger paste (page 353)

5g garlic paste (page 353)

TO GRILL AND SERVE

25g unsalted butter, melted

Coriander sprigs

Red onion slices

Lime wedges

1. Pat the fish as dry as you can, using kitchen paper, then place in a shallow dish. Mix together the ingredients for the first marinade, then brush all over the fish. Cover and refrigerate while you prepare the second marinade.

2. Warm the oil in a small frying pan over a medium heat. Add the garlic and sauté until it is light golden brown, 7–8 minutes. Remove the chopped garlic with a small fine-meshed sieve and drain on kitchen paper; set aside.

3. Warm a dry frying pan over a medium heat. Add the chickpea flour and toast until golden brown, stirring regularly so that it doesn't burn. Tip into a large bowl and allow to cool, then add the fried garlic and all the remaining ingredients for the second marinade. Mix well.

4. Lay the fish on a large plate, skin side down (if it has skin). Apply the second marinade to the flesh of the fish (as a topping), carefully cover with cling film and refrigerate for 2 hours.

5. Heat the grill to high. Transfer the fish to a baking sheet and brush with melted butter. Grill for 3 minutes, brush with butter again, then grill until nicely caramelised and the fish is just cooked, another 3–5 minutes.

6. Serve the grilled fish immediately, with coriander, red onion and lime wedges.

PANEER TIKKA ACHARI

Paneer is a fresh, unsalted, mild cheese, which doesn't need any ageing or culturing. Its soft and forgiving nature means it picks up flavours wonderfully, while not imparting a strong taste of its own. Unusually, it doesn't melt with heat, so it can be added to curries or grilled on its own, as in this recipe, where it's skewered with peppers and marinated beforehand.

SERVES 4 AS A STARTER

~

225g paneer

1 yellow pepper, halved, cored and deseeded

1 red pepper, halved, cored and deseeded

FOR THE FIRST MARINADE

⅔ tsp deggi mirch chilli powder

½ tsp ground turmeric

A large pinch of dried fenugreek, finely crumbled

½ tsp fine sea salt

2 tsp lime juice

FOR THE SECOND MARINADE

1 tsp chickpea (gram) flour

30g mixed pickle (Patak's), ground to a paste

⅓ tsp deggi mirch chilli powder

⅓ tsp ground turmeric

½ tsp fine sea salt

1 tbsp mustard oil

100g full-fat Greek yoghurt

TO FINISH

15g unsalted butter, melted

Kabab masala (page 358)

1. Cut the paneer into 3cm cubes and place in a bowl. Mix the ingredients for the first marinade together with 2 tsp water. Add to the paneer cubes, toss to coat and set aside to marinate while you prepare the second marinade and peppers.

2. Place a dry frying pan over a high heat, add the chickpea flour and toast until golden brown. Tip into a large bowl and allow to cool. Add the pickle, chilli powder, turmeric, salt and mustard oil. Mix until evenly combined, then add the yoghurt and mix again.

3. Cut the peppers into pieces, similar in size to the paneer. Add the peppers and the paneer to the second marinade and leave to marinate in the fridge for 6–24 hours.

4. If you are using wooden skewers, put them to soak 30 minutes before assembling.

5. Heat the grill to high. Thread alternate pieces of pepper and paneer onto metal or wooden skewers and brush with melted butter. Grill the skewers for 8–10 minutes until deep golden and hot right through, turning a couple of times and basting with the melted butter.

6. Dust the kababs with a few generous pinches of kabab masala and serve immediately.

PANEER TIKKA CHAPATI ROLL

Some of the best rolls in Bombay are served at Bademiya. For this version, you need a half quantity of chapati dough (page 368), so if you are making chapatis for dinner one night, you could have chapati rolls the next day.

You need to have everything ready so you can assemble the rolls as soon as the chapatis are cooked. The rolling part is a lot like wrapping up a burrito.

SERVES 4

~

½ quantity chapati dough
(page 368)

Flour, for dusting

FOR THE PANEER FILLING

1 quantity marinated paneer
without peppers (page 278)

1 tbsp vegetable oil

1 small green pepper, finely
sliced

1 small red onion, finely sliced

⅓ tsp ground turmeric

¼ tsp deggi mirch chilli powder

⅓ tsp fine sea salt

1 green chilli, finely chopped

180ml makhani sauce (page 360)

50g baby spinach, washed and
patted thoroughly dry

20 coriander leaves

A few pinches of kabab masala
(page 358)

TO SERVE

70g unsalted butter, melted

Coriander-mint chutney
(page 378)

1. Turn the grill to medium-high. For the filling, place the paneer on a lined baking sheet (no need to skewer) and grill for 8 minutes, turning once or twice, until golden, then cut in half.

2. Heat a medium frying pan over a high heat. Add the oil, then the green pepper and half the red onion and sauté for 3 minutes, stirring often. Turn the heat down and add the turmeric, chilli powder, salt and green chilli and cook for 1 minute. Add the makhani sauce and cook until warmed through and bubbling, then add the grilled paneer, turn to coat and remove from the heat.

3. Divide the chapati dough into 4 portions and roll into neat, round balls. Have ready a clean tea towel to wrap the chapatis once cooked, to keep them hot and soft.

4. Place a large frying pan over a high heat. On a floured work surface, roll out a dough ball as thinly as you can, to a 1–2mm thick round. Place the chapati in the pan and cook for about 1 minute on each side. Roll up into a cylinder and wrap in the tea towel. Repeat to cook the remaining chapatis.

5. To assemble, take a chapati and lay it flat on a clean surface. Arrange the filling components in a neat rectangle in the centre of the chapati: a quarter of the spinach, then a quarter of the remaining sliced onion, 5 coriander leaves, and finally a quarter of the paneer mixture. Sprinkle a big pinch of kabab masala on top of the filling. To roll, fold tightly in half, fold both ends in, then roll tightly into a log shape. Set to one side and form the rest of the chapati rolls.

6. To finish, place the frying pan back over a high heat and brush the rolls all over with melted butter. You should be able to fry two at a time. Add to the hot pan and sear for 30 seconds until golden, then turn and sear for a further 30 seconds.

7. Slice each chapati roll in half, on the diagonal. Serve immediately, with coriander-mint chutney on the side for dipping.

Variation

Chicken tikka chapati roll: Divide ½ quantity chapati dough into 4 even portions and roll into neat, round balls. Grill one quantity marinated chicken tikka (page 270) under a high heat for 12–15 minutes, until browned and cooked through, turning and basting regularly with melted butter. Meanwhile, roll out and cook the chapatis (as left). To assemble each chapati: in a neat rectangle in the centre of the chapati, spread 1 heaped tbsp tomato-chilli jam (page 59). Add 50g baby spinach (as left) and 1 tbsp slaw (page 118). Top with 4 or 5 pieces of chicken tikka. Fold tightly in half, fold both ends in, then roll tightly into a log shape. When the rolls are all assembled, slice in half on the diagonal and serve with extra tomato-chilli jam.

GUNPOWDER POTATOES

A feisty dish of grilled new potatoes tossed with toasted spices, fresh green chillies, spring onions and coriander. It's hard to believe that two of the most everyday ingredients in Indian cookery – potatoes and chillies – were only introduced to the country in the early seventeenth century when the Portuguese arrived. Thankfully, both ingredients thrived.

This potato dish is an excellent accompaniment to lamb raan (page 268).

SERVES 4

~

500g baby new potatoes

½ tsp cumin seeds

½ tsp coriander seeds

½ tsp fennel seeds

1 tbsp vegetable oil, for basting

25g butter, melted

6 spring onions, finely chopped

5g coriander leaves, finely chopped

3 green chillies, very finely chopped

½ tsp flaky sea salt

30ml lime juice

1–2 tsp kabab masala (page 358)

1. Bring a large pan of salted water to the boil. Add the potatoes and cook until just tender, 12–15 minutes, depending on size.

2. Meanwhile, add the cumin, coriander and fennel seeds to a hot dry frying pan and toast for 2 minutes until fragrant. Crush the toasted seeds, using a pestle and mortar; set aside.

3. Heat the grill to high.

4. Drain the potatoes and allow them to steam-dry in the colander for a minute.

5. Place the potatoes on a sturdy baking tray. Brush or sprinkle them with some oil and grill until the upper side is crispy and evenly browned, about 5–7 minutes. Turn the potatoes over and repeat to crisp and colour the other side.

6. Meanwhile, put the crushed toasted spices into a large bowl and add the melted butter, spring onions, coriander and chillies.

7. When the potatoes are thoroughly browned and crisped, remove them from the grill and divide each one in half, using a metal spoon so that you create nice rough edges. Put them straight into the bowl containing the other ingredients and toss until everything is well combined.

8. Add the sea salt, lime juice and at least 1 tsp kabab masala and mix again. Taste for seasoning and add more kabab masala and/or salt if required, then serve.

MARINE DRIVE

"You can take an easy stroll on the wide breezy pavement from
Nariman Point with the dark Arabian Sea at your side. Marine Drive
is lovely, and you could sit on the promenade empty-handed, or indeed
hand-in-hand, as couples do."

PUDDING

"10 o'clock"

AN ICE CREAM AT K. RUSTOM'S
AND THE MAGIC OF MARINE DRIVE

YOU SHOULD NOW HEAD for Nariman Point, to slow down and take the fresh ocean air.

Start at the very end of the sea wall, with the National Centre for the Performing Arts at your back. If you can, go to the tip of the concrete jetty which is shored up by curious brutalist tetrapods piled against one another haphazardly, as if scattered there by a giant god. (No doubt it would have been the monkey god Hanuman, scattering with his usual vim and vigour.) The sun has long since set, but if you're lucky there will be a bright, strong moon. If the man is still there selling raw green mango with chilli powder, then try some. It'll freshen your palate. The waves lap companionably against the concrete shoreline. You may hear the odd murmur or giggle – Bombay's lovers taking advantage of the sheltered quiet of Nariman Point.

You're standing on the youngest part of Bombay, younger in fact than many of its residents: Nariman Point came up from the sea in the 1960s and 70s as part of the controversial Back Bay Reclamation. This idea was first conjured up under British rule but endured beyond Independence. Its many flaws were enthusiastically pointed out back in the 1920s when the modern scheme was conceived by the upstanding Mr Khurshed Nariman, the stalwart of Congress and future Mayor of Bombay.

Embarrassingly for the colonial authorities, Mr Nariman exposed the corruption and favouritism that lay behind the scheme. It was revived in the 1960s, but it was just as contentious as it had been in the 1920s. Most of the proposed reclamation was never actually reclaimed, leaving Bombay with what appears to be a large and obvious jigsaw-puzzle piece missing from its southernmost limb. And poor old Mr Nariman ended up having his name appended to the appendage that he fought so hard against. (There is a lovely short history of Bombay and its development as a city written by our dear friend and great man, Naresh Fernandes, who is another Bombay stalwart. If you ever get

> "Naved used to come here after work (around one o'clock in the morning) and sit sipping chai until sunrise."

to meet him, send him our very best. The book is called *City Adrift* and it's a great read, not the rant that its author says it is.)

You can take an easy stroll on the wide breezy pavement from Nariman Point with the dark Arabian Sea at your side. Marine Drive is lovely, and you could sit on the promenade empty-handed, or indeed hand-in-hand, as couples do. Naved used to come here after work, around one o'clock in the morning, and sit sipping chai until sunrise. A courteous chai-walla kept him topped up all night for 50 rupees. But after a day of mostly savoury eating, it's time for something sweet. Select an ice cream from the freezers of K. Rustom & Co. on Churchgate Street, which opens up onto Marine Drive.

Don't shy away from the stronger seasonal flavours. The guava and jackfruit ice creams are absolutely first-class. Ask them to serve your ice cream as a sandwich – a thick slice between two crunchy wafers. Now make your way back onto Marine Drive, carefully holding your delicate prize in the napkin they provide. (Don't drop it. There might be tears, whatever your age.) Find a spot on the seafront, make yourself comfortable, take your first bite and try not to smile.

K. Rustom & Co. only graduated to being an ice-cream parlour in 1953. The company had started business as "dispensing chemists, tobacconists and general merchants" in the 1940s. (You may notice the black and white photo of the store and its suited management in the early days, with the founder, Mr Khodabux Rustom Irani, seated in the middle.) But business wasn't

"You might argue that this sensuous sweep by the Arabian Sea lined with Art Deco apartments and palm trees is the defining image of Bombay."

booming and the premises had the feel of a stuffy department store. So Mr Irani's brother-in-law, none other than one Mr Bomi Irani of Meher Cold Drink House – where we stopped earlier for a delicious lassi – suggested they start selling curd and he shared with them his trusted recipe.

Bomi Irani's younger brother Soli, who worked at Bertorelli's ice-cream company, then suggested they introduce ice cream. It was all very delicious and a big hit. And so, with a little help from family, K. Rustom & Co. began its journey to becoming Bombay's favourite ice-cream store. Nowadays, it's run by Roda and Aban Irani, Mr Khodabux Irani's daughters.

Finish your ice cream, shake off any crumbs of wafer and turn your attention back to the magical promenade of Marine Drive. You might argue that this sensuous sweep by the Arabian Sea lined with Art Deco apartments and palm trees is the defining image of Bombay. Not the grand and crazy Victoria Terminus, nor the elegant Gothic revival stretch alongside the Oval Maidan, nor the Indo-Saracenic Gateway of India, but the expanse and promise of Marine Drive – open and airy, optimistic and outward-looking. Shamil's grandparents used to take him for walks here as a child back in the 1970s. Back then, to a young boy, it felt impossibly glamorous.

1 View across the Back Bay from Nariman point
2 Perching on tetrapods
3 The sweep of Marine Drive
4 A couple enjoying the view across the bay
5 All variety of seasonal flavours are available at K. Rustom & Co.
6 Early photo of the founder Mr Khodabux Rustom Irani with his employees
7 A not-so-new sign for "new" ice cream

Almost every classic Bombay movie features Marine Drive. In *C.I.D.* the beloved *Bombay Meri Jaan* number is sung by a pickpocket, played by Johnny Walker, who is being driven down Marine Drive in a horse-drawn cart (watch the lovely clip on YouTube). In *Taxi Driver* (in which the "City of Bombay" is sweetly credited as "Guest Artist") Dev Anand is seen driving his black Hillman Minx (number plate 1111) through the scenic stretch. The 1980s classic *Albert Pinto Ko Gussa Kyun Aata Hai* (Why Does Albert Pinto Get Angry), opens on Marine Drive, the view shot through a windscreen, with the passengers temporarily out of sight. Or consider Amitabh Bachchan, stylish

8

9

10

"Shamil's grandparents used
to take him for walks here
as a child back in the 1970s.
Back then, to a young boy,
it felt impossibly glamorous."

and singing on his Suzuki motorbike, in *Muqaddar
Ka Sikandar*. Oh, the motorised romance of
Marine Drive!

They say that the vehicle that really fixed
Marine Drive in the city's collective affections
was the red double-decker 123 bus. This bus
took Bombay's most scenic route, right from
K. Rustom's through the sweep of Marine Drive
to Chowpatty and Gamdevi. Couples would climb
to the upper deck, ambitious commuters would vie
for the best views and students from the colleges
at Churchgate were excited if they got a seat. You
didn't actually need to be going anywhere to get on
the 123. Fare paid to the conductor, and everyone
transported to a seaside retreat, contentedness
guaranteed, only fresh coconut water missing.

That is surely enough star- and sea-gazing for
today. Hop into a taxi back to Colaba, for your
final stop: a very well-earned nightcap at the Taj.

8 Marine Drive and the Air India building
9 Roda and Aban, Mr Khodabux Irani's daughters
10 Fishing boat crossing the Back Bay

The text visible on the wall menus:

Left price chart:

	60/=	70/=	80/=
1- 40	1 - 60	1 - 70	1 - 80
2- 80	2 -120	2 -140	2 -160
3- 120	3 -180	3 -210	3 -240
4- 160	240	4 -280	4 -320
5- 200	5 -300	5 -350	5 -400
6- 240	6 -360	6 -420	6 -480
7- 280	7 -420	7 -490	7 -560
8- 320	8 -480	8 -560	8 -640
9- 360	9 -540	9 -630	9 -720
10- 400	10 -600	10 -700	10 -800
15- 600	15 -900	15 -1050	15 -1200
20- 800	20 -1200	20 -1400	20 -1600
25-1000	25 -1500	25 -1750	25 -2000
30-1200	30 -1800	30 -2100	30 -2400
35-1400	35 -2100	35 -2450	35 -2800
40-1600	40 -2400	40 -2800	40 -3200

Right menu:

29] ROASTED ALMOND CRUNCH
30] WALNUT CRUNCH   70
31] CHOCOLATE NUT   70
32] CHOCO CHERRY
33] PISTA
34] KESAR
35] KESAR PISTA
36] NUTTY DATE
37] KAJU KISMIS
38] ANJEER
39] KAJU KISMIS
40] GAJJAR
41] BLACK CURRENT
42] RUM & RAISIN
        PERU   85
43] SITAFAL   80   70
44] KING MANGO
45] CHOCO BADAM KISMIS
46] VANILLA WITH CHOCOLATE
        SAUCE & BROWNIE
47] PAAN   70
   DOODHI HALWA 70   COLD DRINKS
1] SWEET LASSI   20
2] SWEET LASSI AAM

3] LITCHI   10
4] ORANGE
5] GRAPE
6] PINEAPPLE
7] KOKAM
8] GINGER LEMON

9] SWEET CURD   15

ABOVE: The restaurant of the Ambassador Hotel, as seen from Marine Drive

RIGHT: Marine Drive is also known as the Queen's Necklace, for the glittering lights that wrap around the bay

BASMATI KHEER

This recipe is a sort of *kheer*, a traditional Indian dessert, which is like rice pudding (but much nicer). Basmati rice is soaked, blitzed and then cooked in lots of milk until broken down, to create a thick, creamy pudding that sets when cold. A little sugar is caramelised on top to form a crisp crème brûlée-style top, and the blueberry compote adds fruit and extra tartness. If you do not have a cook's blowtorch for the caramel, scatter a few toasted flaked almonds on top of the kheer instead for a crisp finish.

SERVES 6

~

FOR THE BASMATI PUDDING

110g basmati rice

2 litres whole milk

2 cardamom pods

1 vanilla pod or 3 tsp vanilla extract

100g granulated sugar

90ml double cream

FOR THE BLUEBERRY COMPOTE

125g blueberries

100g granulated sugar

FOR THE CARAMEL TOPPING

2–3 tbsp granulated sugar

1. Tip the basmati rice into a bowl, cover generously with cold water and leave to soak for 2 hours. Drain well, spread out on a baking tray and leave to dry overnight.

2. Transfer the dry rice to a food processor and pulse until coarsely ground (not to a powder).

3. Pour the milk into a saucepan. Give the cardamom pods a sharp bash with a rolling pin to break them open, then add to the milk. If using a vanilla pod, split in half, run a knife down the length to remove the seeds and add the seeds and pod to the milk. If using vanilla extract, add it to the milk. Bring to the boil over a medium heat.

4. Add the rice and bring to a steady simmer. Let simmer for 30–40 minutes, stirring regularly. You will need to keep an eye on the pan to make sure it doesn't boil over. The rice should start to break down completely.

5. Meanwhile, for the compote, put 100g of the blueberries into a small pan and add 200ml boiling water. Bring to a simmer and cook until you have a thick sauce, about 15 minutes. Add the sugar, let it dissolve, then add the remaining blueberries and cook for a final 5 minutes.

6. When the rice has started to break down, turn the heat up and cook at a rolling boil, stirring almost constantly, for 15–30 minutes until reduced to a thick pudding (it needs to be thick enough to set once cold). Remove the cardamom and vanilla pods, then add the sugar and cook for a further 10 minutes, until the kheer is very thick. Take off the heat and stir in the cream.

7. Divide the kheer between 6 ramekins. Allow to cool, then cover and refrigerate for at least 2 hours (up to 24).

8. When ready to serve, remove the puddings from the fridge and sprinkle evenly with sugar. Wave a cook's blowtorch over the surface to melt the sugar and form a caramel topping. Allow to cool and set for a few minutes. Serve with the blueberry compote on top.

MEMSAHIB'S MESS

This is our version of a classic Eton Mess, with the addition of gulkand and rose syrup. We imagine that this is what the well-to-do Memsahibs of Malabar Hill might have made for their fancy parties.

Gulkand is an Indian rose petal jam, apparently good for cooling the body. You can either buy rose syrup or make it at home.

SERVES 4

~

250g strawberries, hulled

45g gulkand

35ml rose syrup (page 332)

250ml double cream

4 meringue nests

1. Blitz 70g of the strawberries with the gulkand and rose syrup.

2. Whip the cream in a bowl to soft peaks.

3. Set aside 1 large or 2 small strawberries for serving. Cut the remaining strawberries into quarters (or smaller pieces if the strawberries are very big) and combine with the strawberry and rose mixture.

4. Finely slice the remaining 1 or 2 strawberries.

5. When you're ready to serve, break the meringues into pieces and drop them into a large bowl. Add the whipped cream and strawberry and rose mixture, and fold until combined but not totally mixed.

6. Divide between serving bowls and top with the sliced strawberries. Serve immediately.

BUN MASKA PUDDING

This is a variation on traditional English bread-and-butter pudding, with lots of nutmeg and a hint of cardamom. You can use good-quality ready-made brioche loaf (or brioche rolls) here; there is no need to make your own. If you can't find charoli seeds, use slivered almonds.

We like to serve our pudding with a scoop of ice cream – cinnamon is particularly nice, but simple vanilla is good too.

SERVES 4–6

~

450ml whole milk

½ tsp ground cardamom

A few generous pinches of freshly grated nutmeg

10g charoli seeds

400g brioche loaf

50g unsalted butter, plus extra for greasing

35g sultanas

2 large eggs, plus an extra 2 yolks

300ml tinned sweetened condensed milk

TO SERVE

Cinnamon or vanilla ice cream (optional)

1. Heat the oven to 190°C/Fan 170°C/Gas 5 and lightly grease a baking dish large enough to accommodate the bread.

2. Pour the milk into a saucepan and add the cardamom and nutmeg. Bring to scalding point, but do not let it boil. Take off the heat and leave to infuse for 10 minutes while you prepare everything else.

3. Put the charoli seeds into a mug, cover generously with boiling water and leave to stand for 2 minutes. Drain and set to one side.

4. Cut or break the brioche into 3cm cubes and place in a large bowl. Melt the butter, drizzle it over the bread cubes, then toss with your hands to coat the bread.

5. Transfer the bread to the greased baking dish and spread out evenly. Sprinkle with the sultanas and charoli seeds, distributing them evenly.

6. In the same bowl, whisk together the eggs, extra yolks and condensed milk. Bring the milk back to scalding point, then slowly pour it onto the egg mixture, whisking as you do so.

7. Carefully pour the warm mixture over the bread and place in the oven. Bake for 20 minutes, or until just set and golden brown.

8. Allow the pudding to stand for 5 minutes before cutting into portions and serving, with a scoop of ice cream if you like.

GULAB JAMUN

A classic dense, rich, sweet Indian pudding. The dough is made with milk powder, fried until golden brown then soaked in sweet syrup, as per Kavi's mum's delicious recipe. We have found that a small mascarpone and pistachio centre creates delight.

SERVES 14–16

~

FOR THE DOUGH

100g semolina

350g milk powder

50g plain flour

25g ghee (or vegetable oil)

FOR THE FILLING

60g mascarpone cheese

30g pistachio nuts, finely chopped

FOR THE SYRUP

800g granulated sugar

TO COOK

Vegetable oil for deep-frying

TO SERVE

Vanilla ice cream (optional)

Chopped pistachio nuts

1. Tip the semolina into a small bowl, add 50ml cold water, stir well and leave to soak for 5 minutes or so.

2. Meanwhile, tip the milk powder and flour into a large bowl and mix well. Add the ghee (or oil) and use your fingertips to rub it into the dry ingredients. Add the semolina and rub with your hands to combine.

3. Add 125ml cold water. Mix to combine and press gently to form a smooth dough (it should be quite stiff and slightly dry rather than sticky). Cover with a clean damp cloth and leave to stand for 30 minutes.

4. For the filling, mix the mascarpone and pistachios together in a bowl. Cover and refrigerate until needed.

5. To make the syrup, tip the sugar into a medium-large heavy-based pan and add 1 litre boiling water. Heat to dissolve the sugar and simmer until you have a clear syrup. Take off the heat and set aside.

6. Lightly grease a large baking sheet. Take the dough from the fridge and put a thumbnail-sized piece to one side (for testing the oil). Weigh the remaining dough into 40g pieces, forming each piece into a ball as you go (they don't need to be neat at this point). Place the dough balls on the prepared baking sheet.

7. Take one dough ball and flatten it onto the palm of your hand. Place ½ tsp of filling in the centre, then fold the dough up around and over it, to seal completely. Roll into a neat ball and place on the baking sheet. Repeat with the rest of the dough and filling.

8. Heat the oil in a deep-fryer or other suitable deep, heavy-based pan to 160°C. To test the temperature, drop in the reserved piece of dough; it should fry very gently, not colour immediately.

9. You will need to cook the dough balls in batches. When the oil is ready, add the first batch, being careful not to overcrowd the pan. Fry gently for 8–10 minutes, slowly building up a very deep golden brown colour. To test whether the jamun are cooked, remove one and split it open; the dough should be cooked throughout, with

no raw patches in the centre. Once cooked, remove the jamun from the pan with a slotted spoon and drain them well on kitchen paper.

10. Warm the syrup over a low heat and add the jamun. Bring to the boil for a moment, then turn off the heat. Allow the jamun to steep for at least 30 minutes; they should soak up a lot of the syrup.

11. Once they have soaked up plenty of syrup the jamun can be served warm or chilled; they are particularly good with a scoop of ice cream. Finish with a sprinkling of chopped pistachios.

MALAI KULFI

This is India's answer to ice cream; it is eaten all around the country – on sticks or cut into cubes. It's a cool treat after a spicy meal.

Malai kulfi is the original: milk is reduced to a thick, saucy consistency and then flavoured with cardamom. Wealthier families would add saffron. Nowadays people make different versions like pistachio (illustrated opposite) and mango.

The kulfis will start to melt very soon after being removed from the freezer, so serve quickly (and have plenty of napkins handy!).

MAKES 4–6

~

410g evaporated milk

80ml double cream

5g milk powder (optional)

40g granulated sugar

½ tsp ground cardamom

1. Pour the evaporated milk and cream into a saucepan, place over a medium heat and slowly bring to a simmer. If using milk powder, add it when the liquid reaches boiling point. Simmer gently for 2 minutes, stirring almost constantly.

2. Add the sugar and cardamom, stir well and simmer, stirring, for another 2 minutes. Allow to cool.

3. Pour the mixture into kulfi or ice-lolly moulds and freeze until completely solid.

4. When ready to eat, remove the kulfi from the moulds and serve straight away.

Variations

Mango kulfi: Prepare as above, reducing the sugar to 30g and adding 120g Alphonso mango purée (available from Indian grocery shops) at the same time as the sugar. Stir well and simmer, stirring, for another 2 minutes, before adding the ground cardamom (as above). Cool, freeze and serve as above. *Makes 6–8*

Pistachio kulfi: Using a blender, blitz 90g skinned, shelled, unsalted pistachio nuts to a smooth paste, adding a splash of evaporated milk (from the 410g listed above). Scrape the pistachio paste into a small bowl. In a saucepan over a medium heat, bring the rest of the evaporated milk and 80ml double cream to a simmer and simmer gently for 2 minutes, stirring almost constantly. Add 60g granulated sugar and the pistachio paste, stir well and simmer, stirring, for 2 minutes. Take off the heat and blitz, using a blender, until smooth. Allow to cool. Freeze and serve as above. *Makes 6–8 (Illustrated opposite)*

GADBAD MITHA

The name means "a sweet mess". This is a fun and fruity concoction, halfway between a sundae and a trifle, and very easy to make. Children will likely take pleasure in assembling their own.

You can include whatever fruits you like. Bananas, blueberries, grapes, mango, peach, strawberries and raspberries will all work well. Do try to use at least three different types for a pleasing variety, and include mango whenever it's in season.

Prepare the ingredients below, then let everyone assemble their own pudding.

SERVES 6

~

200g good-quality ready-made sponge or Madeira cake

250ml good-quality ready-made fresh vanilla custard

50ml whole milk

About 450g fruit (see above)

120g Alphonso mango purée (see note)

50ml double cream

6 scoops of vanilla ice cream

1. Cut the cake into roughly 2cm cubes and place a few pieces in each of 6 sundae glasses or glass serving bowls.

2. Mix the vanilla custard with the milk to loosen it a bit.

3. Prepare your chosen fruit and cut larger ones into bite-sized pieces. Divide between the glasses or bowls.

4. Swirl some mango purée over each portion, then add a drizzle of cream. Spoon a generous amount of custard on top.

5. Finish with a scoop of ice cream and serve immediately.

Note: You can buy good-quality tinned mango purée from Indian grocery shops.

CHOCOLATE MOUSSE

This rich, dark chocolate mousse has a touch of salt and the tiniest hint of chilli. It goes very well with the berry shrikhand on page 311. Both the mousse and the shrikhand can be made in advance, making it an ideal dessert to prepare ahead for a special occasion – serve in pretty bowls topped with a few fresh berries if you like.

SERVES 8

~

100g caster sugar

6 medium eggs (pasteurised or Lion-stamped as they are uncooked)

20g good-quality cocoa powder

½ tsp red chilli powder

A large pinch of flaky sea salt, plus extra to serve

200g dark chocolate, broken into pieces

200ml whipping cream

1. Put the sugar and 40ml water into a small saucepan over a very low heat and let it slowly melt to form a clear syrup. Check the temperature with a sugar thermometer if you have one; it should not go above 120°C.

2. Separate 4 eggs, placing the yolks in a large bowl (or the bowl of a stand mixer fitted with the whisk attachment) and the whites into another large, very clean, bowl.

3. Add the 2 whole eggs, cocoa powder, chilli powder and salt to the egg yolks and whisk for 2 minutes. You don't need to incorporate air at this stage, but the mix should be creamy and light.

4. When the sugar has melted to a clear liquid, allow it to simmer for 2 minutes, then slowly add to the cocoa mixture, whisking as you do so. Continue to whisk vigorously until the mixture is completely cool and you have a smooth, airy sauce consistency; this will take about 5 minutes.

5. Melt the chocolate in a heatproof bowl over a pan of simmering water, making sure the base of the bowl isn't touching the water. Once melted, remove the bowl from the heat and set aside to cool slightly.

6. In another bowl, whip the cream until softly peaking. In a separate, very clean bowl, whisk the egg whites to medium-stiff peaks.

7. Beat the melted chocolate into the egg and cocoa mix. Stir through 1 tbsp each of whipped cream and egg white; this helps to lighten the mixture. Now carefully fold in the remaining whipped cream and egg whites, so as to retain as much air as possible.

8. Transfer the mousse to a clean container, cover tightly with two layers of cling film and refrigerate until ready to serve. (It will keep for up to 3 days in the fridge.)

9. To serve, place a neat scoop in each small serving bowl and sprinkle with a pinch of flaky sea salt.

BERRY SHRIKHAND

Shrikhand is a type of thick, sweetened yoghurt that is especially popular amongst Gujarati families. It is traditionally flavoured with cardamom and saffron, but this berry version goes perfectly with the dark chocolate mousse on page 309.

SERVES 6

~

500g good-quality full-fat Greek yoghurt (see note)

90g icing sugar

25g blackberries

25g blueberries

25g raspberries

TO FINISH

Extra berries

1. Place a sieve over a bowl and line with muslin or thick kitchen paper. (Use a jam straining kit, if you have one.) Pour the yoghurt into the muslin cloth, cover the top loosely with cling film and place in the fridge to strain for 8 hours.

2. Tip the strained yoghurt into a bowl, add the icing sugar and mix nicely.

3. Halve or quarter the berries and lightly fold through the sweetened, strained yoghurt to create a ripple effect. Cover and refrigerate until ready to eat. (Shrikhand will keep for at least 3 days in the fridge.)

4. To serve, scoop the shrikhand into little bowls or glasses and top with extra berries.

Note: If you can get hold of plain labneh, use 300g of it instead of the Greek yoghurt and skip step 1.

PINEAPPLE & BLACK PEPPER CRUMBLE

This is our take on a British classic. You can serve it warm or cold, on its own, or with custard or a scoop of vanilla or cinnamon ice cream. The tang of pineapple and spice of pepper work wonderfully together.

You can prepare the crumble topping in advance, but don't apply it until you're ready to bake.

SERVES 4–6

~

FOR THE FILLING

1 large, fresh ripe pineapple (you need around 750g flesh)

1 vanilla pod or 2 tsp vanilla extract

100g granulated sugar

A few twists of black pepper

FOR THE CRUMBLE

100g plain flour

100g rolled oats

100g granulated sugar

100g salted butter, cubed, at room temperature

TO SERVE

Vanilla ice cream or custard

1. Trim the pineapple of its skin, prising out the "eyes", and cut into 2cm chunks, discarding the hard core.

2. Place the pineapple chunks in a saucepan and add 200ml water. If using a vanilla pod, split in half, run a knife down the length to remove the seeds and add the seeds and pod to the pan. (If using extract, it goes in later.) Simmer over a medium-low heat for 20–25 minutes, or until the pineapple is soft, stirring occasionally. If the pan starts to become dry, add a little more water.

3. Meanwhile, make the crumble. Mix the dry ingredients together in a large bowl. Add the butter and rub in with your hands until fully incorporated; there should be no loose flour left.

4. Heat the oven to 200°C/Fan 180°C/Gas 6.

5. Once the pineapple is soft, add the sugar and simmer for a further 5 minutes. Add the black pepper and vanilla extract, if using. Turn off the heat and set aside.

6. Spread the pineapple mixture in a medium baking dish and top with the crumble mix. Bake for 30–40 minutes, until the topping has formed a lovely golden crust.

7. Allow to stand for 5 minutes then serve, with vanilla ice cream or custard.

THE TAJ MAHAL PALACE HOTEL

"Walk down the sea-facing façade of the hotel along the old Strand Road. Approaching from the south, alongside the sea, you'll notice the enormous oriental domes of the main Taj building."

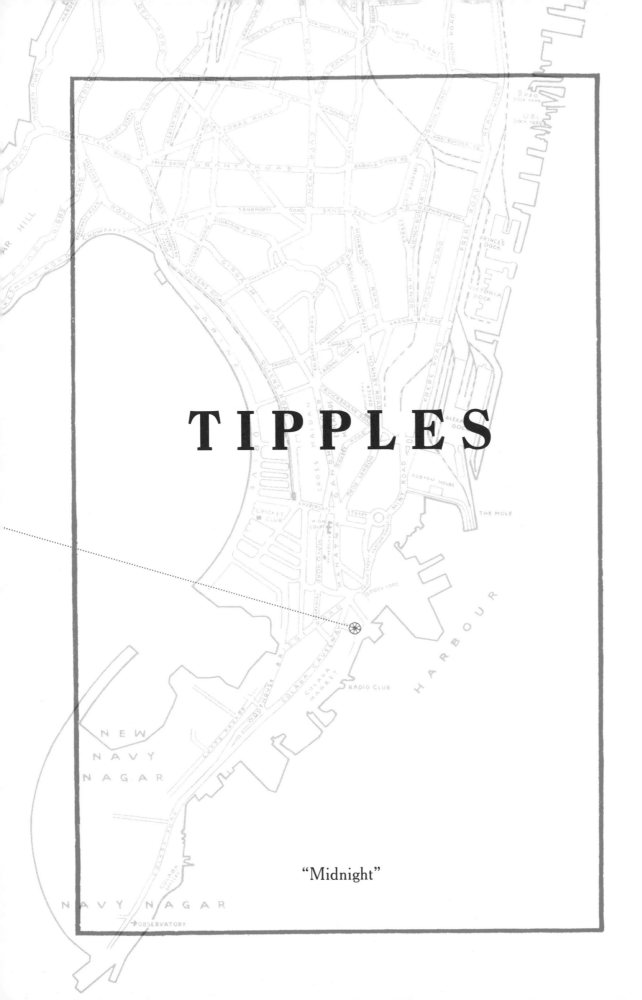

TIPPLES

"Midnight"

TIPPLES AT THE TAJ, AND A STEP BACK IN TIME TO BOMBAY'S JAZZ AGE

IT'S BEEN A LONG DAY. You have much to digest. But before you turn in, you should have a nightcap at the grand old Taj Mahal Palace hotel. This will revive your spirit and encourage deep sleep.

If you were visiting the Taj of the late 1940s when the thrill of India's new independence hung in the air, you'd have first needed to hurry home for a bath, a dusting of talcum powder, a slick of Brylcreem, some cologne and a dress shirt perhaps. You'd have been going to a dinner or a dance. (For Shamil, the smell of Brylcreem so vividly reminds him of his handsome and enterprising grandfather who in 1947 would have been too poor to frequent the Taj hotel.)

Luckily, today everything is less formal. You don't need to be in evening dress to enjoy the happy clink of an ice cube in a tall, strong drink.

Walk down the sea-facing façade of the hotel along the old Strand Road (now apparently called PJ Ramchandran Road). Approaching from the south, alongside the sea, you'll notice the enormous oriental domes of the main Taj building. Look beyond the domes, and you'll see the more modern and much less romantic tower block built in the 1970s, on top of the old site of Green's Hotel.

Were you doing this walk in the 1940s, you would have sauntered into Green's for a long, cool pink gin, and for the innocent pleasure of people-watching. It was by far the more disreputable hotel of the two, once a good spot for moneyed bachelors and lusty sailors in search of gimlets and a wild party with a swing band. The 1940s Louis Bromfield novel, *Night in Bombay*, is a great read for the vivid, sometimes jarring picture it paints of the raffish Bombay of the time. It describes the clientele of Green's: "...sea-faring men who would have been embarrassed by the mid-Victorian imperial elegance of the Taj Mahal dining room; English officers and civil servants and clerks who were there because Green's was Bohemian

"Sadly, not a lusty sailor nor a sleazy tap dancer in sight."

and as wild a place as they dared frequent in a community where everything, every move one made sooner or later became known... and here and there a strange Russian tart or an 'advanced' Parsee or Khoja woman dining alone with a man." (Alone? Goodness!) Today, it's just the much less exciting Tower wing of the Taj that apparently has a slightly more respectable type of person staying there.

As you walk into the air-conditioned lobby of the Taj, the smart little unit of uniformed doormen will smile, nod and namaste. After your long day walking in a much more earthy Bombay, this hotel will feel like a different and rarefied sort of world. It has a gently perfumed coolness, filled with extravagant quantities of freshly cut flowers and heavy, elegant furniture. You'll hear the murmur of music folding in easily with international accents and the posh English of upper-class India. Sadly, not a lusty sailor nor a sleazy tap dancer in sight.

Stand coolly and look at the large red and blue triptych behind the reception desk. It is a beautiful M. F. Husain painting called *Three Stanzas of the New Millennium*, commissioned for the Taj and dealing with India's relationship with tradition and modernity. An interesting and possibly controversial subject.

We thoroughly recommend you stay here sometime if you can. You can often get decent rates. The swimming pool here is a complete treat, a delicious south Bombay oasis. You can also spend a few very pleasant hours wandering the floors of the old section of the hotel enjoying the enormous collection of art. This collection was built up over a few decades from the beginning of the 1960s. The hotel supported young and unknown artists, buying art for the love of it and effectively acting as patron. Over the years, some

DINNER MENU.

❁

POTAGE.
Vermicelle à la Madrilaine.

POISSON.
Filets de Pomfrets aux Huitres. Pommes Nature.

ENTRÉE.
Côte de Bœuf Portugaise.

LÉGUMES.
Flageolets à la Crème.

RÔTI.
Poulets à l'a Broche. Salade.

ENTREMETS.
Pouding Saxon.   Melons Glacés.
Dessert.   Moka.

"Gradually, many talented local musicians emerged. Suave, skilled jazz maestros playing hot sounds every night in steamy Bombay."

of these artists grew to become the most renowned in India; inexpensively bought paintings became valuable and important.

Paying guests can sign up for the hotel heritage tour. As well as hearing about the art collection, you'll be able to admire the inside of the great dome and the beautiful staircase. The tour guides will explain how the industrial baron Jamsetji Tata was refused entry into Watson's Hotel, which had a whites-only door policy. The story goes that in response to this racist slight, he decided to build the Taj, a beautiful hotel that would welcome his countrymen. The tour guides will also very proudly relate how the staff showed tremendous bravery when they dealt with the horrific events of the attack of 2008, when the terrorists took over the hotel and killed thirty-one people in the four-day siege. The sadness with which the staff recall this time is evident in the slight break in their voices as they speak about it, but so, equally, is the pride in how they reacted.

One thing that the tour doesn't spend much time on is the "hot jazz" scene in Bombay, whose heady centre was the ballroom at the Taj. A few years ago, we discovered that Naresh Fernandes (the dear friend, whom we've mentioned before) had written a book, *Taj Mahal Foxtrot*. It brings alive the rich and gloriously colourful jazz age of Bombay, which flourished in the middle decades of the last century. (Jazz is one of Shamil's obsessions. He would say that it has kept him company through the decades, in good times and in bad, over both neat whisky and black coffee. He was utterly overjoyed to learn that Bombay was once boisterously awake late into the nights with loud jazz.)

In these decades, the Taj earned a reputation as the place where the city's smart set would fling their knees up. It was as busy and alive in the wee small hours as it was at midday. It all started in late 1935 when a dapper black American musician, Leon Abbey, performed Bombay's first ever jazz gig in the Taj ballroom. Abbey was a violinist from faraway Minnesota, whose accomplished band had played with Louis Armstrong and Coleman Hawkins. At first, as *The Times of India* reported, the musicians had to "tone down their 'hotting' to meet the less sophisticated taste of Bombay". However, from that moment onwards, and as India marched to freedom, jazz was to become an essential part of the subcontinent's sounds, of the

1 The oriental domes of the Taj hotel
2 An early dinner menu from the Taj
3 Chic Chocolate, India's Louis Armstrong, playing at the Taj with his band
4 Frank Fernand, Rudy Cotton and Chic Chocolate

optimism of the new era. Later on, jazz and swing would even find themselves deeply embedded in the soundtracks of the new Hindi films of the new nation, "leaving India with an appetite for squealing brass, scorching strings and syncopated rhythms". This is all beautifully described in *Taj Mahal Foxtrot*.

Gradually, many talented local musicians emerged. Suave, skilled jazz maestros playing hot sounds every night in steamy Bombay. What a complete delight it must have been! Cool cats like Chic Chocolate, Frank Fernand, Micky Correa and Rudy Cotton all wowed the increasingly hot-stepping audiences at the Taj and made it impossible to sit still. The players usually stayed close by, jamming in Colaba or Dhobi Talao through the early hours.

At the stroke of midnight on 15 August 1947, the combined bands of Micky Correa and Chic Chocolate played the Indian national anthem "Jana Gana Mana" to a beautiful, packed Taj ballroom. Amongst the guests were the young industrialist J. R. D. Tata and Vijayalakshmi Pandit, sister to Jawaharlal Nehru, who was, of course, in

Delhi making the most important speech of his life, broadcast all over India and the world. At midnight, while the world slept, India kept its tryst with destiny and the new nation awoke to life and freedom. Oh, to have been there that evening! It must have been just electric. That night, they opened the doors of the Taj to the crowds in Colaba joyfully celebrating the nation's freedom. They say it was quite a party (although it is also said that not so much as a teaspoon went missing!).

At last, retreat finally to the Harbour Bar. It's a historic sort of place, but has been somewhat rinsed of its heritage. Apparently it used to look like an old maritime clubroom – dark furniture, wooden panels, cigar smoke clouding the air. Now that you've reached the end of this long day, head to the large windows for a view of the bay at night. Ease your weary self into a chair, and exhale.

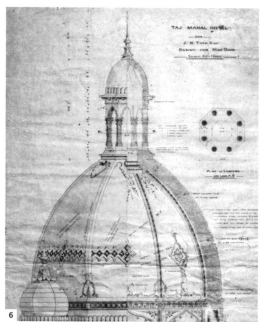

"If we were with you, we'd raise a glass to your hearty appetite and your endless patience."

Order a drink. When it comes, take a long draught of your gimlet or sling, or whatever it is you are having. If we were with you, we'd raise a glass to your hearty appetite and your endless patience. You've listened to our anecdotes and stories of Bombay. You've wandered the city's streets, meandered here and there and eaten its food: from the immediacy of a vada pau so hot from the fryer that it slightly burns your mouth, to a carefully savoured long-simmered nihari on Mohammed Ali Road, to simple bun maska in an Irani café.

We can offer no guarantee that this highly subjective and personal guide has covered the important bits of Bombay, or the most important parts of its history. Some will point out things that we've missed, dishes that we just had to eat but didn't. Others may tell us that it's all a bit incoherent, a mish-mash of stories, foods and cuisines. Still others will say that it's all too rose-tinted a view of a challenging city. Perhaps it is.

We're going to close by quoting our friend Naresh, the chronicler of Bombay, writing in *Taj Mahal Foxtrot*. "Jazz seemed to perfectly embody the spirit of Bombay, a slightly wild port city that knew a tune sounded better when it made room

5   The Taj Mahal Palace hotel in the 1970s, the tower under construction on the site of Green's Hotel
6   An architect's sketch of the proposed Taj hotel, dating from the late nineteenth century

for instruments of all timbres and tones; a city that could be really pretty when it took things slow but that gave you a thrill when it was working at double time; a city that forced you to make it up as you went along; a city that gave everyone the space to play their own melody the way they heard it." For us, this perfectly sums up Bombay at its best.

ABOVE: "From the Harbour in 1933", a signature cocktail of the Harbour Bar at the Taj

RIGHT: Once the reception area, the Palace Lounge is a calmingly beautiful space

ABOVE: The impressive Gateway of India, built to commemorate the visit of King George V to India in 1911

LEFT: The old part of the Taj hotel, still retaining its original elegance

ON COCKTAIL MAKING

Ice (or rather, dilution) is one of the most important ingredients in cocktails. When you shake a drink with ice, you're not just mixing the ingredients together and making them cold, you are diluting them. Certain flavours or aromas will only be detected at a lower alcohol percentage, and so a little dilution is key.

With ice, more is always more. When you're shaking or serving a drink, use as much ice as is sensibly possible. The more ice you use, the colder the drink, and the more controlled the dilution process, whereas one or two ice cubes will melt very quickly.

It is best to use large, solid cubes to slow down and control the dilution of a drink. Avoid ice with a hollow divot in the centre, as it melts very quickly.

When squeezing citrus, a "Mexican elbow" can be useful. Just don't be tempted to squeeze it too hard, as this will release the citrus oils within the skin, which alters the character of the drink, owing to their strong aroma and bitterness.

Use freshly squeezed lemon or lime juice where stated. It's at its sweetest when just squeezed, becoming slightly bitter as it ages.

EAST INDIA GIMLET

The original gimlet was devised to prevent scurvy. When sailors, anxious to avoid death, took to mixing lime cordial with their gin, they created one of the earliest cocktails. Our version adds fresh lime and dill, with a dash of celery bitters.

The cordial must be Rose's. Accept no imitations. Ensure also that your dill is fresh; anything slightly ailing will ruin the flavour of the drink.

This gimlet will go with almost any recipe in this book. But be warned: there's a hefty measure of gin contained within this very easy-drinking tipple.

SERVES 1

~

1 lime wedge

1 small sprig of dill, plus an extra sprig to garnish

40ml Rose's lime cordial

2 dashes of celery bitters

40ml London Dry Gin

Ice cubes

1. Squeeze the lime wedge into your cocktail shaker and discard the spent skin. Place the sprig of dill on one palm and give it a short, sharp slap with the other hand; this helps to release the oils. Add to the cocktail shaker.

2. Add the lime cordial, celery bitters and gin. Top up with lots of ice and shake vigorously for at least 30 seconds. Taste the drink; it should be sour, sweet, fairly strong and very refreshing.

3. Strain into a coupe or martini glass and carefully balance a small sprig of dill on the inside of the glass.

MONSOON MARTINI

This drink takes its name from the Monsooned Malabar coffee that we have served at Dishoom. It has a brilliantly strong, sour and bitter flavour, perfect for an espresso martini.

Ancho Reyes is a Mexican tequila-like liqueur infused with wonderfully smoky ancho chillies. It's a fantastic addition to margaritas and palomas, and in this drink it provides a beautiful, smoky warmth. The walnut bitters are essential; their drying complexity is what really marries the coffee with the chilli heat. The honey will produce a luxurious foam.

SERVES 1

~

½ tsp set honey

30ml cold espresso

25ml Black Cow vodka, or other good-quality smooth vodka

15ml Ancho Reyes liqueur

4 dashes of Fee Brothers black walnut bitters

Ice cubes

TO GARNISH

A tiny dusting of cocoa powder

1 roasted coffee bean (optional)

1. Mix the honey with 2 tsp boiling water. Tip into your cocktail shaker.

2. Add the espresso, vodka, liqueur and walnut bitters. Top up with lots of ice and shake vigorously for at least 30 seconds.

3. Strain into a martini glass. Dust with the faintest drift of sifted cocoa, garnish with a roasted coffee bean, if you have one, and serve immediately.

KOHINOOR FIZZ

We invented this cocktail for the opening of Dishoom Edinburgh. It's a beautifully balanced drink to accompany anything rich or spicy, like Chef Naved's special mutton pepper fry (page 206).

The basics of a classic fizz are simple: gin, citrus and sugar syrup, shaken with ice and topped up with soda water. The addition of an egg white creates a luxurious foam – the "silver fizz". Swapping the soda water for sparkling wine gives you a "diamond fizz". The Kohinoor is the famous and large diamond taken from India by the British (whose name is shared by Mr Kohinoor of Britannia Restaurant).

SERVES 6

~

160g good-quality gooseberry jam (around 50% fruit)

Lots of ice cubes

120ml lime juice (about 4 limes)

210ml London dry gin

30ml Aperol apéritif

2 egg whites

75cl bottle prosecco, cava or champagne, well chilled

Lime slice (dried or fresh), to garnish

1. Put the gooseberry jam into a bowl, add 80ml hot water (slightly cooled from a boiled kettle) and stir well to combine. Pass through a fine sieve into your blender. (Use the back of a wooden spoon to push as much through as you can.)

2. Have 6 tall glasses ready, filled with plenty of ice.

3. Add the lime juice, gin and Aperol to the blender, then the egg whites and 2 large ice cubes. Blitz until smooth and frothy, about 30 seconds.

4. Pour through a strainer and divide equally between the 6 glasses. Top up with chilled sparkling wine – don't pour from too great a height, otherwise you'll get a slightly solid, slightly unsightly foam.

5. Serve immediately, garnished with a lime slice on the rim of the glass.

BOLLYBELLINI

This is a sweet and simple crowd-pleaser of a cocktail. To enjoy it at its best, serve in chilled champagne flutes.

SERVES 8

~

2 green cardamom pods

25ml rose syrup (see below)

30ml sugar syrup (page 138)

100ml raspberry purée

150ml lychee juice (Rubicon)

75cl bottle prosecco, well chilled

1. Using a pestle and mortar, bash the cardamom pods to release the seeds.

2. Pour the rose syrup into a small jug and add the bashed cardamom. Stir well and leave to infuse for 30 minutes.

3. Pour the infused rose syrup through a fine sieve or drinks strainer into a large jug (big enough to hold the other ingredients). Add the sugar syrup and stir well.

4. Add the raspberry purée and lychee juice and mix well.

5. Add the prosecco to the jug and stir gently to combine. Divide between 8 flutes and enjoy immediately.

Note: For the raspberry purée, blitz 175g raspberries with 20ml simple syrup and push through a sieve to remove the seeds. (Or use Funkin Pro or Boiron ready-made purée.)

Rose syrup: Put 150g granulated white sugar, 150ml water, 50ml rose water and 5g dried rose petals or 1 tsp red food colouring into a saucepan and bring to the boil. Turn the heat down and simmer gently for 5 minutes. Take off the heat and allow the syrup to infuse as it cools, then strain it if you've used rose petals. It will keep in a sealed container in the fridge for 2–3 weeks. *Makes about 250ml*

THE DHOBLE

Bombay is technically still under a state of prohibition. The Bombay Prohibition Act of 1949 is a lovely little piece of legislation which allows officials to issue permits for emergency champagne for medicinal purposes. This legislation has never been repealed, so in law, all adults of legal drinking age (twenty-five and above) need a permit if they want to a drink in a bar. Bars in the city are therefore known as "Permit Rooms".

By and large, this law is sensibly forgotten, but not long ago there was a particularly zealous police chief, ACP Vasant Dhoble, who remembered it. He notoriously took to closing down bars and nightclubs in Bombay brandishing a hockey stick. He has since been moved on and has given up raiding bars, but should the "Murderer of Mumbai Nightlife" ever come to London, he might find some amusement in the fact we've named an innocuous-looking breakfast cocktail after him, and all of our bars are adorned with his photo and a hockey stick.

SERVES 1

~

30ml orange juice, from concentrate (see note)

30ml vodka

20ml lemon juice

15ml jaggery reduction (page 339)

4 dashes of orange bitters

Ice cubes

Orange peel twist, to garnish

1. Put the orange juice, vodka, lemon juice, jaggery reduction and orange bitters into a cocktail shaker.

2. Top up with lots of ice and shake vigorously for at least 30 seconds.

3. Strain into a martini glass and garnish with an orange peel twist.

Note: It is important to use orange juice from concentrate to ensure the right balance of sugar.

CHAI PAANCH

Making a milk punch was an old-fashioned way of turning an unpalatable, rough spirit into a smooth, agreeable drink. Fortunately, most spirits have become smoother since the bad old days of the eighteenth century. Nonetheless, marrying strong spirits, tea, citrus oils and sugar with the beautiful mollifying effect of milk clarification is still very satisfying. Replacing the milk with masala chai is our Bombay twist.

The Punch à la Ford, from *Jerry Thomas' Bartenders Guide*, is an essential ingredient. It is an intense citrus syrup, created by drawing the oil out of lemon rinds with sugar. The recipe will make a touch over what you need for chai paanch, but you can turn the leftover syrup into a thirst-quenching drink (see note).

Chai paanch is not a difficult drink to make, but an impressive one that takes a couple of days.

**MAKES ABOUT 500ML
(10 SERVINGS)**

~

FOR THE PUNCH À LA FORD

9–10 unwaxed lemons

100g granulated sugar

50ml lemon juice

FOR THE CHAI PAANCH

300ml warm masala chai (see page 86)

60ml Punch à la Ford (see above)

185ml Gosling's Black Seal or other dark rum

35ml Johnny Walker Black Label or other good-quality blended whisky

35ml Ceylon arrack

35ml ginger liqueur

2 tsp Mozart Dry chocolate spirit

Ice cubes

Nutmeg, for grating

1. To make the Punch à la Ford, use a vegetable peeler to remove the rind from unwaxed lemons in strips (a little pith will not harm the drink); you need 50g lemon rinds. Place them in a bowl, add the sugar and stir well, massaging the sugar into the rinds with your hands. Cover with cling film and leave for 12–24 hours.

2. Add the lemon juice, stir well, and leave while you prepare the masala chai and the rest of the drink. The chai should still be warm (but not hot) when you come to make the drink.

3. Measure the spirits into a large jug and add the chai.

4. Stir the Punch à la Ford, then strain it through a sieve. Measure out the 60ml you need for the drink and add to the jug; the mixture should curdle immediately. Cover the jug with cling film and allow to sit at room temperature overnight.

5. Strain the punch through a double layer of muslin, then through a coffee filter. This last part can take a little while for the liquid to filter through. Pour the strained drink into a sterilised glass container, add a lid and refrigerate until required.

6. To serve, fill rocks glasses with ice cubes, grate a touch of nutmeg onto them and then add a 50ml measure of chai paanch.

Note: Any leftover Punch à la Ford syrup will make an exceptional nimbu pani, or lemon water drink. Simply add a pinch of salt, a little extra lemon juice, plenty of ice and top with soda.

TAJ BALLROOM TODDY

The Taj Mahal Palace hotel was where Bombay's jazz age was born. Its famous ballroom played host to some of the best musicians from the West, and their self-taught and accomplished Indian counterparts.

Apple juice from concentrate is best as it provides the right level of sweetness to counter the punch of the Indian malt whisky, Amrut. If you can't get hold of Amrut, use a single malt Scotch with a bit of body (but not overpoweringly peaty) and a high ABV – around 50% if possible.

SERVES 8

~

320ml medium-dry cider

200ml apple juice, from concentrate

40ml ginger juice (see below)

1 cinnamon stick

2 green cardamom pods

1 clove

120ml agave syrup

200ml Amrut whisky

A dried orange slice or a small strip of orange peel, to garnish

1. Put the cider, apple juice, ginger juice and spices into a saucepan. Warm over a medium-low heat, stirring occasionally, until the liquid reaches simmering point. Let it simmer very gently for 2 minutes.

2. Add the agave syrup and stir well.

3. Measure 25ml whisky into each cup or small heatproof glass.

4. Pour 100ml mulled cider into each cup.

5. Garnish with the dried orange slice or strip of orange peel and serve immediately.

Ginger juice: To make this, grate peeled ginger root into a square of muslin placed in a bowl. Gather up the edges of the muslin and squeeze out the juice. You'll need about 8cm ginger root to give 40ml juice (i.e. 1cm per 5ml).

THE COMMANDER

The Parsi naval Commander, Kawas Nanavati, was a very dashing gentleman. When his beautiful English wife, Sylvia, confessed in 1959 that she was having a torrid affair, Nanavati sped over to her Sindhi lover's apartment on the Nepean Sea Road and shot him three times. The Commander then gave himself up to be arrested at the naval base. The subsequent case became India's most famous murder trial, not least due to the Commander's good looks. Apparently Bombay's women thronged the public gallery for the duration of the trial, dressed in their finest clothes and hoping to get a glimpse of him.

In this drink, we'd like to think that the Navy gin represents the cuckolded commander and the Kamm & Sons (a London aperitif distilled from aromatics including ginseng, grapefruit peel, juniper) his English wife, Sylvia. The absinthe is the naughty spirit, the other man, and the pepper is the gunpowder.

This is a strong, dry drink for sipping, a real palate-livener. Don't have too many. Keep it in the freezer and serve it so cold that the liquid turns syrupy.

MAKES 70cl bottle

~

10g black peppercorns

345ml Navy strength gin

1½ tsp absinthe

110ml Kamm & Sons

1. Roughly crack the black peppercorns, using a pestle and mortar; they should be nicely broken up but not ground to a powder.

2. Place a sieve over a large measuring jug or bowl and line with a double layer of muslin. Put the bashed peppercorns in the centre, then very slowly, in a thin trickle, pour the gin through them. The gin should take on a faint brown tint, and have a very pleasing warmth to it, without being too peppery. If the gin hasn't picked up much flavour, simply pour it through the pepper again. If it's too strong, dilute with a little extra gin (if you add extra gin, only use 345ml to make the batch). Discard the peppercorns.

3. Pour the peppery gin into a measuring jug and let it settle for 10 minutes.

4. While the gin is settling, pour the absinthe into a 70cl bottle (ideally, use the Navy gin bottle, then you won't need to sterilise it). Put the lid on and turn the bottle over a few times to thoroughly coat the inside of the bottle.

5. Take the lid off and slowly pour the gin into the bottle, being careful not to pour in the pepper sediment at the bottom.

6. Add the Kamm & Sons and 250ml water. Finally, seal with the lid, invert a few times to mix well and chill thoroughly in the freezer. Serve small measures extremely chilled, with no extra ice.

BOMBAY PRESIDENCY PUNCH

Arrack – made from the sap of coconut flowers – is one of the oldest spirits in the world, and Ceylon arrack is a particularly fine example. It tastes a little like tequila, only lighter, with deliciously nutty hints.

We use a green Darjeeling tea, brewed reasonably strong, along with the bay leaves. This can be a tricky tea to find, but first flush Darjeeling is a fine substitute.

SERVES 4–6

~

400ml cold Darjeeling green tea, brewed with 4 dried bay leaves (see above), bay leaves retained

300ml Ceylon arrack

100ml jaggery reduction (see below)

150ml lime juice (about 6 limes, squeezed gently to avoid releasing bitter aromatic oils)

1 lime, sliced

Bay leaves (from the tea infusion)

Lots of ice cubes (at least 25)

Nutmeg, for grating

1. Put the tea, Ceylon arrack, jaggery reduction and lime juice into a large jug. Stir well to ensure the jaggery is completely mixed in. If you leave this drink for any length of time, it'll settle again and need stirring again before serving.

2. If you have a punch bowl and tea cups, decant the drink into the punch bowl. Add the lime slices and bay leaves, then the ice. Grate plenty of nutmeg over the top and ladle into punch cups to serve. Otherwise, fill tall glasses with ice and add a lime slice. Pour in 100–150ml punch and grate over lots of nutmeg just before serving.

Jaggery reduction: With its complex date and toffee notes, this give a roundness to drinks that cannot be achieved with sugar syrup alone. An essential ingredient in this punch, it is excellent in cocktails too, especially in those made with darker spirits. It can also be mixed with tamarind, lime juice and soda for a delicious summer cooler.

To make it, you will need 400g jaggery – the darker the colour, the stronger and richer your reduction will be. Put the jaggery and 200ml hot water (cooled for 5 minutes after boiling) into a small pan and melt gently over a low heat, stirring regularly. Once melted, turn the heat up to medium-high and let bubble to reduce to a thick, dark brown caramel; this should take around 10 minutes. To test to see if the reduction is ready, drop a tiny amount onto an ice cube; it should thicken up immediately to the consistency of treacle. If it sets completely, you've gone too far and need to incorporate a little water (be careful, it will steam and bubble – let cool a little first). When you're satisfied with the reduction, decant into a sterilised jar. It will keep for 1 month in a cool cupboard, or at least 6 weeks in the fridge.

CYRUS IRANI

A drink to honour a fictional hero. We named it after the leading character in the one-off immersive theatre production that we created in Dishoom Kensington. Cyrus Irani is the charismatic but wayward Irani café-owner who sought and found redemption.

The turmeric syrup used in the cocktail is a play on the medicinal turmeric milk that many Indians turn to when they're feeling below par.

SERVES 1

~

10ml lime juice

35ml turmeric syrup (see below)

35ml Centenario or other good-quality reposado tequila

Ice cubes

Lime wedge, to garnish

1. Measure the lime juice, turmeric syrup and tequila into your cocktail shaker.

2. Add lots of ice and shake vigorously for 1 minute.

3. Pour through a strainer into a sours or sherry glass, and serve with a lime wedge on the rim.

Turmeric syrup: Mix 200g set honey with 100ml hot water. Add 1 tbsp ground turmeric and 1 tbsp cayenne pepper and stir well to combine. Add 200g full-fat Greek strained yoghurt and mix until smooth. Pour into a small saucepan and place over a very low heat. Heat to 80°C and hold it at that temperature for 2 minutes (check with a cook's thermometer); you may need to lift the pan off the heat source occasionally; stir regularly to prevent the mixture from catching. Add 60ml freshly squeezed lime juice, stir lightly just twice, then take off the heat. Allow the mix to settle and curdle for 1–2 hours. Tip the curdled mixture into a muslin-lined sieve set over a bowl and leave to drain for 2–3 hours. Pour the liquid into a sterilised bottle or jar and store in the fridge for up to 2 weeks; it will soften as it ages. *Makes about 200ml*

Note: The yoghurt solids that you get when you strain the turmeric syrup are fantastic; use them to marinate chicken, lamb or pork, or add to a tomato-chickpea curry.

BLOODY MARY

For best results, make the Bloody Mary mix up in advance and give the flavours a few hours to mingle – though the longer you leave it, the more peppery it will get. Those with foresight might decide to prepare it the night before the morning after.

Enough ice is absolutely essential to a good Bloody Mary, so you need plenty of room in the glass, which should be filled almost to the top with ice cubes.

The tomato purée helps the juice along a little, so there is no need to buy an expensive tomato juice. We use a smoke powder, but at home you can use smoked paprika, or replace the Tabasco with the smoked version.

SERVES 4

~

FOR THE BLOODY MARY MIX

540ml tomato juice

65ml tomato purée

25ml Tabasco sauce

65ml Worcestershire sauce

40ml lemon juice

40ml distilled white vinegar

3 tsp ground pink Himalayan salt (or flaky sea salt)

3 tsp crushed black pepper

2 tsp jaggery reduction (page 339)

¼ tsp smoked paprika

TO SERVE

100ml vodka

Bloody Mary mix (see above)

Ice cubes

4 celery sticks

4 pickled silverskin onions

Flaky sea salt and freshly ground black pepper

1. For the Bloody Mary mix, combine all the ingredients in a jug and stir well to ensure the salt and spices are well distributed. Store in a sealed bottle or jar in the fridge and use within 4–5 days.

2. When ready to serve, add the vodka to the Bloody Mary mix, stir to combine and pour into 4 tall glasses. Add as much ice as will fit in the glass.

3. Garnish with the celery and silverskin onions and sprinkle with a little salt and pepper. Serve immediately.

Note: For a single serving, pour 165ml Bloody Mary mix into a glass and add 25ml vodka and plenty of ice.

VICEROY'S OLD-FASHIONED

A strong and smooth Old-fashioned, well-rounded by a month in the bottle – treat it as you would any good whiskey. Drink it neat or on the rocks; if the latter, use plenty of ice so that it dilutes much more slowly. We'd like to think that Dickie Mountbatten would have found much-needed repose in this strong drink.

There are two ageing stages to this drink. The first (and longest) is to marry the whiskey with a dark, thick green tea and brown sugar reduction. The longer you age at this stage, the bigger the flavour will be. We recommend a month, though we've left it as long as a couple of years, and it only improves with time.

The second stage comes after the addition of water, which allows the drink to round and soften a little; for this you need at least a day, and the longer the drink is left in this finished state, the softer it becomes.

MAKES 70cl bottle

~

FOR THE REDUCTION

2 green teabags

220g dark brown sugar

8 dried bay leaves

TO FINISH

460ml dry, spicy bourbon
(such as Woodfood Reserve),
or rye whiskey

2 tsp Angostura orange bitters

115ml filtered water

1. For the reduction, put the teabags into a measuring jug and pour on 200ml boiling water. Stir, then leave to infuse for 5 minutes to make a strong tea.

2. Put the sugar and bay leaves into a small heavy-based stainless-steel saucepan (or other heavy pan with a pale interior). Give the teabags a squeeze then dispose of them. Pour the green tea into the pan and stir well.

3. Place over a low heat and heat gently until the sugar has dissolved, then turn the heat up. Allow to bubble and reduce to a thick, dark brown caramel; this should take around 10 minutes. To test whether it is ready, drop a tiny amount onto an ice cube; it should thicken at once to the consistency of black treacle. If it sets completely, you've gone too far and need to incorporate a little water (it will steam and bubble, so let it cool a little first).

4. When the caramel reduction is ready, discard the bay leaves and allow to cool; it doesn't need to be completely cold, but it should be left for at least 30 minutes.

5. Pour the whiskey into a large jug or bowl and then add 115ml of the green tea reduction. Stir well to combine, then pour into a sterilised bottle. (Better still, empty the whiskey bottle and use that.) Leave in a cool, dark place for at least 1 month.

6. When the month is up, slowly invert the bottle several times to mix well.

7. Add the Angostura bitters and filtered water; this should more or less fill a 70cl bottle to the top. Let it stand for at least 24 hours to soften a little before drinking.

INGREDIENTS &
COOKERY GUIDANCE

Those new to Indian cookery should take the time to digest the following information. It will be invaluable in helping you to make sense of, and then master, some of the recipes in this book.

INGREDIENTS

There is an ever-expanding range of spices and exotic ingredients in supermarkets these days, particularly the larger ones and particularly those in cities. You can also buy an excellent range of products online from websites such as Spices of India, Red Rickshaw, Sabadda and, of course, the ubiquitous Amazon. But if you don't know one already, we urge you to hunt out a good Indian grocery shop. You should find everything you need for this book there, and plenty more besides.

Amchur

Amchur is dried unripe mango powder. It has an unmistakable, mouthwateringly tangy flavour which pairs well with grilled meat and fish.

Asafoetida (hing)

A highly pungent spice, derived from a giant fennel, which must be used in very small quantities owing to its strong flavour. Use the powdered yellow version, which is slightly less intense.

Atta (chapati flour)

A wholewheat flour with a slight grainy texture, this is perfect for creating flavoursome breads. It is used in many of our bread recipes and is easy to find in larger supermarkets and online.

Cardamom

Black cardamom is a headier spice than its delicate green cousin, and more suited to savoury dishes. The pods are dried over open flames, giving strong smokiness and great depth, so use them sparingly. Try to pick out the pods once the dish is cooked, as biting into one will be an unwelcome surprise. Green cardamom is used in drinks, desserts and savoury dishes that call for a more subtle flavour.

Charoli seeds

Charoli seeds look a little like a pine nut but have the flavour of an almond. They are used in our bun maska pudding (page 300). You should be able to find them at an Indian grocery shop, but if not you can use flaked almonds instead.

Chickpea flour (gram flour, besan)

Used for thickening, and to make some breads, this is gluten-free, and available in most supermarkets.

Crispy fried onions and shallots

Used as a garnish, these are crunchy and sweet. They are sold in packets in Asian and Southeast Asian grocery shops. Crispy fried onions are an essential finish for biryanis; to prepare your own, see page 230.

Curry leaves, fresh

Fresh curry leaves are much more aromatic than their dried equivalent, and are definitely worth the trip to an Indian grocer that stocks fresh produce. Buy plenty, as they freeze well.

Deggi mirch chilli powder

A medium-hot chilli powder with a vibrant red hue, thanks to Kashmiri chillies. It is available from most Indian grocery shops and well worth seeking out for the authentic flavour it imparts. If you can't get hold of it you can use regular chilli powder instead, reducing the amount by one-third to half as regular chilli powder tends to be hotter.

Fenugreek leaves, dried (kasoori methi)

This is a spicy dried herb, which adds a final touch of savour to many dishes. It is also a key ingredient in our kabab masala.

Fine sev

Very fine and delicate fried chickpea noodles, perfect for garnishing plates of dahi bhalla chaat (page 180), or for tumbling with chutneys, onions, herbs and pomegranate for bhel (page 163).

Green chillies

Indian green chillies have a distinctive flavour, a good level of heat and a lovely astringent character. They are incorporated fresh into many recipes and garnishes, or fried lightly and then salted slightly, for careful nibbling. They are available to buy by the handful in Indian grocery shops, and they will freeze well. You can substitute green chillies from a supermarket, but they may not be quite the same.

Jaggery

This is an unrefined cane sugar with a beautifully rich, complex and almost caramel-like flavour. We use it in some dishes and to make jaggery reduction (page 339), an intense syrup used to flavour cocktails and drinks.

Kewda water (kewra water)

This is an extract distilled from the pandan leaf – quite aromatic, with a floral, oddly sweet characteristic. We use it to finish the lamb for our awadhi lamb biryani (page 234) and nihari (page 240).

Limes

We use fresh limes a lot more often than you might expect: in savoury dishes, drinks, and as a garnish for squeezing at the table.

Onion seeds (kalonji, nigella seeds)

An earthy, almost nutty seed that pairs beautifully with turmeric dishes.

Papaya paste

A paste of unripe (green or raw) papaya, this is used to tenderise meat, rather than for flavour. It is not always easy to find, though you should be able to get it in a larger Indian grocery shop.

Rose syrup

This is used for finishing rich and savoury sauces, or to make a syrup for desserts and drinks. It is available from Indian or Middle Eastern grocers (Natco and Rooh Afza are good brands); avoid cheaper rose syrups, as they tend to have a lot of added colour but not much flavour. If you prefer, you can make your own rose syrup (see page 332).

Rose water

This has many applications in Indian cookery. We use it mainly for finishing rich and savoury sauces or to make a syrup for flavouring desserts and cocktails.

Saffron

Saffron is widely available, though a little expensive to buy. It has a distinctive, aromatic flavour that is absolutely essential to our biryanis. See page 230 for how to prepare saffron water.

Spice masalas, ready-prepared

Several ready-prepared spice masalas are used in this book, because their lengthy ingredient lists make them impractical to prepare, namely chana masala, pav bhaji masala and chaat masala. These should be easy to find in most Indian grocery stores and online. MDH and TRS are good brands.

Tamarind

This has a delightfully sour-sweet tang to it and is a key ingredient in the chutneys that accompany so many of our fried dishes. It is available in several different forms.

Tamarind paste is the easiest to use – avoid any with added spices or other flavours.

Tamarind block is a concentrated form that comes with or without seeds. The seedless version is excellent if you can find it. If it does have seeds, you will need to double the quantity to allow for their removal (they will need to be sieved out).

Tamarind syrup is a little thin for making chutneys, and more commonly used for drinks.

Whole tamarind takes a fair amount of time and effort to prepare, as it needs to be de-shelled, steeped in boiling water, mixed vigorously, then pushed through a sieve, and the stones removed.

Urad daal

As far as lentils are concerned, the recipes in this book rely solely on urad daal. You'll need whole (black) urad lentils to make house black daal (page 214); split (white) urad lentils are used in dahi bhalla chaat (page 180), haleem (page 246) and bedmi puri (page 370).

Yoghurt

Our recipes call for full-fat Greek yoghurt; lower fat yoghurts just don't give the same eating quality or characteristics when cooking.

USING SPICES

Our recipes rely heavily on judicious spicing. There are various ways to introduce spices to a dish, from the subtlety of the potli in our nihari (page 240), to the pleasing punch in the mutton pepper fry (page 206).

Making a spice masala

A small number of the recipes in this book call for their own specific blend of spices, but most of them use our house garam masala (page 356). This is a versatile and reliable combination of spices, adding essential heat and flavour to almost any dish. (*Garam* simply means hot.) Once you start making your own garam masala, you will not look back.

For the very best results, bake the spices in a low oven at 50°C for 2–3 hours, to tease out the flavour. It's also possible to make a good spice masala by toasting the spices for just a minute or two in a dry frying pan. Once cooled, the spices need to be ground to a fine powder.

Potli

This is like a bouquet garni, but with spices instead of herbs. Whole spices are wrapped in a square of muslin, tied with food-safe string and added to the cooking pot. This allows for easy removal at the end of cooking, and produces a more subtle flavour compared to adding loose spices.

Tempering spices

Where used, this technique – also known as *tadka*, *tarka* or *baghaar* – helps to set the tone for the dish. Whole spices, bay leaves and often curry leaves are dropped into hot oil and allowed to sizzle for 5–10 seconds, creating an aromatic base and anchoring the ingredients to come. The leaves will crackle due to the moisture content. Do not allow the ingredients to burn.

MAKING SAUCES & CURRIES

There are techniques and processes that are common to many of the recipes. For example, a lot of the dishes in the book involve creating a rich, flavoursome sauce. For the most part, these use familiar ingredients, but the cooking methods differ from those that the majority of non-Indians have grown up with. The following guidance is intended to give you the best chance of achieving authentic deliciousness.

Starting with a bowl of water

Many dishes involve frying vegetables and spices over a medium or high heat for a reasonably long time, but the ingredients must not be allowed to burn. Before you begin, place a bowl of water by the hob. You can add a tablespoonful of water if the ingredients start to cook too quickly. This will allow you to sauté them for longer periods, enough to achieve the required depth and robustness of flavour, and darker colour.

Stirring

Most of the curries and sauces in this book demand a lot of stirring. The ingredients must not be allowed to stick; it is important to lift and scrape the caramelised flavour from the base of the pan. The high heat under the pan creates flavour, while the stirring helps you to work that flavour back into the body of the sauce. A heatproof rubber spatula is excellent for getting into the corners of the pan, though the rubber may retain the flavour (keep a spatula solely for this purpose).

Using oil

Oil is used in varying amounts throughout our recipes, not only for sautéing and deep-frying, but as an essential ingredient required to build up the character and colour of sauces. Do not be tempted to reduce the quantity at the start of the recipe. If you are concerned about the finished dish being too oily, skim some off at the end instead.

Caramelising onions

In comparison to European methods, our process for caramelising onions is hotter, faster and oilier. The onions should be diced finely – a greater surface area allows for more caramelisation. The process takes 15–20 minutes, and the heat should be fairly high. Pay attention, and stir the onions very frequently. They need to cook evenly, without any parts of the mixture beginning to stick or burn.

If this begins to happen, add a spoonful of water, and loosen any stuck pieces. This will help the mixture to achieve a uniform caramelisation. The end result should be a dark, savoury, rich brown (not a light golden colour) with plenty of depth as well as sweetness (pic 1).

Adding ginger and garlic pastes

Ginger and garlic pastes are used in almost every savoury dish in this book. When used as part of a sauce base, they should be added at the point when the onions are caramelised and the oil is still hot. The paste needs to be stirred almost constantly so that it does not burn. Add a splash of water if the paste gets sticky or appears to take on too much colour too quickly. Ginger and garlic pastes should cook to a light golden brown colour in 2–4 minutes, and smell sweet and fragrant rather than raw or burnt.

Cooking powdered spices

Spices, along with any salt, are generally added once the onions, ginger and garlic are nicely browned. The spices need to be cooked for at least 3 minutes (pic 2), and up to 10 minutes for larger spice masalas (such as the mutton pepper fry, page 206). Add a couple of tablespoonfuls of water when the spices start to stick. This will allow you to keep cooking them a little longer.

Cooking tomatoes

Once the spices are cooked through, many recipes call for chopped tomatoes. Use fresh tomatoes if they are in season and flavourful, or good-quality tinned if not. Tomatoes need cooking for longer than you may expect, and have three distinct stages. First, all the water must leave the tomatoes; then they need to be cooked until they disintegrate completely; finally, they need to caramelise in the oil (pic 3). The mixture tends to dry up before the latter stages are complete. Although it may seem counterproductive, when this happens, add a tablespoonful or two of water, so that you can continue the process.

Cooking meat

In many of our recipes, the meat is caramelised in its sauce, rather than fried beforehand (as is more usual in European cookery). This is one reason why oil is so important; it gives the meat some colour. Regardless of when the meat is added, it generally needs to be simmered until very tender.

Adding yoghurt

Yoghurt is frequently added to a curry or sauce. The aim is to cook the water out of the yoghurt and slightly caramelise the dairy. At a medium-high heat, it should takes a little over 5 minutes for yoghurt to completely cook down. It will first split, then fry, then become a rich and oily part of the masala, as the sugars in the milk brown to create flavour.

Adding water or stock

It is advisable to add just enough water or stock to cover the meat, and then top up the liquid a few times during cooking (pic 4), rather than drowning your masala and leaving the meat to boil. Keep the heat low, for a healthy simmer, and stir regularly.

Finishing the dish

After all this frying, stirring and simmering, you should have a very rich, deep and flavoursome dish. It now demands a final flourish before you serve it. This could be a sprinkle of garam masala (page 356) and a generous squeeze of lime; perhaps some fresh ginger matchsticks, coriander or mint; or a dash of coconut milk. Some dishes call for a more complex combination, like the heady mix of rose water, kewda water, cardamom, mace, lime and garam masala that we use to finish the nihari (page 240).

If you wish to, you can skim off any excess oil before finishing the dish.

Garnishing

The garnish is the final touch, a way to brighten flavours at the table. It can be diced or sliced red onions, wedges of lime, a selection of fresh green herbs, fresh or fried green chillies, a chutney, or a bowl of kachumber (page 121), or any combination of these. The garnish often serves to cut through a particularly rich dish.

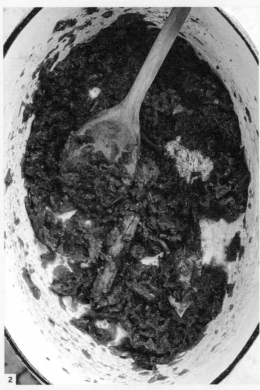

Cooking finely diced onions to a dark, rich, even caramelisation.

Cooking the powdered spices with the caramelised onions until cooked through.

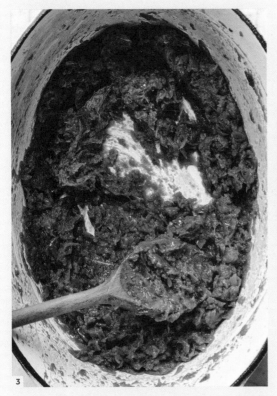

Cooking the tomatoes until they disintegrate and caramelise in the oil.

Topping up the liquid to keep the meat just covered during cooking.

PREPARATORY RECIPES

These preparatory recipes are the key to many of the dishes in this book. Some of the spice masalas are ready in minutes, while there are a few sauces which call for lengthy simmering. The garlic and ginger pastes are in almost every recipe; an Indian kitchen is never without them.

GARLIC & GINGER PASTES

The recipe is the same for either paste. You can start with whole garlic cloves or ginger root each time, but it is much easier to keep pre-prepared jars of paste in the fridge. Home-made pastes will yield a more satisfying result than supermarket-bought (but won't keep for quite as long).

The quantity given below is sufficient for a mini food processor or blender. You can, of course, make more, or less.

Providing you start with garlic and ginger that is fresh (not stale or dry), pack the paste into sterilised jars and cover the surface with a layer of oil, these pastes should keep in the fridge for 10 days.

MAKES ABOUT 170g

~

3 garlic bulbs or 180g fresh root ginger

25ml vegetable oil, plus extra to store the paste

1. Peel your garlic or ginger completely and roughly chop.

2. Using a mini food processor or blender, blitz the garlic or ginger with the oil to a smooth paste. The oil should be enough to loosen the mixture; if it seems too thick add 2–3 tsp water.

3. Place in a clean, sterilised jar and cover the surface with a thin layer of oil. Store in the fridge and use within 10 days.

ONION-TOMATO MASALA

This masala is the foundation of a number of our recipes – masala beans (page 48), mattar paneer (page 106), chole (page 100) and rajma (page 102), for example. It is also an excellent ingredient to keep in your fridge or freezer. Just a couple of tablespoonfuls can provide unparalleled depth, aroma and flavour, the kind that can only be yielded from slow, careful cooking.

Before you make this for the first time, read the notes on caramelising onions (page 349) and take care: if you burn the onions, you will need to start again.

Do not be tempted to reduce the quantity of oil, as it is necessary for the proper caramelisation of the onions. The oil is also useful for storing the masala in the fridge, as it forms an airtight barrier on the surface. This can be skimmed off when you come to use the masala. You could discard the oil at that point, or keep it to make something else – first-class fried eggs, for example.

This onion-tomato masala will keep for about a week in the fridge, and for several months in the freezer.

MAKES ABOUT 650g

~

300ml vegetable oil

1.2kg Spanish white onions, finely and evenly diced

35g garlic paste (page 353)

30g ginger paste (page 353)

1¾ tsp deggi mirch chilli powder

30g tomato purée

2 tsp fine sea salt

600g chopped tomatoes (flavoursome ripe fresh, or good-quality tinned)

1. Warm a deep, heavy-based frying pan over a medium-high heat. Add the oil, let it warm for a few seconds, and then add the onions. They should simmer quite rapidly in the oil, without sizzling too much; don't allow them to burn. As the onions begin to cook, they will release some water, which will quickly evaporate due to the heat of the oil.

2. Let the onions caramelise to a deep brown colour, stirring very frequently and almost constantly. Add a splash of water, if needed, to prevent them burning. The onions are ready when they are soft in texture and deep brown in colour, with no hints of burn or bitterness. This should take around 20–40 minutes.

3. Add the garlic and ginger pastes and sauté until light golden brown, stirring almost constantly.

4. Add the chilli powder, tomato purée and salt, and sauté for 2 minutes.

5. Add the chopped tomatoes, stir well and cook for about 20 minutes, stirring very regularly. The tomatoes need to completely break down and caramelise a little in the oil; if the pan starts to dry up before this happens, add 1–2 tbsp water, and carry on cooking.

6. Transfer any masala that you're not using straight away into a clean jar, cover and allow to cool, then store in the fridge and use within a week. (Or freeze in useful quantities once cool.)

GARAM MASALA

We use garam masala in almost every savoury dish we make. We give two methods for this spice mix: a quick recipe using a pan, and a longer recipe using the oven. The longer one will yield a richer, fuller flavour.

As with all masalas, freshly grinding your spices produces the best results. For an especially rich garam masala, add a large pinch each of saffron and grated nutmeg along with the poppy seeds and rose petals.

The garam masala will keep an airtight container in a cool, dark cupboard for up to a month.

MAKES ABOUT 50g

~

1 black cardamom pod

4 cloves

5g black peppercorns

2 large cinnamon sticks

10g coriander seeds

5g cumin seeds

4g fennel seeds

2g star anise

1 bay leaf

2g mace blades

10g poppy seeds

2g dried rose petals

OVEN METHOD

1. Heat the oven to 50°C (lowest Gas). Spread everything apart from the poppy seeds and rose petals on a baking sheet. Place in the oven for 2½ hours.

2. Add the poppy seeds and rose petals to the tray, place it back in the oven and turn the oven off. Allow the mixture to cool in the switched-off oven for 30 minutes.

3. Transfer the cooled spice mix to a spice grinder and grind to a fine powder.

PAN METHOD

1. Put everything apart from the poppy seeds and rose petals into a cold, dry frying pan and place over a medium heat to warm, shaking the pan occasionally. Toast for 2 minutes, then turn off the heat.

2. Add the poppy seeds and rose petals, and let the mixture cool in the pan.

3. Transfer the cooled spice mix to a spice grinder and grind to a fine powder.

"MAGIC" MASALA

Flavoured with plenty of tangy amchur (dried unripe mango powder) and bright red chilli powder, this finishing salt is so-named because we sprinkle it onto dishes to add a little sparkle, a touch of magic. Sprinkle it onto salli (page 173) or okra fries (page 179); or add it to cut fruit for fruit chaat – sour-sweet green mango works a treat.

MAKES ABOUT 20g

~

10g fine sea salt

10g amchur

4g deggi mirch chilli powder

1. Mix the ingredients together in a bowl.

2. Store in an airtight container or jar in a cool, dark cupboard. It will keep for up to 2 months.

GHATI MASALA

A delicious sprinkle you'll want to dust over everything. This makes a generous quantity and it keeps for at least a week. The garlicky oil you are left with is delicious for cooking sauces, vegetables or eggs.

MAKES ABOUT 90g

~

100ml vegetable oil

40g garlic (9–10 cloves), finely chopped

30g desiccated coconut

10g deggi mirch chilli powder

4g fine sea salt

1. Heat the oil in a small pan over a medium heat and add the chopped garlic. Fry until it is very lightly browned; do not allow it to colour too much or burn, as it will taste bitter. Remove with a slotted spoon and place on a tray lined with kitchen paper to cool and drain. The garlic should be quite crispy.

2. Heat a frying pan over a medium-low heat. Add the desiccated coconut and toast slowly, stirring regularly, until light golden brown. Transfer to a plate and allow to cool completely.

3. Combine the garlic, toasted coconut and chilli powder and blitz to a reasonably coarse powder using a spice grinder. The masala will be a little clumpy owing to the oil in the garlic and coconut.

4. Store on a layer of kitchen paper in an airtight container and use within a week.

KABAB MASALA

This is a key spice mix that finishes many a dish: kababs, vegetables, meat and more. It will keep for a while, but is best used freshly ground.

MAKES ABOUT 35g

~

10g dried fenugreek leaves

22g chaat masala

2g deggi mirch chilli powder

1g garam masala (page 356)

1g fine sea salt

1. Heat the oven to 100°C/Fan 80°C/lowest Gas. Sprinkle the dried fenugreek leaves onto a foil-lined baking sheet and bake for 20 minutes. Allow to cool completely.

2. Blitz all the ingredients together in a spice grinder and decant into an airtight container or jar. Store in a cool, dark cupboard and use within 2 weeks.

CHILLI DRIZZLE

This is a sweet-sour-spicy syrup to add tang to your dishes. Drizzle it on anything that needs a bit of livening up. Or combine it with tamarind chutney to make a tamarind drizzle (see below).

Take good care while preparing this drizzle, and do not stand over the pan, as the steam will sting your eyes. It will keep in the fridge for up to a couple of months, in a sterilised container.

MAKES ABOUT 300ml

~

300ml sherry vinegar

30g jaggery

¼ tsp deggi mirch chilli powder

½ tsp dried chilli flakes

1 tbsp lime juice

150g soft dark brown sugar

2 tsp coriander seeds

1. Put everything apart from the coriander seeds into a small saucepan. Add 60ml water and heat, stirring, until well combined, then cook over a high heat until reduced by half, about 15–20 minutes.

2. Meanwhile, warm a dry frying pan over a medium heat. Add the coriander seeds and toast for 2 minutes, then transfer to a bowl and allow to cool.

3. Tip the toasted coriander seeds into the drizzle and mix well. Pour into a clean jar and leave to cool. Cover and refrigerate until serving. For longer storage (see above), use a sterilised bottle or jar.

Tamarind drizzle: This is used as a dressing for vada pau (page 174), salads and chaats. To make it, simply mix 4 tsp chilli drizzle with 3 tsp tamarind chutney (page 377). *Makes 35ml*

LAMB STOCK

This lamb stock is a crucial part of the flavour and depth of our nihari (page 240) and awadhi lamb biryani (page 234). It sets to a very thick, opaque jelly once it has cooled. Ask your butcher for a combination of shank/leg and shoulder bones, cut to 5–7cm lengths.

The exact weight of bones and quantity of water will depend on the capacity of your stockpot. The stove method is slightly quicker, whereas the oven or slow-cooker method calls for less attention (and milder cooking smells emanating through your house).

MAKES ABOUT 1.5 LITRES

~

1–1.5kg lamb bones

1–2 garlic cloves

STOVE METHOD

1. Place the lamb bones in your stockpot and pour on enough boiling water to cover completely (2–3 litres). Bring to the boil over a high heat and allow to boil for 2 minutes. Drain, discarding the liquid.

2. Return the lamb bones to the stock pot, cover them with fresh cold water and add the peeled, whole garlic cloves. Bring to the boil, again over a high heat, and skim off any foam and impurities that float to the surface.

3. Lower the heat to a simmer and cook for 4–5 hours, topping up with a little water if the bones become exposed above the surface of the liquid.

4. Remove the bones and let the stock bubble to reduce by half.

OVEN OR SLOW-COOKER METHOD

1. If using an oven, heat to 120°C/Fan 110°C/Gas ¼. If using a slow cooker, set it to low.

2. Place the lamb bones in your cooking pot or slow cooker and cover completely with cold water. If cooking in the oven, put the lid on and place in the oven. If using a slow cooker, simply position the lid. Cook for 8 hours.

3. If using a slow cooker, transfer the stock and bones to a stockpot.

4. Now, bring to the boil over a high heat and boil steadily for 20 minutes, then remove the bones and let the stock bubble to reduce by half.

MAKHANI SAUCE

This rich, creamy sauce is used for the chicken ruby (page 208), phaldari kofta (page 210) and paneer tikka chapati rolls (page 280).

MAKES 1 QUANTITY

~

35g garlic (8–9 cloves)

175ml vegetable oil

20g fresh root ginger

800g chopped tomatoes (fresh or good-quality tinned)

2 bay leaves

6 green cardamom pods

2 black cardamom pods

2 cinnamon sticks

2 tsp fine sea salt

1½ tsp deggi mirch chilli powder

30g butter

1 tsp garam masala (page 356)

20g granulated sugar

1 tbsp runny honey

1 tsp ground cumin

1 tsp dried fenugreek leaves, crushed to a powder between your fingers

½ tsp fresh dill fronds

80ml double cream

1. Take 15g garlic and finely dice it. Warm a large saucepan over a medium-high heat and add the oil. Toss in the chopped garlic and fry until light golden brown and slightly crispy, about 7–8 minutes. Remove with a slotted spoon and drain on kitchen paper.

2. Grate the remaining garlic and the ginger to a fine paste on a microplane, or grind using a pestle and mortar.

3. Using a blender, blitz the chopped tomatoes to a fine consistency.

4. Place the saucepan containing the oil back over a medium-high heat and add the bay leaves, green and black cardamom pods and the cinnamon sticks. Let them crackle for 1 minute, stirring regularly.

5. Turn the heat down and add the garlic and ginger paste. Cook for 5 minutes, allowing the paste to brown but not burn.

6. Add the tomatoes, salt and chilli powder to the pan. Bring to a rapid simmer and cook until reduced by half, stirring regularly so that it doesn't catch. This should take about 30 minutes.

7. Add the butter and simmer for a further 5 minutes.

8. Add the garam masala, sugar, honey, cumin, crispy garlic, dried fenugreek and fresh dill fronds and cook for a further 15 minutes.

9. If the sauce is to be used straight away, add the cream and simmer gently for 5 minutes; it is then ready to use. If not using immediately, allow to cool, cover and refrigerate; add the cream when you reheat the sauce to assemble your dish.

RICE

This is a lengthier process than some rice cooking methods, but the end result will be perfectly fluffy rice, with each grain intact.

You will need a large pan with a lid (which is only positioned for step 5).

SERVES 4

~

360g basmati rice

2 tsp fine sea salt

A generous squeeze of lime juice, or 1 tbsp spirit vinegar

25g salted butter (optional, but recommended)

1. Fill a large bowl with cold water and gently add the rice. Move the rice around with your hands to help release the starch, then let the rice settle to the bottom. Pour out the water, then repeat this process until the water is clear (usually 3–4 times). Cover the rice with fresh cold water and leave to soak for 1 hour.

2. Pour 3 litres boiling water into a large pan and add the salt and lime juice or spirit vinegar. Bring to the boil.

3. Cut a piece of foil large enough to comfortably cover the top of your pan.

4. Drain the rice and add it to the boiling water. Cook, stirring regularly, until almost done; this should take 4–5 minutes, and the rice should still be slightly firm in the centre.

5. Tip the rice into a sieve immediately; don't shake off all the excess water. Return the rice to the still-hot pan, shake the pan gently to create an even layer, then dot with butter, if using. Place the foil over the top of the pan and tightly crimp the edges around the edge of the pan. Place the pan over a high heat until you see the foil dome up (inflate a little), about 1 minute.

6. Position the lid to seal. Turn off the heat and leave to stand, covered, for 15–30 minutes before serving.

BREADS

Indian breads require varying levels of skill, but some of the most impressive are quite easy. Even a novice can make a fine chapati, while bhature and paratha are only a small step up, and as satisfying to make as they are to eat. Sadly, pau is not included – as hard as we tried we couldn't recreate its pillowy deliciousness at home.

PURI

Puri is one of the most common north Indian breads, often eaten on its own with chai, either plain or sprinkled with sugar. It also goes well with chole (page 100), rajma (page 102) and aloo sabzi (page 105).

The dough can be challenging to work with as it is dry and crumbly. Keep your hands and the dough well oiled, work quickly and do not overwork the mix. The result will be beautiful, crisp breads ready in under an hour.

MAKES 10

~

350g atta (wholewheat chapati flour)

70g semolina

7g fine sea salt

45ml sunflower oil, plus extra for oiling

Vegetable oil for deep-frying

1. Mix the flour, semolina and salt together in a large bowl. Stir in the sunflower oil, then make a well in the centre.

2. Add 240ml water and knead for 5 minutes, or until you have a stiff, slightly rough dough. If the dough is too dry, add more water, a little at a time, until it comes together.

3. Pour a little oil into your hands and rub over the surface of the dough. Wrap in cling film and rest for 30 minutes.

4. Cut off a 50g piece of dough, roll into a ball and flatten on an oiled surface. Using an oiled rolling pin, roll out to about the size of a saucer, about 2mm thick. Set aside (on another oiled surface) while you roll the rest. The rolled, oiled breads can be stacked on top of each other.

5. While you shape the puri, heat the oil in a deep-fryer or other suitable deep, heavy-based pan to 180°C. To test the temperature of the oil, drop in a small piece of dough; it should immediately start bubbling.

6. To fry the puri, slip one into the oil. When it comes to the surface, lightly push it back under the oil by tapping it gently; it should inflate like a cushion. Once inflated, fry for 20 seconds, then turn over and cook for a further 20 seconds until golden brown all over, and holding its crispy shape. Remove and drain on kitchen paper while you fry the remaining puris. Serve while still warm.

NAAN

At Dishoom, every naan is baked by hand, to order. And the truth is, unless
you have a tandoor oven to hand, making naan at home will not be easy. The
temperature in a tandoor can reach almost 500°C, twice what can be achieved in
a domestic oven. These instructions, however, will allow you to give home-made
naans a go. They won't be as soft and fluffy as tandoor naans, but they'll still be
gratifying. If you have a ceramic barbecue and a pizza stone, you can use them
to bake your naan – just make sure the barbecue is as hot as it can (safely) be.

The dough can be prepared in advance, but must be stored in the fridge and
allowed to return to room temperature before cooking. Naans take a little effort
to knead and some time to rest, but then cook in under a minute. You will need
a large heavy-based frying pan that is suitable to use under the grill.

Naan goes well with all kinds of grills, curries and salads. It is also used to make
our bacon naan roll (page 47) and variations.

MAKES 10

~

560g maida flour, plus extra
for dusting

10g fine sea salt

5g baking powder

8g caster sugar

150ml milk

1 large egg

1 tbsp vegetable oil, plus extra
for oiling

Melted butter, for brushing

1. Sift the flour and salt into a large bowl and make a well
   in the centre.

2. Put the baking powder, sugar, milk, 135ml water and
   the egg into a large jug and whisk to combine. Pour into
   the well in the flour mixture and gradually draw in the
   flour with a round-bladed knife. Then knead with your
   hands to a soft, smooth dough; this should take about
   5 minutes. The dough will be quite soft and slightly
   sticky as you knead it, so you may want to dust your
   hands with a little flour before you begin. Set the dough
   aside to rest for 10 minutes.

3. Trickle the 1 tbsp oil over the surface of the dough, then
   knead aggressively for 30 seconds, thoroughly squashing
   the oil into the dough. Bring the dough back to a neat,
   smooth ball and place in a clean bowl. Drape a clean,
   damp tea towel gently over the surface of the dough and
   leave to rest for 2 hours.

4. When the resting time is up, take a 70g piece of dough,
   roll it into a neat ball and place on an oiled baking sheet.
   Repeat with the rest of the dough, then cover with cling
   film and leave to rest for a further 30 minutes.

5. Lightly oil an area of clean work surface. Take a ball
   of dough and flatten it into a round on the oiled surface,
   then roll into an oval, about 2mm thick, using oil rather
   than flour to prevent sticking, if necessary. Allow the
   naan to rest for 1 minute.

6. When you are ready to cook the naan, turn the grill to
   its highest setting. Position the grill rack so that your

Illustrated overleaf, with variations

frying pan will be close to the heat source, but not so close that the dough touches it when it puffs up. Have a clean tea towel ready to one side. Heat a large heavy-based frying pan (suitable to use under the grill) over your highest heat on the hob, as hot as it will go.

7. Lay the naan in the hot pan. Count to 20, then place the pan under the grill. The naan should puff up and brown in patches in about 30 seconds. Be vigilant: you should let it colour a little, but remove it from the pan before it becomes crispy. When you remove the naan from the pan, wrap it in the tea towel, so that it softens in its own steam for a minute or so before serving.

8. Place the empty pan back over the hot hob to reheat for the next naan. Continue until you've cooked all the naan. Brush with melted butter and serve while still warm.

Note: To store cooked naans, leave to cool in the tea towel, then keep in an airtight plastic bag for up to 2 days. To reheat, rub them with wet hands to moisten slightly, then place in the toaster or under a grill for a couple of minutes.

Variations

Crispy sesame & onion seed naan: Roll the dough as thinly as possible. Top each rolled naan with 1 tsp black sesame seeds and ½ tsp onion seeds, pressing them in with your fingers. Cook for a little longer than above, until crispy.

Garlic naan: Roll the dough into rounds. Sprinkle each with ½ tsp finely chopped garlic and 1 tsp finely chopped coriander leaves, pressing them in with your fingers. Cook and serve as above.

Cheese naan: For each naan, you will need 15g grated Cheddar, ½ tsp finely chopped green chilli and 1 tsp finely chopped spring onion. Mix together in a bowl. Take a ball of dough in the palm of your hand. Using your other hand, flatten the dough into a disc. Pinch the edges, using your forefinger and thumb, to create a well in the centre surrounded by slightly thinner edges. Press the cheese filling into the well and crimp the edges of the dough together around the filling to seal it in, then carefully work back into a ball shape. Leave to rest for 5 minutes. Roll the stuffed dough ball into a round flatbread, 3–4mm thick. Cook as above, but allow about twice as long under the grill; the naan should still puff up, even with the filling inside. Wrap in a clean tea towel for 1 minute before serving.

CHAPATI

At Dishoom we serve roomali roti, a soft, thin, unleavened "handkerchief" bread. The dough is flipped and stretched by hand until it resembles fine cloth. The saying goes that the test for a good roomali is whether you can read a newspaper through it. This technique takes years to master, so we suggest you use our recipe below to make slightly thicker (and much more straightforward) chapatis.

It takes only a couple of minutes to cook a chapati, and the dough will keep, well wrapped, in the fridge for up to 2 days.

Chapatis go well with just about everything – grills, curries, etc.; they also form the basis of the chapati rolls on page 280.

MAKES 10

~

125g plain flour

375g atta (wholewheat chapati flour)

8g fine sea salt

¼ tsp granulated sugar

125ml milk

1 medium egg

1 tbsp vegetable oil

1. Sift the flours and salt into a large bowl. Mix in the sugar and make a well in the centre.

2. Combine the milk, egg, oil and 120ml water in a jug and whisk with a fork to combine. Pour into the well in the flour mixture and gradually draw in the flour with a round-bladed knife, then knead with your hands for 8 minutes to create a soft dough.

3. Cover with a clean, damp cloth and leave to rest for 30 minutes.

4. When the resting time is up, knead the chapati dough for a further 2 minutes, then weigh into 70g portions and roll each into a neat ball.

5. Heat your biggest frying pan over a high heat. It needs to be very hot. Take a clean tea towel and fold it into a thick rectangle.

6. Take a dough ball and, on a floured work surface, roll out as thinly as you can, to a thickness of about 1mm.

7. Place the chapati in the pan and cook for 1–2 minutes on each side. While it is cooking, carefully use the folded tea towel to press down onto the bread in brief little dabs, moving over the surface. You should be left with a soft, slightly charred bread, perfect for mopping up sauce or making wraps. Repeat to shape and cook the rest. Serve warm.

BHATURE

This is a puffed-up deep-fried bread which hails from the Punjab, in the north of India. It is the typical accompaniment to chole (page 100).

The dough needs at least 3 hours to rest, but is perhaps better with 10–12 hours. The warmer the room is, the sooner the dough will be ready.

MAKES 10

~

250g maida or strong white bread flour

80g atta (wholewheat chapati flour)

80g coarse semolina

7g fine sea salt

4g caster sugar

4g baking powder

45g full-fat Greek yoghurt

85ml whole milk

20ml vegetable oil, plus extra for oiling and deep-frying

1. Mix the flours, semolina, salt, sugar and baking powder together in a bowl and make a well in the centre.

2. In a jug, mix together the yoghurt, milk, 20ml oil and 90ml water. Pour into the well in the flour mixture and gradually draw in the flour with a round-bladed knife, then knead with your hands – just until a smooth dough is formed that leaves the side of the bowl clean. This should only take a couple of minutes.

3. Pour a little oil into your hands, then rub over the surface of the dough. Cover loosely with cling film and leave to rest at room temperature for 3–12 hours.

4. Tip the dough onto a clean work surface. Weigh into 30g pieces and roll each piece into a ball. Let them sit at room temperature for 30 minutes.

5. Pour enough oil into a large, wide pan to just under half-fill it and heat to 190°C. Have a large metal spatula close to hand for frying.

6. Lightly oil the palms of your hands and press a ball of dough between them to flatten it. Using a rolling pin, roll the dough as thinly as possible – no thicker than 1mm. You may need to add a little extra oil to the rolling pin to prevent it from sticking.

7. Carefully slide the rolled dough into the hot oil. As it slides in it should immediately start to bubble; if not, your oil is not hot enough. Keep pressing the bhatura back into the hot oil with your spatula, using short, sharp taps. Do not hold it under the oil, or it will be too greasy. It will puff up in around 10–15 seconds.

8. Carefully flip the bhatura over in the pan, and then it should puff up some more to create a "cushion". Flip it every 10–15 seconds or so, until it is a rich golden brown on both sides. The total frying time should be no more than a minute. Drain on kitchen paper while you roll and fry the rest. The bhatura will keep its shape and crispness if it has been fried for the right amount of time; if it starts to collapse on removing from the oil, it's not quite ready. Serve while still warm.

BEDMI PURI

These crispy deep-fried breads are stuffed with a heavily spiced lentil mix – an extra flavour to enjoy as you scoop up your curry. The best examples in Bombay can be found at Pancham Poori-walla just outside Victoria Terminus, but the dish originated in Agra in the north of India, where it's often eaten for breakfast.

Allow time to soak the urad daal before you start cooking. You need to work quickly with puri dough, as it can become quite crumbly. Keep the dough you aren't working with covered with lightly oiled cling film to prevent it drying.

MAKES 8

~

1 quantity puri dough (page 363)

FOR THE DAAL PEETHI

60g split (white) urad daal, soaked for 2–3 hours in cold water

1 tsp fennel seeds

1½ tsp ground coriander

1½ tsp deggi mirch chilli powder

⅔ tsp garam masala (page 356)

⅔ tsp asafoetida

1g bicarbonate of soda

TO SHAPE AND COOK

Vegetable oil, for oiling and deep-frying

1. While the puri dough is resting, prepare the daal peethi. Drain the soaked daal. Using a pestle and mortar, grind the fennel seeds to a coarse powder. Combine the daal with the ground fennel and all the other ingredients.

2. Pulse the mixture, using a mini food processor or stick blender, to a coarse paste; don't make it too smooth. Weigh the daal peethi into 16g pieces, then shape into balls in the palm of your hand.

3. Working with oiled hands, take 50g puri dough and roll into a ball (pic 1). Flatten into a disc in the palm of your hand (pic 2) and place a ball of filling into the centre (pic 3). Bring up the edges of the dough (pic 4) and pinch them together to seal (pic 5). Work the dough into a ball, smoothing the sealed part as best you can. Place the ball on an oiled surface, sealed part down, and flatten slightly into a disc (pic 6). Ensure the surface is coated with oil. Repeat with the rest of the dough.

4. Using an oiled rolling pin, roll a disc of dough out to a round, 2–3mm thick (pics 7 and 8). Set aside on an oiled surface while you roll the rest. The rolled, oiled breads may be stacked on top of each other, interleaved with oiled baking parchment, and stored in the fridge for 3–4 hours if you wish to make them in advance.

5. Heat the oil in a deep-fryer or other suitable deep, heavy-based pan to 180°C. To test the temperature of the oil, drop in a small piece of dough; it should immediately start bubbling.

6. To fry the breads, slip one carefully into the oil. When it comes to the surface, lightly push it back under the oil with a series of short, gentle taps. It should inflate like a cushion. Let it fry for 20 seconds once inflated, then turn over and cook for a further 20–30 seconds. The bread should be a nice light brown colour all over and hold its crispy shape. Remove and drain on kitchen paper while you fry the rest. Serve while still warm.

Cooked bedmi puri illustrated on page 104

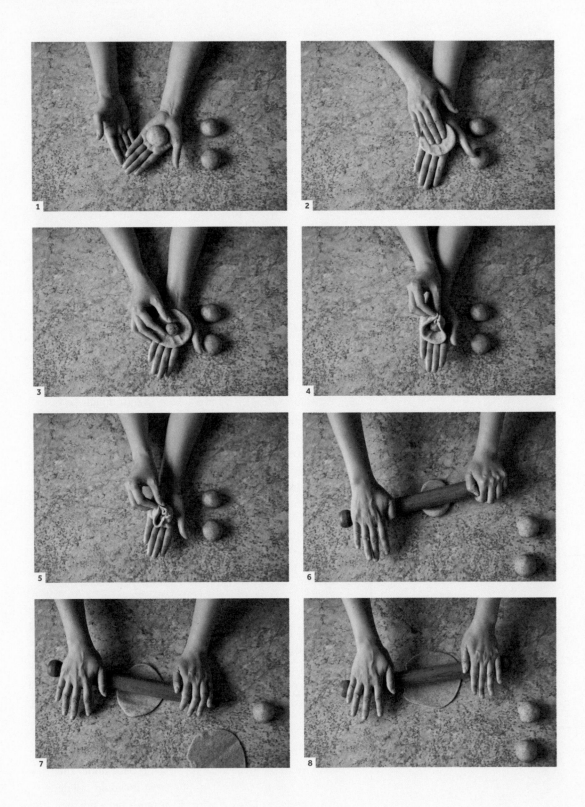

MALABAR PARATHA

An oily, flaky bread from Kerala, paratha accompanies any south Indian-style dish very nicely. In parts of south India and Sri Lanka, past-their-best parathas are often chopped up and fried on a hotplate with vegetables and eggs to make a filling dish known as *kotthu*.

Paratha goes particularly well with butter garlic crab (page 198), soft-shell crab masala (page 202) and mutton pepper fry (page 206).

MAKES 10

~

500g strong white bread flour

7g fine sea salt

10g granulated sugar

50ml whole milk

2 tbsp vegetable oil

TO SHAPE AND COOK

Vegetable oil, for oiling

Plain flour, for dusting

50g butter, melted

1. Put the flour, salt and sugar into a large bowl and mix to combine. Make a well in the centre.

2. In a jug, mix together the milk, 190ml water and the oil. Pour into the well in the flour mixture and gradually draw in the flour with a round-bladed knife, then knead with your hands until you have a smooth, elastic dough. Pour a drop of oil into your hand, then lightly oil the surface of the dough. Cover loosely with cling film and leave to rest at room temperature for 1 hour.

3. Divide the dough into 70g pieces, roll into balls on a lightly floured surface and shape the parathas (as shown overleaf). Leave the dough discs to rest for 15 minutes before cooking. The first dough ball will probably be ready to cook by the time you've finished rolling the last.

4. To cook the parathas, warm a large non-stick frying pan over a high heat and have the melted butter and a pastry brush to hand.

5. Place a paratha in the pan and press down to flatten. The dough should sizzle a little as it hits the pan, and after 30–45 seconds you should see air starting to inflate it. Turn the dough over and repeat the process, watching it puff up a little more.

6. As soon as the second side has puffed and you can see no more raw dough, brush the surface with melted butter, flip it over and brush the other side. Transfer to a warmed plate and serve immediately.

Shaping illustrated overleaf

Roll out one ball of dough as thinly as possible to a rough rectangle, about 20 x 14cm.

Brush the entire surface of the finely rolled dough with oil.

Sprinkle the surface of the dough very lightly with plain flour.

Starting at one side, fold the sheet of dough concertina-style, making 1–2cm pleats.

5

Continue to fold in a concertina fashion until you have a 20cm long strip of many layers.

6

Starting at one end of the strip, roll the dough up into a disc.

7

Place the second end of the strip across the centre of the disc and place this side down to "hide" the end. Press the disc to flatten slightly with oiled fingers.

8

Repeat the rolling and shaping with the remaining dough balls to form the rest of the parathas.

CHUTNEYS, PICKLES & DRESSINGS

Along with fresh garnishes (see page 350), chutneys, pickles and dressings enhance many Indian dishes. Our chutneys are mostly quick to make and very fresh-tasting, and as such they are meant to be eaten within a few days. Easy come, easy go, very fine and moreish.

TAMARIND CHUTNEY

This is an excellent accompaniment for anything that calls for a bit of sour and spice. You can buy tamarind in many forms (see page 348); some have added salt and/or sugar, and some do not. Here we recommend the pure blocks of pulp and seed. If you can find the tamarind paste that has no seeds, only flesh, then use half the quantity suggested.

Tamarind chutney is used in vada pau (page 174), aloo tikki chaat (page 183), dahi bhalla chaat (page 180), bhel (page 163), soft-shell crab masala (page 202) and chilli pomelo salad (page 115); it also goes very well with fried dishes and snacks, such as okra fries (page 179), samosas (pages 166 and 172) and prawn koliwada (page 201).

MAKES 350ml

~

150g tamarind paste

55g Medjool dates, stoned

⅔ tsp cumin seeds

90g jaggery

⅓ tsp fine sea salt

2 pinches of deggi mirch chilli powder

1 tsp ground ginger

1. Break up the tamarind and roughly chop the dates. Place them both in a large bowl, pour on 500ml boiling water to cover, stir well and leave to stand for 1 hour.

2. In the meantime, warm a dry frying pan over a high heat. Add the cumin seeds and toast until they crackle. Tip the toasted seeds into a mortar and crush lightly with the pestle. Set aside.

3. Strain the soaked dates and tamarind through a sieve into a pan, pushing as much of the flesh through as you can with the back of a wooden spoon.

4. Add the jaggery, salt, chilli powder and ground ginger to the pan and simmer over a low heat until reduced to a thick pouring consistency, about 1 hour. The mixture will become more viscous as it cools.

5. Remove from the heat, add the crushed cumin seeds and stir well. Pour the chutney into a warm sterilised jar, put the lid on and allow to cool before sealing. It will keep for up to a week in the fridge.

CORIANDER-MINT CHUTNEY

This fresh, slightly spicy chutney is used in vada pau (page 174), aloo tikki chaat (page 183), dahi bhalla chaat (page 180) and bhel (page 163); it also goes well with okra fries (page 179) and prawn koliwada (page 201).

MAKES 70g

~

½ tsp cumin seeds

20g coriander leaves and stems

20g mint leaves

1 tsp granulated sugar

5g green chilli (1–2), roughly chopped

25ml lime juice

Coriander-mint chutney and chilli chutney illustrated on page 376

1. Warm a dry frying pan over a medium-high heat. Add the cumin seeds, toast for 2–3 minutes then tip onto a plate and leave to cool.

2. Using a mini food processor or stick blender, blitz all the ingredients together with 25ml water until smooth. Transfer to a jar, unless serving straight away.

3. The chutney will keep for 1–2 days in the fridge, though it will lose colour as it oxidises – press cling film onto the surface, before putting the lid on, to deter oxidation.

Coriander-mint dressing: This is used as a dipping sauce and as the dressing for chana chaat salad (page 112). Prepare as above, increasing the sugar to 15g, replacing the fresh chilli with 25g pickled jalapeños (drained weight) and adding 25g sunflower seeds and ¼ tsp ground turmeric before blending the sauce. *Makes 110g*

CHILLI CHUTNEY

A moreish, spicy, garlicky dip, this goes well with fried dishes and snacks like okra fries (page 179), samosas (pages 166 and 172) and prawn koliwada (page 201).

MAKES 150ml

~

25g dried red chillies

4 tsp coriander seeds

2 tsp cumin seeds

35g garlic (8–9 cloves), chopped

80ml olive oil

80ml malt vinegar

2 tsp fine sea salt

80ml lime juice

40g jaggery

1. Put the dried chillies into a bowl and pour on enough boiling water to cover. Leave to soak for 10 minutes.

2. Meanwhile, put the coriander and cumin seeds into a dry frying pan and place over a medium heat. Let them warm up and toast for 1–2 minutes, until fragrant.

3. Drain the chillies and squeeze out any remaining water (wearing gloves, or do this between two spoons, to protect your hands).

4. Blitz all the ingredients together in a blender or mini food processor to a smooth, thick liquid. Cover and refrigerate until ready to serve. The chutney will keep for up to 5 days in the fridge.

CARROT & GREEN CHILLI PICKLE

This is an addictive home-style pickle which gets along very well with chole bhature (page 100) and aloo sabzi (page 105).

SERVES 4

~

120g carrots

2 tbsp mustard oil

1¼ tsp split mustard seeds

¾ tsp onion seeds

¾ tsp fennel seeds

12 green chillies

¾ tsp ground turmeric

½ tsp deggi mirch chilli powder

1 tsp fine sea salt

50ml rice vinegar

1. Cut the carrots into batons, approximately 4 x 1cm, and set aside.

2. Warm the oil in a small saucepan over a medium-high heat. Add the mustard, onion and fennel seeds and sauté for 20 seconds. Add the green chillies, ground spices and salt and sauté for 20 seconds.

3. Add the carrot batons and rice vinegar to the pan and stir well. Turn the heat down slightly, put the lid on and simmer for 4 minutes.

4. Transfer to a bowl or jar and allow to cool completely before serving. Ideally, let the pickle sit in the fridge for a day before serving to allow the flavours to mingle. It will keep in the fridge for 2–3 days.

LIME & CHILLI DRESSING

This dressing is used in our salads and greens recipes, including paneer and mango salad (page 116) and bowl of greens (page 123). It is also delicious drizzled over avocado or served with grilled fish.

MAKES 175ml

50ml lime juice

5g ginger paste (page 353)

5g green chilli (1–2), chopped

½ tsp fine sea salt

30g granulated sugar

25ml rice vinegar

60ml olive oil

35ml vegetable oil

4g mint leaves

1. Using a mini food processor or stick blender, blitz everything until completely homogenised.

2. Transfer to a bowl and refrigerate until ready to serve. It will keep in the fridge for 3–4 days.

MENU SUGGESTIONS

Below we provide some crowd-pleasing menu ideas. Your popularity with family and friends will be guaranteed. If you'd prefer to build your own menu, we'd recommend you approach the main event as follows: a grill, a curry or daal (something with a sauce) and/or a raita alongside, plus breads or rice, and a vegetable dish.

A SUNDAY LUNCH

Prawn koliwada (page 201)

Coriander-mint chutney (page 378)

~

Lamb raan (page 268)

Gunpowder potatoes (page 283)

Bowl of greens (page 123)

~

Chocolate mousse (page 309)

A DIWALI FEAST

Dahi bhalla chaat (page 180)

Aloo tikki chaat (page 183)

Okra fries (page 179)

~

Phaldari kofta (page 210)

Paneer tikka achari (page 278)

Chana chaat salad (page 112)

Chapati (page 368)

~

Gulab jamun (page 302)

AN EID FEAST

Lamb samosas (page 166)

~

Haleem (page 246)

Chicken berry Britannia (page 232)

Lamb boti kabab (page 264)

Crispy sesame and onion seed naan (page 365)

Raita (page 124)

~

Gadbad mitha (page 306)

A VEGETARIAN MEAL

Pau bhaji (page 160)

~

Mattar paneer (page 106)

Chole (page 100)

Puri (page 363)

Raita (page 124)

~

Berry shrikhand (page 311)

A VEGAN MEAL

Bhel (page 163)

Chilli pomelo salad (page 115)

~

Bedmi puri (page 370)

Aloo sabzi (page 105)

Carrot & green chilli pickle (page 379)

Bowl of greens (page 123)

~

Pineapple & black pepper crumble
(page 312)

A LAVISH FEAST

Masala prawns (page 274)

Lamb sheekh kabab (page 263)

Raita (page 124)

~

Mutton pepper fry (page 206)

Butter garlic crab (page 198)

House black daal (page 214)

Malabar paratha (page 372)

Kachumber (page 121)

~

Selection of kulfis (page 304)

MIDWEEK SUPPERS

These recipes take 30 minutes to cook after
marinating, making them excellent options
for a prepare-ahead midweek meal. Serve
with kachumber (page 121) or a salad.

Lamb boti kabab (page 264)

Spicy lamb chops (page 267)

Lamb sheekh kabab (page 263)

Paneer tikka achari (page 278)

Murgh malai (page 273)

Chicken tikka (page 270)

Masala prawns (page 274)

Macchi tikka (page 277)

भोजन का कमरा
DINING ROOM

AFTERWORD: DESIGNING DISHOOM

If you're still here with us, digging around in the last dregs of this book, then we salute your stamina. By now, you may have cooked up a few of our recipes and eaten our food in your own kitchen. Perhaps you have read patiently through some of our guided walks around Bombay. We may even have managed to convey some of our profound affection for the city.

Our relationship with Bombay, like the best sort of relationship, continues to mature and deepen with the passage of time. Admittedly, the city is not always easy to love. It is that most utterly imperfect of cities; it is full of the best and the worst, the extremes of human existence cohabiting cheerfully, hemmed in tight against each other by the ocean on three sides. (Of course, this book hasn't attempted to travel down the darker alleyways of the city.)

Endless wanderings in Bombay have brought us more knowledge, to be sure. However, each extra wandering, each extra delving into the history of this or that building, and each extra meeting with some Bombay character full of stories to tell, has brought much more than that. As our knowledge has grown, so has our obsession with and love for the city, and we had to put our learning to use.

When we create a Dishoom restaurant, we always imagine it as an Irani café deeply rooted in some aspect of Bombay history. In Carnaby, the setting is Bombay's rock 'n' roll scene, which flared up briefly in the late 1960s and early 1970s. In King's Cross, the setting is in a notional godown in the vicinity of Victoria Terminus, the Independence movement a backdrop. We then sit down and write a story – a different founding myth – for each Dishoom.

Literally every single aspect of the design (no detail too small) is informed by this story. We spend weeks and months researching the Bombay of that era. We meet people with memories of that period. We comb the city for the right antique furniture. We mine archives, museums and libraries and find ourselves in long derelict warehouses, railway offices, old cinemas and wherever else our story leads us. (Our designers, John and Ian, are stalwart and expert companions on this journey.)

"When we create a Dishoom restaurant, we always imagine it as an Irani café deeply rooted in some aspect of Bombay history."

The fictional proprietor of our new restaurant may have views on the politics of the time, or perhaps specific tastes in art and literature. The proprietor, like any person, has quirks which would naturally be expressed in the restaurant. We like to think that you walk across the threshold of our restaurants and into our stories, into our imagining of some facet of Bombay.

Someone who grew up in Bombay might recognise the large clock in Covent Garden as a close replica of the one in Victoria Terminus. The panelling and Art Deco styling in Kensington (housed in the famous Art Deco Barkers Building) are directly inspired by the utterly gorgeous Liberty Cinema. The staircase in Carnaby is a close echo of the one in the Jehangir Art Gallery. The green stained-glass windows in Edinburgh are uncannily like those in the David Sassoon Library.

Even the shades of paint on the walls have their ancestry in Bombay. We have "Britannia Ochre" in Manchester named for the ceiling of Britannia Restaurant and "Chilli-man-green" in King's Cross named for the wall behind a chilli vendor in Null Bazaar. We once changed all of the screws in the lobby of Carnaby to flat-headed ones, to correctly reflect those available in the 1960s.

Each detail has a reason, and each restaurant has its own fifty-page guide for the team who work there, which documents each reason, as well as the stories and the relevant historical background. (Pity our teams who are asked to digest this stuff!)

Glance now across the walls of the restaurants. In King's Cross, the graffiti and tattered fly-postering on the walls are copies of original anti-colonial graffiti and posters that we found in archives. There is a row of photos taken by India's first female photo-journalist Homai Vyarawalla,

"Is our motivation that we enjoy telling all these stories? Absolutely. Do we love combing through Bombay as we do? Certainly."

documenting the events of Indian Independence in chronological order. There is a wall (the Chilliman-green wall, as it happens) that has portraits of the major figures of the Independence movement. We had never seen a wall like this before, and jumped at the chance to create one.

Finally, of course, in the spirit of the old Irani cafés, there are many old family portraits. (If you look carefully, you might notice a slim sixteen-year-old girl in a Bombay studio in 1944, gazing confidently from a picture. This photograph is of Shamil and Kavi's grandmother and was sent to their grandfather before their engagement was agreed. It can be said without exaggeration that the entire Dishoom enterprise owes its existence to this photograph.)

Sometimes we have taken this even further. For example, when we were opening Dishoom Carnaby we discovered the surprising East-West relationship that had flourished in the 1960s, when Western influences kicked off a rocking music scene in Bombay. We were drawn in by this cul-de-sac of history, and became friends with Sidharth Bhatia, who chronicles this era in his great little book *India Psychedelic*, as well as with many of the musicians of the time (and we were delighted when some of them made it to the launch). Many of their photographs are on our walls in Dishoom Carnaby, alongside gig posters and replica works of art from the period. As the Carnaby project evolved, we were so enamoured of the sounds and stories that we decided to release an album and a single on vinyl as part of the launch. We named the album *Slip-Disc*, after the grungy Bombay club in which Led Zeppelin played an impromptu gig in 1972 (see page 253).

A few years later, we came upon the book *Taj Mahal Foxtrot* by our friend Naresh Fernandes, which paints a joyfully vivid picture of Bombay's jazz scene (see page 318). We were thrilled to discover that Bombay had a rich and colourful history of jazz. It had to be brought to life. We began to wonder whether we could actually welcome our patrons into our story in a much more literal sense. Could our characters meet our guests, the plot unfolding around them? It was then that we conceived *Night at the Bombay Roxy*, an immersive theatre production that took place in Dishoom Kensington. Guests in the first two weeks of the restaurant's life were invited not to a new Dishoom, but to the opening night of the Roxy, a jazz club housed in a former cinema in Bombay in 1949. There was a charismatic but wayward hero, Cyrus Irani, a glamorous heroine who sang beautifully with her jazz band, an escaped prisoner, crooked policemen, and much Dishoom food and drink.

Thus, we think of each restaurant as a vividly imagined and detailed love-letter to Bombay. Why go to such extreme lengths? Common sense would dictate that we should limit ourselves to looking after people well and serving them decent food and drink in pleasant surroundings. Is our motivation that we enjoy telling all these stories? Absolutely. Do we love combing through Bombay as we do? Certainly. Does it make our restaurants better? It must, surely, although few will consciously notice or understand all the details (when they do, we rejoice!). In the end though, a lover doesn't need reasons to write love-letters.

(You can find the story – the founding myth – for each Dishoom restaurant on our website: www.dishoom.com/journal)

Footnote: Why Bombay, not Mumbai? This might seem an odd choice after the official name was changed in the 1990s. You will have noticed our overpowering nostalgia for that wild port city of migrants seeking their fortunes, bringing with them their myriad cultures and beliefs and stories and food, until all of it was woven completely into the fabric of the city. To us, this joyfully crazy, open-hearted, cosmopolitan place will always just be Bombay.

RECOMMENDED READING

Below is a short list of books that we have loved and treasured over the years. Some have inspired us with their wisdom, others have guided us through Bombay and the rest we simply admire. We are grateful for them all.

... ...

A Suitable Boy
by Vikram Seth

A doorstop of a novel that will immerse you completely in 1950s India. When you finish this book, you will feel as if you are saying goodbye to dear friends.

... ...

Bombay Art Deco Architecture
by Navin Ramani

Endless pictures of beautiful Art Deco balconies, balustrades and bas-reliefs. Hours of joy (if you like that sort of thing).

... ...

Bombay Deco
by Sharada Dwivedi and Rahul Mehrotra

More hours of Art Deco joy.

... ...

Bombay Gothic
by Christopher London

A wonderful, charming guide to Bombay's great Gothic buildings.

... ...

Bombay: Meri Jaan
by Jerry Pinto and Naresh Fernandes

A rich anthology of prose and poems on Bombay from a number of distinguished contributors, including V. S. Naipaul, Salman Rushdie and Khushwant Singh. Lovely.

Bombay: The Cities Within
by Sharada Dwivedi and Rahul Mehrotra

The authors walk you around the city with enormous knowledge and understanding, thus revealing the different layers of the palimpsest that is Bombay. Our copy is well thumbed.

... ...

Bombay Then and Mumbai Now
by Jim Masselos, Pramod Kapoor, Naresh Fernandes and Chirodeep Chaudhuri

A sizeable visual treat of beautiful photography.

... ...

City Adrift: A Short Biography of Bombay
by Naresh Fernandes

This book, and its author, are the best sort of Bombay companions. Naresh refers to it sometimes as a pamphlet, sometimes as a rant. It is neither, but is a short, delicious history of Bombay with a sharp analysis of the issues it faces today.

... ...

In Hot Blood: The Nanavati Case That Shook India
by Bachi Karkaria

"I've shot my wife's lover and I'm handing myself in." Learn about the dashing Parsi naval officer, his English wife, her murdered lover and India's most famous murder trial.

... ...

India Psychedelic
by Sidharth Bhatia

A colourful chronicle of Bombay's brief, intense infatuation with 1960s rock. This book was the inspiration for our restaurant in Carnaby and for the LP that we released in 2015.

Jerry Thomas' Bartenders Guide: How to Mix Drinks
by Jerry Thomas

Unchanged since 1862 and still a lot of fun to read. A serious bon vivant's life companion.

... ...

Laughter in the House: 20th Century Parsi Theatre
by Meher Marfatia

Photographs and anecdotes from the old troupers of Parsi theatre. If you want or need to laugh, this will do the trick, quickly.

... ...

Love and Longing in Bombay
by Vikram Chandra

The narrator of this collection of short stories is sitting in a smoky Bombay bar with a strong drink in his hand. We recommend the same.

... ...

Maximum City: Bombay Lost and Found
by Suketu Mehta

If our perspective on Bombay seemed excessively rose-tinted to you, we would understand. This is the antidote. The Bombay of this book is real and might slap you in the face a couple of times and it wouldn't be wrong to do so. A brilliant journalistic exploration of the city today. We are in awe of Suketu's work.

... ...

Midnight's Children
by Salman Rushdie

Surely one of the best books written in English. This won the "Booker of Bookers" prize in 2008. Hang a "Do Not Disturb" sign on the door and escape into a magical Bombay world. So many voices saying so many things all at once.

Mumbai Fables
by Gyan Prakash

The author has very kindly entertained us and our obscure ideas. We would recommend his work any day.

... ...

Night in Bombay
by Louis Bromfield

You'll be happy to have picked this up for its vivid picture of a raffish 1930s Bombay. Find an armchair and sip a Gin Sling while you read.

... ...

Taj Mahal Foxtrot: The Story of Bombay's Jazz Age
by Naresh Fernandes

This book is a real treasure — it inspired endless conversations, late-night jazz sessions, Dishoom Kensington and our one-off immersive theatre production.

... ...

Words: From Here, There and Everywhere or My Private Babel
by Farrukh Dhondy

Joyful and mischievous musings on words, Indian and non-Indian, from our friend Mr Dhondy, who has a permanent glint in his eye.

... ...

bombaywalla.org

Not a book but a website that provides an ever-charming source of obscure Bombay knowledge, written by the ever-patient and kind Dr Simin Patel, DPhil (Oxon).

GRATITUDE

First, we must surely thank you, O big-hearted patrons of our livelihoods. You have risked spraining your wrists by picking up this cumbersome cookery book. You dine with us, and inevitably leave us with your wallets slightly lighter and waistlines slightly heavier than when you arrived. It is you who allow us to do what we do. We are literally nothing without your patronage and you have our most genuine gratitude.

We owe a profound debt of heartfelt thanks to our endlessly conscientious and hard-working team who conjure up a kind welcome and nourishment each day and each night in our restaurants. Our suppliers, who steadfastly come on this journey with us, we also give you a wholehearted thanks.

Our families (none more than Saloni, Maria and Rabab) put up with so much and here we acknowledge it; you have cheerfully suffered our exhaustion, our tempers, our elation and too often our absence these past years. Your unwavering love and support is humbling.

Natalie and Richard, you have been the most patient and thoughtful editors and guides in this weighty venture of the Dishoom book, sagely reining us in and yet never raining on our zeal. Janet, you are a superwoman of quiet and diligent editing. Dave, you are a colossus of design and to our (admittedly biased) eyes this book is surely among the most beautiful ever to roll off a press. Kitty, we give thanks for your tireless behind-the-scenes organising. Liz and Max, your photographs speak for themselves. It is a joy to look at our beloved Bombay through your eyes that see and understand so much. There cannot exist a more unflagging agent than Louise, who repeatedly rescued this project from its contented smouldering on the backburner. And thank you to you and Luigi for finding us a publisher as wonderful as Bloomsbury has been.

Carl, our *Daru-walla* extraordinaire, has taught us the history of cocktails and slaked our thirst with drinks too tasty for comfort. His mixology is contained within this book and he deserves an enormous thank you. Rishi, you have been a stalwart support to Chef in shaping up his food

recipes for the book. And Nicola, we acknowledge your remarkable dedication to the proper browning of onions and your enthusiastic testing and re-testing of Naved's recipes in your cosy kitchen. Aneeta and SPK, we have gratitude in our hearts for your hard work in 2009, creating our first recipes when there was no menu, no nothing.

Sara and Ginny, it must here be honestly recorded that you have taken much of the weight of this bookish endeavour on your sturdy backs. You have heroically marshalled, corralled, researched and composed until jottings became drafts, lists became photographs and a manuscript became a book. You are both champions and this book is yours as much as it is the authors'.

Our friends who companionably made their way through our drafts have our sincere appreciation for the slip-ups they spotted and the richness they added. Naresh, Sidharth, Sidin and Roly, we are looking at you. And most of all in this regard, and for even more still, Simin, who never ceases to delight us with her encyclopaedic knowledge of everything that ever happened in Bombay.

We also must salute the hard work of the good Amar and Adarsh who co-founded Dishoom with us back in 2010. And, remembering the times when the sum of our knowledge could be written on a small roti, thanks are due to the wise and generous Karen for helping us to think, to research, to taste and to recruit, to the ever-effervescent Robbie who was and is endlessly full of the best ideas, and to Afroditi for patiently designing the very first Dishoom.

Ed, you have always been our wisest counsellor. Shilen, you gave your profound and unstinting support when we really needed it. To Shamil's Mum who prayed at our first 'havan' that guests should want to keep returning to Dishoom but may not know why, we are very grateful. Robert, you have helped us understand what Dishoom was and to distil it into an essence, maybe even into an elixir. Elise, you have helped Dishoom to speak a lovely and unexpected poetry. And John and Ian, over six restaurants and many years you have made countless trips to Bombay with us, and your skill in designing all of this Bombay-ness and our stories into actual physical spaces here in the UK is completely unrivalled.

Brian, old friend, you have carried much on your broad shoulders these past years. Without you, and without Andy, Stephen, Nina, Jon, Arun and Yash, there would be no Dishoom, let alone a book.

We need also to express heartfelt appreciation to Bhawani at Akshaya Patra, Carmel at Magic Breakfast and everyone at Seeds of Peace for all their fantastic and valuable work. It's a true privilege to work with you and support you.

Finally, we must mention those in Bombay who have helped us so generously for this book and before. Pooja, for always being at the end of a phone to help and for knowing so much. Chiki, for helping us find the most gorgeous antique furniture. Rafique-bhai and Farrokh-bhai, for being expert guides. And for all their help to us and all that they do for the city, Amir-bhai at Koolar & Co., Farokh-bhai at Kyani & Co., Danesh-bhai at Paris Bakery, Zend-bhai at Yazdani, the Sequeira family at Karfule petrol pump, Dinshaw-bhai at Meher Cold Drink House, Nayeem-bhai at Surti Bara Handi, Hatim-bhai and Aamir-bhai the Icecreamwalas, Roda-ben and Aban-ben of K. Rustom & Co. and finally that legend, Mr Kohinoor at Britannia Restaurant.

INDEX

C

cabbage
  slaw 118, *119*
Café Coffee Day 18
Café Naaz 18
Café Samovar 191
Calcutta 19
Cambridge, Duke and Duchess of
  91, *93*
caramelising onions 349–50, *351*
cardamom pods 347
  Bollybellini 332
  chai syrup 143
  masala chai 86, 87
  rose & cardamom lassi 140
carrots
  carrot & green chilli pickle 379
  pau bhaji 160, *161*
  phaldari kofta 210–12, *211, 213*
  vegetable samosas *167*, 172
cashew nuts
  granola 52, *53*
Catherine of Braganza 16
cauliflower
  pau bhaji 160, *161*
  phaldari kofta 210–12, *211, 213*
Censorship Act (1878) 94
chaat
  aloo tikki chaat *182*, 183
  chaat masala 348
  dahi bhalla chaat 180–1, *181*
chai *70*
  chai paanch 334, *335*
  chai syrup 143
  masala chai 86, 87
chana chaat salad 112, *113*
chana masala 348
chapati flour 347
chapati 368
  chicken tikka chapati roll 281
  paneer tikka chapati roll 280–1,
    281
Charles II, King 16
charoli seeds 347
cheese
  cheese & masala sticks 78, 79
  cheese naan 365
  chilli cheese toast 184, *185*
  kejriwal *40*, 41
  lamb sheekh kabab 262, *263*
  murgh malai 272, *273*
  see also mascarpone cheese; paneer
Chhatrapati Shivaji Maharaj Terminus
  see Victoria Terminus (VT)
Chic Chocolate 319, *319*
chicken
  chicken berry Britannia 232, *233*

chicken ruby *208*, 209
chicken tikka 270, *271*
chicken tikka chapati roll 281
keema per eedu 42–3, *43*
murgh malai 272, 273
chicken livers
  chicken livers on toast 44, *45*
  keema per eedu 42–3, *43*
chickpea flour 347
chickpeas
  aloo sabzi *104*, 105
  aloo tikki chaat *182*, 183
  chana chaat salad 112, *113*
  chole bhature 100, *101*
chilli 348
  aloo sabzi 105, 105
  butter garlic crab 198, *199*
  carrot & green chilli pickle 379
  chilli cheese toast 184, *185*
  chilli chutney 378
  chilli drizzle 358
  chilli pomelo salad *114*, 115
  chilli powder 347
  chilli-topped kharis 81
  fried chillies 100, 175
  gunpowder potatoes 282, 283
  kejriwal *40*, 41
  lamb samosas 166, 167–71
  lime & chilli dressing 379
  mutton pepper fry 206–7, *207*
  prawn moilee *204*, 205
  soft-shell crab masala 202–3, *203*
  tomato-chilli jam *46*, 59
Chisti, Hazrat Fida Mohammed
  Adam 251
chocolate mousse *308*, 309
chole bhature 100, *101*
Chor Bazaar 219, *220*
Chowpatty 17, 148, 151–4, *152–5*,
  290
Churchgate 290
chutney
  chilli chutney 378
  coriander-mint chutney 376, 378
  dahi bhalla chaat 180–1, *181*
  tamarind chutney 376, 377
C.I.D. (film) 289
cider
  Taj ballroom toddy 336
cinnamon sugar sticks 79
cocktails 326
  Bloody Mary 341
  Bollybellini 332
  The Commander 337
  Cyrus Irani 340
  The Dhoble 333
  East India gimlet 326, *327*
  Kohinoor fizz *330*, 331

monsoon martini 328, *329*
Taj ballroom toddy 336
Viceroy's Old-fashioned 342, *343*
see also drinks
coconut
  ghati masala 357
  granola 52, *53*
coconut cream
  Colaba colada *142*, 143
  prawn moilee *204*, 205
coconut milk
  breakfast lassi 54, 55
  prawn moilee *204*, 205
  soft-shell crab masala 202–3, *203*
coffee
  monsoon martini 328, *329*
Colaba 17, 251–4, 319
Colaba colada *142*, 143
The Combustibles *254*
The Commander 337
condensed milk
  bun maska pudding 300, *301*
  falooda 146, *147*
coriander
  bhel *162*, 163
  coriander-mint chutney 376, 378
  kachumber *120*, 121
corn-on-the-cob
  butter-bhutta *164*, 165
Correa, Micky 319, *319*
cotton 64–5
Cotton, Rudy 319
couscous
  chana chaat salad 112, *113*
crab 189–90
  butter garlic crab 198, *199*
  soft-shell crab masala 202–3, *203*
cracked wheat (bulgur)
  haleem 246–7, *247*
cranberries
  chicken berry Britannia 232, *233*
cream
  chocolate mousse *308*, 309
  gadbad mitha 306, *307*
  malai kulfi 304, *305*
  Memsahib's mess *298*, 299
crisps, salli 173
crumble, pineapple & black pepper
  312, *313*
cucumber
  kachumber *120*, 121
  raita 124, *125*
cumin seeds
  jeera biscuits 82, 83
curry leaves 347
custard
  gadbad mitha 306, *307*
Cyrus Irani (cocktail) 340

D

daal *see* urad daal
dabba-walla service 102
dahi bhalla chaat 180–1, *181*
Daily Herald (UK) 66
dates
    banana & date porridge *50*, 51
    chilli pomelo salad *114*, 115
    tamarind chutney *376*, 377
David Sassoon Library 192, *192*,
    196–7, 385
Dawoodi Bohra Muslims 224
deggi mirch chilli powder 347
Delhi 19, 319
designing Dishoom restaurants 385
Dhobi Talao 27–30, 319
The Dhoble 333
Dhoble, Vasant 254, 333
Dishoom Carnaby 254, 385, 386
Dishoom Covent Garden 205, 385
Dishoom Edinburgh 192, 331, 385
Dishoom Kensington 340, 385, 386
Dishoom King's Cross 385–6
Dishoom Manchester 385
Dishoom Shoreditch *19*
Diwali 20, 198, 210
doodhpati chai 86
dough seal, biryani 230
dressing, lime & chilli 379
drinks
    Bombay Presidency punch *338*, 339
    breakfast lassi 54, *55*
    chai paanch *334*, 335
    Colaba colada *142*, 143
    falooda 146, *147*
    fresh lime soda 138, *139*
    masala chai 86, *87*
    passion fruit sharbat 145
    salted lassi 140, *141*
    watermelon sharbat *144*, 145
    see also cocktails
dumplings
    phaldari kofta 210–12, *211*, *213*
Dwivedi, Sharada *Bombay: The Cities
    Within* 132
Dyer, General 66

E

East India Company 16
East India gimlet *326*, *327*
Edward VII, King 186, 190
eggs
    akuri 36, *37*
    egg naan roll 47
    keema per eedu 42–3, *43*

kejriwal *40*, 41
    Parsi omelette 38, *39*
Eid 20, 240
Elizabeth II, Queen 91, *92*
Elphinstone, Lord 66
Elphinstone Circle 66
Elphinstone College 130
The Elphinstonian Amateurs 130
Esplanade Mansions 191–2, *192*
espresso
    monsoon martini *328*, 329
evaporated milk
    falooda 146, *147*
    malai kulfi 304, *305*

F

falooda 146, *147*
fennel seeds
    khari *80*, 81
fenugreek leaves 347
Fernand, Frank 319, *319*
Fernandes, Naresh
    City Adrift 19, 287
    Taj Mahal Foxtrot 318, 319, 320,
    386
films 289, 319
fine sev 348
Fire Temples 30, *30*
fire toast 48, *49*
Flora Fountain 67–8, *67*
Fort 63, 67
Frere, Sir Henry Bartle 63, 65, 66,
    67
fruit
    gadbad mitha 306, *307*
    see also blackberries, pineapple *etc*

G

gadbad mitha 306, *307*
Gaitonde, V. S. 191
Gamdevi 290
Gandhi, Mahatma 29, 129
Ganesh 20, 152
garam masala 356
garlic
    butter garlic crab 198, *199*
    garlic naan 365
    garlic paste 350, 353
    ghati masala 357
    makhani sauce 360
garnishes 350
Gateway of India 91, 251, 252, 288,
    325
George V, King 91, 325
ghati masala 357

gimlet, East India 326, *327*
gin
    The Commander 337
    East India gimlet *326*, *327*
    Kohinoor fizz *330*, 331
ginger
    bhel *162*, 163
    ginger juice 336
    ginger paste 350, 353
    masala chai 86, 87
    prawn moilee *204*, 205
    Taj ballroom toddy 336
    tomato-chilli jam *46*, 59
Girgaum Chowpatty 17, 151–4,
    152–5
Goan restaurants 29–30
gooseberry jam
    Kohinoor fizz *330*, 331
Gothic architecture 17, 132
gram flour 347
granola 52, 53
green beans
    pau bhaji 160, *161*
    phaldari kofta 210–12, *211*, *213*
Green's Hotel 317
grilling 260
Gujarat 17
gulab jamun 302–3, *303*
gulkand
    Memsahib's mess 298, 299
gunpowder potatoes 282, 283

H

haleem 246–7, *247*
Hamlet No Omelette (play) 131
Hanuman 287
Harbour Bar, Taj Mahal Palace hotel
    319–20, *322*
Hawkins, Coleman 318
hing 347
honey
    granola 52, 53
Horniman, Benjamin 66, 129
Horniman Circle 63–4, *65*, 66
house black daal 214, *215*
Husain, M.F. 27, 191, 221, *223*
    *Three Stanzas of the New
    Millennium* 317

I

Ibrahim Merchant Road 222
ice cream 220, 287–8, 289
    see also kulfi
Icecreamwala, Hatim and Aamir 220,
    223